Perspectives on Public Relations Research

Edited by Danny Moss,
Dejan Verčič and Gary Warnaby

Routledge
Taylor & Francis Group

LONDON AND NEW YORK

First edition published 2000
by Routledge
11 New Fetter Lane, London EC4P 4EE

Simultaneously published in the USA and Canada
by Routledge
29 West 35th Street, New York NY 10001

Reprinted 2001

First published in paperback 2003

Transferred to Digital Printing 2004

Routledge is an imprint of the Taylor & Francis Group

© 2000, 2003 Danny Moss, Dejan Verčič and Gary Warnaby
editorial matter and selection; individual chapters, the contributors

Typeset in Garamond by Taylor & Francis Books Ltd
Printed and bound in Great Britain by Selwood Printing Ltd, West Sussex

British Library Cataloguing in Publication Data
A catalogue record for this book is available
from the British Library

Library of Congress Cataloging-in-Publication Data
A catalogue record for this book has been applied for

ISBN 0–415–31618–9

Contents

Illustrations

Figures

Tables

Contributors

Professor **Barbara Baerns** is Head of the Centre of Public Relations Studies in the Institute of Media and Communications Research at the Department of Communications Science at the Free University of Berlin. Having obtained her doctorate in 1967 from the Free University of Berlin, Barbara Baerns completed a second doctoral thesis in 1982 leading to recognition of 'venia legendi' status (Ruhr University of Bochum). She is political editor of the *Neue Hannoversche Presse* and the *Neue Ruhr/Neue Rhein Zeitung*. She has also worked in the Department of the US Information Center, Hanover, and was head of the Public Relations Department of Coca-Cola Central Europe in Essen.

James E. Grunig is now a professor at the College of Communications at the University of Maryland. He has published over 150 articles, books, chapters, papers and reports. His most influential publications include: *Managing Public Relations* (co-authored with Todd Hunt) and *Excellence in Public Relations and Communication Management* (editor). He has won the three major awards in public relations: the Pathfinder Award for Excellence in Public Relations Research awarded by the Institute of Public Relations Research and Education; the Outstanding Educator Award from the Public Relations Society of America (PRSA); and the Jackson, Jackson and Wagner Award for Behavioral Science Research made by the PRSA Foundation. James Grunig directs a $400,000 research project for the International Association of Business Communicators Research Foundation on excellence in public relations and communication management.

Dr Larissa A. Grunig, is now a professor at the College of Communications at the University of Maryland. In 1989 Dr Grunig received the Pathfinder Award for Excellence in Research, sponsored by the Institute of Public Relations Research and Education (USA). She was founding co-editor of the *Journal of Public Relations Research* and has written more than one hundred articles, book chapters, monographs, reviews and conference papers on public relations, activism, science writing, feminist theory, communications theory and research.

Toby MacManus is a senior lecturer at the Department of Communication and Marketing, Bournemouth University. He lectures in public relations and media marketing strategy, and is currently engaged on a doctoral dissertation about international public relations. He has produced many papers and articles on European, cultural and sociological aspects of public relations, and contributed to the teaching of the MA programme in European Public Relations at the Free University of Berlin, and Hogeschool Eindhoven. From 1991–4 he was President of the CERP Education Research Committee.

Danny Moss is Principal Lecturer and Co-Director of the Centre for Corporate and Public Affairs at the Manchester Metropolitan University (MMU). Prior to moving to the MMU in 1992, he held the post of Director of Public Relations Programmes at the University of Stirling for some six years, where he was responsible for the introduction of the UK's first dedicated master's degree in public relations. Danny Moss is the co-founder and organiser of the International Public Relations Research Symposium which is held annually at Lake Bled in Slovenia. He is the author of several books, including *Public Relations in Practice: A Casebook, Global Sources* and *Public Relations Research: An International Perspective* (co-edited with Toby MacManus and Dejan Verèiè) and has written widely on the theme of public relations and management.

Karl Nessmann holds a master's degree and Ph.D. and is an assistant professor at the University of Klagenfurt (Austria) in the Institute of Media and Communication Science. He is responsible for two public relations programmes at the university: public relations studies for media and communication students, and a post-experience public relations course for practitioners. Karl Nessmann's research interests include public relations theory, evaluation, education and film. He has published a number of articles and books in these subject fields.

Elizabeth L. Toth, Ph.D., APR, is Associate Dean of Academic Affairs and full Professor at the S.I. Newhouse School of Public

Communications at Syracuse University. She has co-authored a number of notable books including *Rhetorical and Critical Approaches to Public Relations*, *The Velvet Ghetto* and *Beyond the Velvet Ghetto*. Elizabeth Toth has published over fifty articles, chapters and papers on public relations theory, gender, and public affairs. She is also editor of the *Journal of Public Relations Research*.

Dejan Verčič is partner in Pristop Communications and Assistant Professor for Public Relations and Communication Management at the University of Ljubljana. Among his clients are governments, domestic and international corporations and associations. He holds an M.Sc. in communications science from the University of Ljubljana. He coordinates the European Public Relations Body of Knowledge Project, and since 1992 has organised the annual International Public Relations Research Symposium at Lake Bled. In 1997 he co-edited *Public Relations Research: An International Perspective* (with D. Moss and T. MacManus).

Robert I. Wakefield has twenty years of experience in public relations and has been practising, writing and lecturing on international communications for more than a decade. For six years he directed global public affairs for Nu Skin, a Utah-based multinational firm with annual revenues of $1 billion plus. He has a Ph.D. from the University of Maryland, and has practised or lectured on public relations in twenty-five countries. His work emphasises strategic planning, recruitment and management of global communication resources, PR agency usage, issues management, and qualitative research. He has been actively involved in PRSA, including two years as chair of the international section and judge of PRSA's prestigious Silver Anvil awards.

Gary Warnaby is Senior Lecturer in the School of Management at Salford University. He teaches and researches in the areas of retail strategy, public relations strategy and the marketing of place.

Jon White is a consultant in management, organisational development and public affairs. Previously he worked at Cranfield University School of Management, where he was responsible for the School's teaching and research activities in public relations, public affairs and corporate communications.

Jon White has written extensively on public affairs, public relations and corporate communications, and has published *How to Understand and Manage Public Relations*, *Strategic Communications Management: Making Public Relations Work* (co-authored with Laura

Mazur), and has worked with James Grunig and others on the writing of *Excellence in Public Relations and Communication Management*. He has also written a number of management case studies. Jon White holds a doctorate from the London School of Economics and Political Science, where he has also taught corporate communications. He is an honorary professor in public affairs at the University of Birmingham's School of Business and an associate faculty member at Henley Management College. He contributes to graduate programmes in management at the Cass Business School, City University, and strategic communication management at USI Lugano.

Preface

The past two decades have witnessed a remarkable expansion of interest within Europe in the study of public relations both as an academic discipline and professional practice. While the roots of the public relations profession as we know it today in Europe can arguably be traced to the post-Second World War period, it is perhaps only in the past two decades that public relations has begun to assume significant importance as a recognised business function within Western European countries. Indeed, public relations is still at a comparatively nascent stage in its development within many parts of Europe. A fact which at least partially accounts for the diversity of views about precisely what the practice involves and how it can be managed effectively.

The International Public Relations Symposium was founded as a response to the recognition that no forum existed within Europe to bring together scholars, often working in different disciplinary and cultural traditions, who have over the years begun to explore the emergence of public relations practice across Europe. Here it was recognised that there was a need for some counter-balance to the traditionally dominant American perspective of public relations. Thus one of the underlying aims in establishing the symposium was to explore whether a distinctive European perspective on public relations could be said to have emerged and, if so, how this might differ from that found within the United States in particular. Moreover, it was recognised that in order to enable the study of public relations to expand and gain wider acceptance amongst the academic community within Europe, it was necessary to promote the development of a distinctive European body of knowledge in this field, rather than relying primarily on the work of US scholars. Of course, the founders of the Symposium acknowledged that European thinking about public relations would inevitably be influenced by the body of work that has emerged in the USA over the past two decades in particular. However, they recognised the potential for considerable cross-fertilisation of ideas between US and European researchers which might help enrich the discipline as a whole and strengthen its theoretical base. In this sense, the establishment of an annual Public Relations Symposium at Lake Bled was seen as a valuable step in building what is expected to become a strong and distinctive European body of knowledge in the still evolving field of public relations.

Acknowledgements

The organisers of the Second Bled Symposium wish to thank the following organisations for their generous sponsorship which helped ensure that it was possible to attract a distinguished international group of scholars to the Symposium:

Pristop Communications, Ljubljana, Slovenia

Government of the Republic of Slovenia: Public Relations and Media Office and Ministry of Science and Technology

HIT, Nova Gorcia, Slovenia

Mobitel, Ljubljana, Slovenia

SKB Bank, Ljubljana, Slovenia

Telekom Slovenije, Ljubljana, Slovenia

PR Plus RM, Maribor, Slovenia

Introduction

Public relations research: interdisciplinary perspectives

Danny Moss, Dejan Verčič and Gary Warnaby

One of the prerequisites of any profession that wishes to be taken seriously is the existence of a recognised body of knowledge, and professional standards that bind its members and governs their conduct. While European academics and practitioners have begun to work towards the establishment of a distinctive European body of knowledge in public relations, as was noted in the introduction to the first volume of papers from the International Public Relations Symposium (1994), much of this work has tended to take place in a very fragmented manner and has been the product of quite different research traditions. Thus while the foundations of a distinctive European body of knowledge in public relations have undoubtedly begun to be laid, there is still much work to be done before it will be possible to claim that a substantive and distinct European body of knowledge exists. The fact that the majority of the research into public relations within Europe continues to be based largely on models and theoretical frameworks which have been developed by US scholars, highlights the relatively immature state of the discipline within Europe. Indeed, the reliance on theoretical frameworks developed as a result of research conducted largely within US organisations and within US society, might arguably militate against the development of a genuinely European perspective of public relations practice. While US models might arguably provide an adequate basis for explaining public relations practice within the UK (because of relatively close socio-cultural, linguistic and business ties), there is little reason to assume that such models can necessarily be applied, for example, in southern and central European countries which have their own distinct culture and traditions. However, without further research into how public relations is understood and practised within such countries, it is impossible to reach any firm conclusions about the adequacy of current conceptualisations of public relations in terms of their application across Europe.

Establishing the disciplinary boundaries of public relations, and thus delineating what constitutes the body of knowledge in public relations, has proved a challenging task for scholars not only in Europe but also within the US, where such academic study has a far longer lineage. Indeed, the task of defining a distinctive body of knowledge in public relations has been complicated by the multi-disciplinary roots and boundaries of modern public relations theory and practice. Here, for example, Hazelton and Botan (1989) locate public relations within the domain of the social sciences, seeing it as an applied social science which uses communication to exchange meaning between organisations and their publics. Other public relations scholars (e.g. Grunig and Hunt 1984; Grunig and Grunig 1992) broadly accept that public relations is perhaps best located within the social sciences, but differ in the particular theoretical framework which they see as most useful/appropriate to help explain and understand modern public relations practice. These differences are reflected, to some degree, in the location of public relations teaching and research within different academic institutions. Here, for example, Hazelton and Botan (1989: 13) suggest that the academic roots of modern public relations theory are found in schools and journalism and the empirical and humanistic social sciences concerned with the study of communication. While this may be true of the US experience, in the UK for example, the study of public relations has emerged largely within schools of management and business, which has undoubtedly influenced the emphasis and focus of scholarly work conducted by UK academics in this field.

Indeed, as Hazelton and Botan (1989) emphasise, theories (relating to public relations) only have practical utility insofar as they contribute to solving problems associated with the understanding, teaching or practising of public relations. Hazelton and Botan go on to suggest a number of ways in which theories can be useful to both practitioners and scholars:

- theories can perform a descriptive function, describing the phenomena associated with public relations;
- they can help promote greater understanding of concepts such as what role public relations can or should play;
- theories may also have a predictive role, allowing us to anticipate the future and sometimes intervene to control future outcomes;
- and finally, theories can also have a heuristic role, serving to stimulate debate and further theory building.

A further view of the theoretical foundations of modern public relations practice is offered by Ehling *et al.* (1992) who argue that the theoretical foundations upon which public relations management rests can be traced to at least four conceptual systems: inter-organisational theory; management and decision theory; communications theory and conflict resolution theory. First, inter-organisational theory provides insights into the type of social interrelationships, interactions and interdependencies that may affect groups and sub-clusters of organisations and institutions. Management and decision theory offers a better understanding of the type of management responsibilities and decision-making processes which may affect the operation of the public relations function. Communications theory provides insights into the various elements and processes involved in both one-way and two-way communicative interaction between individuals, groups and organisations. Finally, conflict resolution theory suggests ways of interpreting and dealing with a variety of confrontational situations that may arise under different social settings. Ehling *et al.* go on to suggest that drawing on these theoretical foundations leads to the conclusion that social conflict and social cooperation should constitute the central units of analysis for public relations executives. In short, in their managerial role, public relations executives must understand how to assess the potential impact of disputes and conflicts of interest through analysis of the social settings and inter-organisational networks in which conflict and cooperation are made manifest. Furthermore, they must appreciate where communication in the form of negotiation can be used to help mitigate or mediate potential conflict in order to resolve disputes and arrive at common agreement and cooperation.

Thus, as can be seen from even this brief review of the debates surrounding the disciplinary foundations of modern public relations theory and practice, our understanding of public relations, particularly when viewed from an international perspective, is still continuing to evolve. While current thinking about public relations theory remains dominated by the work of a relatively small number of largely US-based scholars, their work has come under increasing critical review from an emerging body of international scholars, often working from different disciplinary traditions, who are bringing fresh and sometimes challenging insights to bear on existing conceptual frameworks and models of public relations. Thus, as Hazelton and Botan (1989) have recognised, there is a need for a continued concerted and systematic effort to build the body of knowledge in this field. Arguably, the introduction of new and increasingly international perspectives of public relations can only help to broaden and strengthen our understanding of how public relations is practised throughout the world, and thus expand the overall body of knowledge available to both scholars and practitioners alike.

Introduction to the chapters

This second volume of papers from the annual International Public Relations Research Symposium reflects something of the diversity of research traditions amongst scholars working in the field of public relations both within the USA and Europe. Part I of the book contains chapters by Verčič and Grunig (Chapter 1) and Moss and Warnaby (Chapter 2) which both examine public relations from a management perspective, locating public relations as a discipline within the management domain, and exploring where and how public relations can contribute to the strategic management function. Verčič and Grunig examine the origins of public relations theory, exploring the utility of public relations concepts and practice from the perspective of industrial economics and strategic management theories. Here the authors argue that only by locating public relations within these domains is it possible to explain fully the potential contribution which public relations can make to the overall management of organisations. Moss and Warnaby offer a critique of existing theories of public relations management, and consider how such theories relate to current theories of strategic management practice. Here the authors suggest that current conceptualisations of the concept of strategy and the strategic management of public relations within the public relations literature, fail to reflect fully how thinking about strategy within the management field has evolved in recent years.

Part II of the book contains three chapters which complement one another in the sense that they each examine public relations from different contemporary perspectives. Collectively these chapters challenge the reader to reassess their understanding of contemporary public relations theory and practice, and thus they broaden the boundaries of contemporary thinking about public relations. Larissa Grunig (Chapter 3) analyses the public relations literature of the past two decades from the perspective of feminist phase theory and examines the implications for the role of postmodern women in the new millennium. Her chapter provides a challenging analysis of gender bias in contemporary public relations research, and highlights how largely male-dominated scholarship has influenced the social construction of thinking about gender issues. Elizabeth Toth (Chapter 4) examines the development and application of rhetorical theory in public relations.

Here Toth explores the development of rhetorical theory, how rhetoric can be defined from a humanistic, symbolic, critical and dialogical perspective, and how rhetorical theory can be used to understand the types of problems that public relations encounters and the type of response strategies employed by practitioners. Jon White (Chapter 5) suggests that public relations can be seen as a form of applied social psychology, which focuses on relationships between groups and the use of communication as a means of influencing group interaction. The chapter charts the development of social psychology theory, and explores the extent to which developments in this field have infiltrated public relations thinking.

Part III focuses on international perspectives of public relations, and contains two chapters which explore how public relations practice varies in the international context. Toby MacManus (Chapter 6) examines the relationship between the concepts of societal and organisational culture and public relations practice in organisations today. The chapter explores how the concept of culture has been defined, and considers the extent to which culture, both at the societal and organisational level, may influence the way public relations is understood and practised. Robert Wakefield (Chapter 7) reviews the results of an exploratory Delphi study into the characteristics of effective multinational public relations programmes. The study explores the extent to which multinational public relations programmes exhibit generic or specific localised characteristics, and reveals some interesting patterns in terms of the variables that account for multinational programme effectiveness.

Finally, Part IV of the book contains two chapters by German-speaking authors which examine public relations from a historical perspective. In examining public relations from this angle, these chapters reflect the strong historical tradition within Austria and Germany. The value of such studies is that in examining the historical development of public relations within the European context, they may help to explain both how and why the pattern of theoretical and practical development of public relations may differ in Europe compared to the USA. Karl Nessmann (Chapter 8) examines how the concept of public relations has evolved during the nineteenth and twentieth centuries in German-speaking countries. The chapter highlights the problems of transferring the American understanding of the concept of public relations to the German context, and emphasises the fact that Germany and Austria have their own traditions in terms of the practice and conceptual understanding of public relations. Barbara Baerns (Chapter 9) charts the historical development of the relationship between advertising and journalism in the German media, and explores the implications for the role of public relations in this context. The chapter examines the principles underlying the separation of advertising and editorial material in the German media, and considers the implications of the failure of German media owners to implement these principles effectively.

Collectively, these chapters reflect something of the breadth and diversity of research being undertaken within the field of public relations both in Europe and the USA. This diversity of perspectives can be seen to reflect the fact that public relations is still emerging as a distinct academic discipline, particularly within Europe, hence the boundaries of the discipline remain relatively fluid. This second volume of research papers from the International Public Relations Research Symposium represents a further step forward towards the establishment of a European body of knowledge in public relations, and marks a further advancement in understanding the practice of public relations in a European context.

References

Botan, C. H. and Hazelton, Jr, V. (eds) (1989) *Public Relations Theory*, Hillsdale NJ: Lawrence Erlbaum.

Ehling, W. P., White, J. and Grunig, J. E. (1992) 'Public relations and marketing practices', in J. E. Grunig (ed.) *Excellence in Public Relations and Communications Management*, Hillsdale NJ: Lawrence Erlbaum.

Grunig, J. E. and Grunig, L. A. (1992) 'Models of public relations and communication', in J. E. Grunig (ed.) *Excellence in Public Relations and Communications Management*, Hillsdale NJ: Lawrence Erlbaum.

Grunig, J. E. and Hunt, T. (1984) *Managing Public Relations*, New York: Holt, Rhinehart and Winston.

Part I

Public relations and management theory

1 The origins of public relations theory in economics and strategic management

Dejan Verčič and James E. Grunig

Introduction

Most definitions of public relations included in textbooks and professional literature state that public relations is an integral part of management, and that the function of public relations in management is different from other management functions such as marketing or human resources (e.g. Cutlip *et al.* 1994; J. Grunig and Hunt 1984). However, most scholars and practitioners of public relations have failed to make the theoretical connections to theories of economics and management that are necessary to explain the contributions that the management of public relations makes to the overall management of organizations.

Because public relations is part of management, this chapter argues that it is necessary to study public relations within that framework. Only in this way can those characteristics of public relations that developed from the management environment of the discipline be identified, thereby exposing the real value of public relations concepts. This does not mean other academic disciplines do not contribute to our understanding of public relations. Instead, it means that we have to be clear about the phenomenon of public relations and its place in social reality.

We maintain, however, that if public relations practitioners and researchers are to explain and demonstrate the utility of public relations concepts and practices, they have to do it within the home ground of management – in theories of economics and management and in the application of these theories in managerial practice. Even further, as we try to explicate in this chapter, it is precisely via social science theories, such as public relations theory, that economic and managerial theories can gain practical relevance for everyday applications, a relevance that they often miss.

Microeconomics, management and public relations

Mintzberg (1983) traced the origin of management theory to neoclassical microeconomics, a theory based on the assumption of a rational, economic man (women did not exist in classical theory) who maximized some criterion important to him – utility in the case of consumers and profits in the case of entrepreneurs. In the first sentence of the first chapter of his book *Microeconomics and Behavior*, titled "Thinking like an economist," Frank said, "Microeconomics is the study of how people choose under conditions of scarcity" (1994: 3). To make such decisions, he added, people compare the costs and benefits of their choices and, by doing so, maximize their self-interest by making choices that produce the greatest benefits for the least cost.

J. Grunig opened his 1966 monograph 'The role of information in economic decision making', therefore, with a statement on the centrality of decision making to economic theory:

> The process of decision making is a central feature of most economic analyses. Assumptions about the way in which economic actors make basic decisions underlie theories of the firm, consumer demand, welfare economics, market structure, location, and other basic economic theories.
>
> (1966: 1)

It does not take much of an effort to identify a progression from the two central components of neoclassical microeconomic theory, the theory of consumer demand and the theory of the firm, to today's theories of marketing, which assume an exchange relationship,[1] and to theories of management decision making.

Both sets of problems, the behavior of consumers and the behavior of managers, are related to two core theoretical problems in public relations – the behavior of publics and the contribution of public relations to management decision making. Although public relations theory is connected to these two core economic theories that developed into contemporary theories of marketing and management, public relations theory adds another dimension to those theories – the social and political dimensions of management. Our central focus at the beginning of this chapter will be on management theory, but we shall also discuss the relationship of theories of publics and markets to economic theory.

The microeconomic approach to management was a simple one: a rational, economic actor made decisions that would maximize one goal, profitability, of a firm. The assumption of one actor and one goal quickly ran into theoretical difficulty, however (Mintzberg 1983). Firms obviously consist of more than one decision maker, so important questions arose: Who is the actor? and How do multiple actors come together to produce a single decision?[2] Likewise, both economists and sociologists objected to the idea that profit is the only goal of firms. Thus management theory developed from the idea that a single economic decision maker pursued a single goal, to the idea that multiple actors pursue multiple goals or even no goals at at all. (When there are no goals, the organization becomes a complete political arena.)

Mintzberg summarized the transition in this way:

> Management theory, in particular the theory about the goals of the business firm, has done a complete about-face in the last three decades or so, from a reliance on classical economic theory to an increasing attention to newer sociological themes, from the notion of given organizational goals to that of fluid power in and around the organization with no set goals, from an organization devoid of influencers to one in which virtually everyone is an influencer, from the view of the organization as society's instrument to that of it as a political arena.
>
> (1983: 8)

Today, in fact, pure theories of rational behavior in management continue only in operations research – normative management theory that specifies with a great deal of mathematical and statistical detail how, for example, firms can maximize profits, minimize the costs of transportation, or identify the optimum location for plants or distribution centers (J. Grunig 1966). However, as we shall see below, theories of monopoly in the microeconomic theory of market structure have surfaced in reverse in contemporary theories of strategic management.

Even though economic theories of management decision making have been challenged and revised extensively, they still provide the core concepts of management theory. If we can trace the origins or connections of key concepts of public relations theory to economic theory, therefore, we can identify the connection between public relations theory and management theory. And in doing so we can identify the unique contribution that public relations makes to management.

American cultural biases in management and public relations

Before beginning a search for the origins of public relations concepts in economics and management, it is necessary to address a possible American ethnocentrism in our quest for theory, and to discuss the constraints and advantages of an American bias in both bodies of theory. Historically, management has been an American concept; and so has public relations (Sriramesh and White 1992). Both terms, for example, cannot be translated easily into other languages – even into British English. The American aspect of the term 'management' has already been mentioned by Drucker (1993). As Thurley and Wirdenius noted in their book *Towards European Management*, "Until this century there was no special concept of management used in European languages" (1989: 25).

For public relations, the problem is even more obvious and acute. In Slavonic languages, the introductory literature on the subject uses the term in its original form (e.g. for Slovenian usage see Gruban *et al.* 1990; for Serbian usage see Đurić 1992; for Czech usage see Nemec 1993). In Germanic languages the term had been translated, but the original is being used more widely (e.g. Avenarius and Armbrecht 1992). In romance languages, such as French or Italian, it has been possible to translate the term in words close to the original (*relations publiques, pubbliche relazioni*). Nevertheless, the translation has not eliminated problems in explaining the meaning of public relations (e.g. Boiry 1989; Roggero 1993). Dunn (1988) even complained that the British misunderstand the term public relations and even confuse it with advertising. Finally, as we will see later, public relations has an ambiguous and changing meaning even in American English.

If we are to understand public relations in its full potential, we have to think beyond two historical accidents that are misleading. First, Bernays' (1923) claim that public relations counsels are the heirs of publicists from the previous century. Second, the location of the public relations curriculum in US universities and its arrangement primarily within schools and colleges of journalism (see Hess *et al.* 1986).

The American concept of public relations is the only global concept of public relations available currently (see Verčič *et al.* 1995). So, to criticize public relations on the conceptual level, we have to criticize the American conceptualization of public relations. This is not a claim that other conceptualizations are not possible or even emerging. It is a simple but accurate statement that other conceptualizations have not yet been developed to a level that allows disciplined criticism.

Our search for the origins of public relations theory in economics and management, therefore, will be largely a search in the American literature of management and public relations. We begin that search by examining the fundamental questions addressed in economic and management theory.

Industrial economics, strategic management and public relations

There are three fundamental questions defining management and public relations as part of it:

1   Why are there firms?
2   Why are firms different?
3   How are firms possible?

We could ask the same questions for all formal organizations, but the problem is that there are no organizational theories that would allow us to develop the argument with the same precision as we are developing it for firms. For that reason, we propose here to read the argument on two levels: first, literally as about firms, and second, in a parallel manner, as concerning formal organizations in general. In the final instance, the general argument stays the same.

Why are there firms?

For most of its history, economics, or more precisely neoclassical microeconomics, which is supposed to deal with "the application of economic paradigms to the study of the individual, the firm, or the family" (McCormick 1993: 2), under the title of the theory of the firm, has not dealt with the behavior of firms but rather with the behavior of markets (Kay 1994; Rumelt *et al.* 1994b). For this reason it is more correct to call microeconomic theory "price theory" (DeSerpa 1988: 3). For example, in the major textbook of Anglo-American economics, Samuelson and Nordhaus's *Economics* (1985), the word "firm" does not appear in the index.

For traditional (and later neoclassical) economics, as we said in the introduction, a human being is a rational, evaluating and maximizing person: *homo economicus*. He or she can forecast and make the right decisions concerning the maximization of his welfare (McCormick 1993: 116–18). The same concepts of self-interest are also "the fundamental building blocks of the theory of the firm" (McCormick 1993: 299). It is assumed that the firm is a "black box" that behaves as if it were a human individual, rational in its maximization of profit (McCormick 1993: 299).

The second assumption of neoclassical microeconomics is that firms in the market are governed by "the invisible hand," which brings supply and demand into an equilibrium that determines prices (McCormick 1993). If the supply of an article is greater than demand, prices signal to firms to produce more or that other firms should enter production. If supply is below demand, prices signal to companies to produce less or to stop the production of that particular article. The market, therefore, allocates resources optimally – both for society and for its individual members (including companies).

In the nineteenth century, first in railways and then in other industries in the United States, the number of companies started to decline as a result of mergers. New big economic entities emerged, corporations, and control over them moved into the hands of newly emerging experts for efficiency – "organizational engineers" – managers. The trend of corporatization of the North American economy even strengthened in the twentieth century. In 1932, Adolf A. Berle and Gardimer C. Means published their famous study *The Modern Corporation and Private Property*, in which they pointed to the seriousness of problems of concentration of economic power in corporations, and of separation of ownership and management. In 1937, Ronald Coase published an article in the review *Economica* in which he posed the fundamental question: Why are there firms?

The size of corporations and control by managers became the basic problems of new industrial organization economics. "The original objective of industrial organization economics was the identification of the structural attributes of industries that either facilitated or prevented the development of perfect markets" (Barney 1994: 66).

In the 1970s, the two questions of traditional industrial organization economics were again under the spotlight in the United States. The reason was new competition from Asia and, to a lesser extent, from Europe. The new institutional economics emerged with two major streams, transaction cost and action. Transaction cost theory focused on the question of the limits (of size) of companies, and action theory on the question of control (Doz and Prahalad 1994).

Here, we are interested in transaction theory as developed primarily by Williamson. Following Coase, Williamson saw markets and firms (hierarchies) as alternative methods of economic governance. People are self-interested and inclined to strategic behavior, to "opportunism" as Williamson said following Knight, and to "bounded rationality," as he said following Simon (Williamson 1992). These two factors interact, and because of them "transaction costs" emerge, which make some transactions more costly in some institutional contexts (e.g. in markets) than in other institutional contexts (e.g. in hierarchies). These costs are the result of the search for information, control and the like. Williamson (1992) proposed that firms should be analysed in their production function as one of the alternative forms of governance, and not as instruments for maximization of profit as assumed by neoclassical microeconomics. The firm is "first and foremost an effi-ciency instrument" (Williamson 1992: 95), "the product of a series of organizational innovations that have had the purpose and effect of economizing on transaction costs" (1992: 75).

Therefore Williamson (1994) explained the reorganization of the railway business (and the emergence of the corporation) as a conse-quence of the inability of old organizational structures to coordinate the complexity of traffic, which explained why railroads adopted a military hierarchy. In the same way, he explained the development of modern corporations, starting with DuPont in 1921, from centralized, functionally organized (such as production, finance and legal affairs) unitary companies (U-form) into partially decentralized companies with headquarters and (partially) autonomous units (M-form: multi-regional, multibusiness or multinational). Williamson based his explanations on Chandler's (1962) research, and to Chandler's dictum, "structure follows strategy," he (1994) added his own: "economy is the best strategy."

Rumelt *et al.* summarized the value of the transaction theory in these words: "Today, we know that advising managers to run a firm as if it were a set of markets, is ill-founded. Firms replace markets when *nonmarket* means of coordination and commitment are superior" (1994b: 548).

The transaction cost theory has some shortcomings. Hammond (1994) commented that it is not clear which transaction costs are the most critical for a firm to minimize. Doz and Prahalad (1994) added that it is impossible to explain the relationship between Japanese companies and their suppliers, which is "a relationship built on mutual trust." This is because the basic terms of transaction theory, self-interest and opportunism, are culturally bounded and rooted in the economic and legal tradition of the US.

Nevertheless, transaction theory is of key importance, for it enables us to observe all forms of economy (from a perfectly decentralized, competitive market, to a militarily organized, hierarchical firm) on the same continuum of more or less costly modes of exchange (Robins 1987). It tells us that every form of exchange has its costs. Thus, for example, the question of organization of the flow of information in a company is no longer a question of how to bring perfect information to the top of the company, but "becomes a question of choosing among different kinds of biases" (Hammond 1994: 112).

Why are firms different?

The microeconomic theory of the firm, which in the nineteenth century gave the concept of maximization of profit at the level of firms, and equilibrium of prices in the perfect competition at the level of society, does not need firms, decision making and management (Ansoff 1987; Rumelt *et al.* 1994a). Markets using prices behave as automatic signalization systems which alone allocate resources for the benefit of society (Kay 1994). Using the medium of (maximization of) profit, firms direct resources where returns are higher, and through time profits should fall to zero. That is not so. In 1967, Dun and Bradstreet published data indicating that the five-year survival rate of newly established firms is 33 per cent (Kahneman and Lovallo 1994). Sidney Winter estimates that the size ratio between the smallest and the biggest US companies is 1:100,000, and that this and other indexes of difference are increasing (Williams 1994).

Rumelt has calculated that the variance in return on capital among businesses in the FTC Line of Business is 0.8 per cent due to corporate effects, 8.3 per cent due to stable industry effects, and 46 per cent due to stable business-unit effects; the differences between business units in the same industry are eight times higher than those between industries (Rumelt *et al.* 1994a).

In the past twenty years, economic analysis included terms such as "uncertainty," "information asymmetry," "bounded rationality," "opportunism" and "asset specificity" (Rumelt *et al.* 1994a: 26). But because the question, Why are firms different? put into question some of the basic principles of neoclassical economics, Rumelt *et al.* (1994a), consciously following Coase, identified it as the fundamental question of the study of management and, in particular, of its strategy.

How are firms possible?

The third question is, in a certain way, already present in the assumptions of the preceding questions: "Why are there firms?" and "Why are firms different?", which, without presupposing that firms are possible, would not even be possible to be raised; and in that sense it looks almost absurd. But despite, or rather because of this, it has to be raised.

McCormick says: "The firm is a legal fiction. In the strictest sense of reality, no such thing exists except in our minds" (1993: 298). But Wallace (1982) warns that some are not even legal fictions! Multinationals are not firms, neither as limited liability companies, nor as corporations, rather as groups or networks of entities which have been established under different national legal regimes and have different nationalities and legal forms.

But firms which are legal fictions, or not even that, have become the cornerstones of social order in the twentieth century. At least from the second half of the twentieth century, different authors agree on this, both from left and right, modernists and postmodernists, "realists" and "futurists" (e.g. Chomsky 1989; Schiller 1989; Gandy 1992; Drucker 1993; Emmott 1993; Kennedy 1993; Linstead 1993; Maynard and Mehrtens 1993).

Vernon (1968) reminds us that entrepreneurs have had "the right" to establish companies without scope or size limitations only from the end of the nineteenth century; and only from the beginning of the twentieth century have the majority of legislations allowed companies to be owners of other companies.

Berle and Means (1968 [1932]) say that the corporation came into the US legal system from the British tradition where a corporation in the eighteenth century was treated as a "franchise" (in Norman French "privilege"); the existence of a corporation was conditioned upon a grant from the state. The grant established the corporation and gave it its legal person independent of associates: the right to operate under its own name, to sue or be sued, and to persist independently of changing associates – and this was also the origin of their limited liability. The grant had been given first by the British crown and, in America after the Revolution, from states as its successors. It was only in 1837 that Connecticut, as the first state, approved a general law that established the right of incorporation.

In the first hundred years, from 1837 when Connecticut adopted the law, to the recession of the 1930s, the legitimacy of private enterprise was beyond any serious doubt: at the time of industrialization and the birth of the modern company, which began in the 1820s with the building of the railway system, thus so economically unifying the US (Ansoff 1987), in the spotlight was the entrepreneur who brought together newly emerging technologies with an emerging social need. The linking body was a new social entity – the firm (*ibid.*). That it served both the individual owner and society was obvious and self-evident. To be against entrepreneurship was to be against progress. In the time of the emergence of public relations in the 1920s, its purpose was exactly to remove the "social barriers" in the way of progress, which were there in the form of uneducated masses. In 1928, the founding father of the new profession, Edward L. Bernays, in the very first "scientific article" on the subject, which was published in *The American Journal of Sociology* under the title "Manipulating public opinion: the why and the how," wrote: "Public opinion is slow and reactionary, and does not easily accept new ideas" (1928a: 959).

Hannan and Freeman (1989) explain the existence of firms as a consequence of two core competencies: reliability and accountability. The first relates to the capacity of firms to make products of equal quality repeatedly. The second relates – to put it simply – to the capacity to make more from less and to be able to document it: "The modern world favors collective actors that can demonstrate or at least reasonably claim a capacity for reliable performance and can account rationally for their actions" (*ibid.*: 74). Organizational structures make their operations reliable with continuous reproductions of their own structures which must be nearly the same today as they were yesterday. They can achieve this with institutionalization and with the creation of highly standardized routines. It is reliability which is also the source of danger in the form of inertia. And for the creation of inertia two things are necessary: legitimacy of existence and living space (niche).

Reliability as defined by Hannan and Freeman corresponds strongly with the more fundamental concept of trust. Erikson (1963) under-lined the importance of trust for the feeling of ontological security of a child. Garfinkel (1963) experimentally demonstrated the psychological consequences of implicit and not even articulated aspects of social norms, negation of common sense and everyday routines. In sociology, Giddens' (1986) structuration theory argues that trust is one of the basic notions incorporated in the central concept of routines. These have a central place also in an ecological economy (Hannan and Freeman 1989: 81–116), evolutionary economy (Nelson 1994) and management, where they form one of the major sources of competitive advantages of firms (Porter 1994).

Trust is in an interpersonal world based on familiarity and is there-fore limited (Luhmann 1979). In the organizational world, where the breach of trust can usually be observed only after the fact (as for example in politics or management), the preservation of trust becomes of the utmost importance. Trust is therefore partially object-mediated (as for example in money). In general, the person whose trust has been abused can punish the offender with his future acts. Trust is possible only because of the ability of a human being to have free will. Those who stand behind their public presentations are worthy of trust.

Therefore, the general moral is: give trust when there is no need for it (Luhmann 1979).

Following Hannan and Freeman, we can say that the inability to ¬etain trust equals the loss of one of two major capacities that make ĩrms possible. Therefore we can say that companies are possible because they are trustworthy, and if they are not, they become improbable (this does not necessarily mean that they immediately die; it is a possible hypothesis that the loss of this basic capacity first raises transaction costs, which, in the final consequence, undermines also the other basic capacity – efficiency).

Summary

This discussion of the fundamental questions in economics and management began with the question, Why are there firms? This is the fundamental question of the institutional economics. The question, Why are firms different? is the fundamental question of strategy. The question, How are firms possible? emerges finally as the fundamental question of public relations. This last question also adds a social dimension to management theories that essentially developed from economic theories. Before developing the answer to the final question more deeply, we explain in the next section how two of J. Grunig's middle-level theories of public relations also originated from theories of economics and management.

Microeconomics, publics and models of public relations

In the 1960s in the United States, very little research had been done on public relations, and practically no theory had been developed (J. Grunig 1992a). At the time, most research consisted of biographies of leading practitioners, case studies of public relations practice, and highly applied studies on questions such as the factors leading to the acceptance of news releases, or the proportion of content in the news media that came from public relations sources. However, public relations educators considered much of communication research to be relevant to public relations, although they did little of this research themselves. Communication research relevant to public relations at the time was on the effects of the mass media, public opinion, attitudes and persuasion, effects of information campaigns and – to a lesser extent – interpersonal and organizational communication.

Most communication scholars at the time had their intellectual roots in the social and political sciences – sociology, social psychology and political science. Economic theory essentially was unknown to communication scholars. Within this context, then, J. Grunig (1966) wrote a monograph that traced the role of information in economic theories of decision making. His purpose was, first, to show economists why information is a limiting variable in economic decisions but, more importantly, to "show communication specialists the types of information needed by decision makers so that more effective communications strategies may be planned" (1966: 1).

In essence, he suggested that for the mass media or other sources of messages to have an effect, they must be relevant to the decision situations of the recipients of messages:

> A theoretical role for information in decision making would be an addition to both economic and communication theory. The understanding gained would also have considerable heuristic value for students of communications. For example, communicators working in information services, public relations and advertising provide information for decision makers, although in the latter two cases the information is not intended to be as objective as in the former. Information services such as the information divisions in government or the Cooperative Extension Service in colleges of agriculture exist primarily to provide relevant technical information.
>
> Public relations practitioners provide information to executives about the effects of their decisions on the public and provide stockholders, employees and others what they hope is relevant information of the kind needed to make decisions about the company. Advertising workers provide consumers information needed to make decisions about purchases of the advertised products. Instrumental economic information is also provided by more strictly journalistic information sources, such as trade publications, and by the general news media.
>
> (J. Grunig 1966: 1–2)

Although he did not know it at the time, this monograph was the forerunner to the situational theory of publics (J. Grunig 1997) and the models of public relations (Grunig and Grunig 1989; 1992) that are major components of the model of excellence in public relations developed by the IABC research team (J. Grunig 1992b). Both theories, therefore, have roots in microeconomic theory, although other social and behavioral science theories have contributed to their full development.

J. Grunig (1966) began the monograph by reviewing the way in which economic man was assumed to make decisions in the theory of consumer behavior and the theory of the firm. Classical microeconomic theory treated information as a given, not as a variable, by assuming that consumers and entrepreneurs possessed perfect knowledge. Given perfect knowledge, consumers made choices that maximized their satisfaction (utility) in the case of consumers, or their profits in the case of entrepreneurs.

Beginning with Knight, economists began to ask what would happen to microeconomic theory if the assumption of perfect knowledge were relaxed. Perfect competition required perfect knowledge, Knight said: "perfect, continuous costless intercommunication between all individual members of the society" (1921: 78). Because perfect communication does not exist, Knight concluded, most economic decisions are made under conditions of risk and uncertainty. Relaxing the assumption of perfect knowledge led to such economic concepts as Simon's (1948) bounded rationality. Bounded rationality means that economic decision makers are unable to maximize their pleasure or profit but that instead they satisfice – make the best decision they can with the information they have.

In addition to assuming that limited information and knowledge limits the rationality of decision making, other economists developed rational theories of when it would be in the self-interest of economic man to search for additional information. Most of these economic theories of the search for information were normative theories, many of which now have been incorporated into operations research. The premise of the normative theory is simple: decision makers should search for information as long as the cost of the search does not exceed the increase in value of the pleasure or profit produced by the search (J. Grunig 1966). In addition, however, many economists have used such theories of rational behavior as positive, descriptive theories of *why* people search for information, even though they acknowledge that few people actually think in this rational way. (In his contemporary textbook, similarly, Frank (1994) devoted a chapter to the economics of information.)

In this descriptive sense, then, J. Grunig treated the search for information as a dependent variable and looked for theories in economics, psychology and sociology to conceptualize two kinds of decision situations – what Katona (1951; 1953) had called genuine decisions and habitual decisions. Most economic decisions, J. Grunig said, "are made on the basis of habit, genuinely rational decisions are made in new situations where the decision maker has little previous decision experience and in important, 'crossroads' decisions" (1966: 41). To explain why people react to some decision situations habitually and to others rationally, J. Grunig used Dewey's (1938) concept of problem recognition. When they recognize a situation as problematic, they engage in genuine decision behavior; when they do not, they engage in habitual behavior.

In habitual situations, J. Grunig concluded, people need less information than in genuine decision situations. Thus they are more likely to communicate in the search for information in a genuine decision situation. If outside sources such as public relations practitioners provide information free of charge, their activities reduce a genuine decision maker's cost of search for information, as long as the information is relevant. Thus decision makers are most likely to seek out or use information from public relations sources when it is relevant to them – the essential assumption of J. Grunig's contemporary situational theory of publics.

From economic decisions to a theory of publics

J. Grunig (1968) developed this economic theory of information seeking in his dissertation study of large landowners in Colombia, and in a subsequent study of peasant farmers in Colombia (J. Grunig 1969a; 1969b; 1969c; 1971). This research in Colombia suggested the second variable of the situational theory, constraint recognition – a variable that also has part of its roots in the normative economic method of linear programming (J. Grunig 1966; J. Grunig and Repper 1992) – to explain communication behavior in situations in which people have few, if any, alternatives from which to choose. Later, J. Grunig (1976a) added Krugman's (1965) concept of level of involvement to explain why people actively search for information in genuine decision situations, but passively attend to information in non-decision situations.

The full theory, then, was presented in J. Grunig and Disbrow (1977) and in J. Grunig and Hunt (1984). The latter authors integrated the earlier theory of economic decision making and the search for information with Dewey's theory of publics to produce a full theory of the behavior of publics and their importance in public relations theory.

The situational theory of publics shares two variables, problem recognition and level of involvement, with many theories of consumer behavior in marketing (see Assael 1987). The reason, no doubt, is because both theories had a common root in the microeconomic theory of consumer behavior. However, J. Grunig and Repper[3] distinguished between publics and markets, an essential difference in their view:

> Organizations can choose their markets, but publics arise on their own and choose the organization for attention. [Market] segments that fit the company's capabilities are chosen for penetration. Those segments that do not suit the company's capabilities are left for others to serve. Publics, in contrast, organize around issues and seek out organizations that create those issues – to gain information, seek redress of grievances, pressure the organizations, or ask governments to regulate them.
>
> (1992: 126)

Another way of looking at the difference is that individual decision makers become members of markets because of economic circumstances – the demand for goods and services – whereas decision makers become members of publics because of the social and political *externalities* that are byproducts of the economic behavior of firms. We will explore the concept of externalities in more detail, then, in the next section as we discuss the social and political contributions that public relations theory supplies to management theory. The motivation for communication behavior by members both of publics and markets, however, is similar – essentially the three independent variables of the situational theory.

From individuals to organizations and models of public relations

We saw earlier in this chapter that Mintzberg (1983) described the move from microeconomic theory to organization theory in management as a move from one actor with a single goal to multiple actors with many goals or no goals. J. Grunig made a similar theoretical move in the 1970s when he expanded the theory of economic decision making and communication behavior from the individual level of members of publics to the level of the organization, in an attempt to explain the communication behavior – especially the public relations behavior – of different types of organizations.

In J. Grunig (1976b), he reasoned that organizations would engage in genuine and habitual decisions in much the same way as members of publics. He found analogs for these concepts in theories of open and closed systems and in mechanical and organic structures of organizations. He then reasoned that problem-solving organizations (open-system, organic) would engage in what Thayer (1968) had called diachronic communication, and that habitual, fatalistic organizations (closed-system, mechanical) would engage in Thayer's synchronic communication.

The J. Grunig (1976b) study provided preliminary support for the new organizational theory and, in turn, led to a lengthy program of research on the public relations behavior of organizations and on the structural, environmental, cultural and power-control explanations for differences in this communication behavior (Grunig and Grunig 1989; 1992). J. Grunig replaced Thayer's concepts of diachronic and synchronic communication with his concepts of symmetrical and asymmetrical communication, and then with his four models of public relations – press agentry, public information, two-way asymmetrical, and two-way symmetrical.

The two-way symmetrical and two-way asymmetrical models have become a critical component of the general theory of excellent public relations developed by the IABC research team (J. Grunig 1992b). The picture of the development of public relations theory is not complete, however, until we place the middle-range theories of publics and models of public relations into the broader picture of management theory and of strategic management in particular.

American conceptualization of management

The word "organization" comes from the Ancient Greek "organon" which means a tool or instrument. The firm as a tool is one of the possible modes of performance of economic activities. It exists if it is reliable and efficient.

Efficiency

Organizations are established with a certain purpose. The purpose of a hospital is to cure, of a school to educate, and of a firm to produce something that somebody else is prepared to pay for. No formal organization can justify its existence if it does not perform its primary purpose (Drucker 1993). For firms it is easy to control performance because they are the only form of organization with an inbuilt mechanism to measure performance at least negatively: with profit. The profit has a function of (negative) feedback: there is a need for minimum necessary profit which enables the firm to stay in business. The first task of management is to care for the performance of basic purpose. The second task of management is to care for efficiency, which is revealed in the productive use of resources (Drucker 1993).

Productivity is a concept borrowed from engineering principles and is a ratio between inputs and outputs (McCormick 1993).

The first to successfully use engineering principles for planning a mechanical (social) organization was Frederick the Great of Prussia, who ruled from 1740 to 1786. He inherited an army of mainly criminals, paupers, mercenaries and unwilling conscripts. He borrowed some ideas from the ancient Roman legions and some from the European armies of the sixteenth century, and was inspired by the mechanistic philosophers of his time. He introduced ranks and uniforms, strict regulations, specialization of tasks and equipment, a command language and systematic training. He separated advisory and command functions. His (human) machine worked on orders. His men were more afraid of their officers than of their enemies (Morgan 1986).

Following the same principles, the classical theorists of management (Henri Fayol, F. W. Mooney and Lyndall Urvick) created management as "a process of planning, organization, command, coordination, and control" (Morgan 1986: 25).

Until Taylor published *The Principles of Scientific Management* in 1911, the term "scientific management" was generally attributed to a reform attorney, Louis Brandeis from Massachusetts, who, in court in 1910, leveled against the railroad interests with the idea that travelers would pay lower costs of transportation if the railroads were managed according to new principles of efficiency (Banta 1993).

But Taylor had been using the phrase "scientific management" at least since 1903, and in 1909, in a lecture at the new Harvard Business School, he explained what it was all about very simply:

First: Holding a plum for them to climb after.

Second: Cracking the whip over them, with an occasional touch of the lash.

Third: Working shoulder to shoulder with them, pushing in the same direction, and all the while teaching, guiding, and helping them.

(quoted in Banta 1993: 3)

If such an approach would seem outmoded to some people, the following sentence in McCormick's *Managerial Economics* shows how common this view is: "In general, there are two basic approaches to combating the incentive problem: the stick and the carrot" (1993: 564).

Taylor's major contribution is that he has demonstrated it is possible to improve "natural" practices with careful observation and analysis (Rumelt *et al.* 1994a). The effect of the use of Taylor's scientific management has been an enormous increase in labor productivity.

Using roughly the same principles as those with which Taylor founded the "scientific management" of workers, Edward L. Bernays founded public relations as the scientific management of relations between firms and their environments – as crystalizing, manipulation and finally as engineering of public opinion (Bernays 1923; 1928a; 1928b; 1955a; 1955b). Yet in 1976, he labeled a public relations specialist "a social technician" (Bernays 1976: 25). The ideal of the profession is efficiency: "to eliminate the waste and the friction that result when industry does things or makes things which its public does not want, or when the public does not understand what is being offered it" (Bernays 1928b: 44). Even today much conceptualizing of public relations is done within that framework, as in a book on the use of management of objectives in public relations (Nager and Allen 1984).

Effectiveness

By the mid-1950s, it became obvious that aggressive competition could not stop the slowing down of growth in some industries, and even the decline of others; industrial leadership was moving from "first generation" industries to technology and rich newborns (pharmaceuticals, computers, etc.); and the one-way race for profit produced unwanted side effects.

> Neglect by the firm of the environment and of changing social values became progressively unacceptable to society. Anti-trust legislation, safety legislation, consumer pressures, pollution constraints, price and wage controls – all increasingly showed that the firm was losing both its immunity from outside influence and its privileged position as the principal instrument of social progress.
>
> (Ansoff *et al.* 1976: 43)

It came to a "strategic problem" (Ansoff and Hayes 1976: 1), not befitting the firm and the environment. "Strategic planning" emerged as a first solution, which related only to the production process and its immediate environment: "The social and political dynamics both within and outside the organizations are assumed to be irrelevant and unaffected" (Ansoff and Hayes 1976: 1).

That proved to be insufficient. Now "strategic management" emerged, which is "pertaining to the relation between the firm and its environment" (Ansoff 1987: 24n). Its major decisions are about the "selection of the products-mix which the firm will produce and the narkets to which it will sell" (*ibid.*: 24).

It was recognized that the firm

> relates to its environment in two distinctive ways. (1) Through *competitive* (or operating) behaviour in which it seeks to make profitable the goods/rewards exchange with the environment. It does this by attempting to produce as efficiently as possible and to secure the highest possible price and market share. (2) Through *entrepreneurial* (or *strategic*) behaviour in which it replaces obsolete products/markets with new ones which offer higher potential for future profits.
>
> (Ansoff *et al.* 1976: 42)

Yoshihara (1976) names these two modes "(1) exploitative adaptation and (2) strategic adaptation."

In contrast to the mechanical view on organizations, the organic view developed (Morgan 1986). This second direction was popularized by Peters and Waterman (1982) with their book *In Search of Excellence*. Other views followed. Morgan (1986) gives an overview using eight metaphors through which one can examine organizations: machines, organisms, brains, cultures, political systems, psychic prisons, flux and transformation, and instruments of domination.

Success of the firm is therefore dependent on entrepreneurship, rationalization and matching the organization to its environment. Therefore it is not surprising that the past president of the British multinational ICI, Sir John Harvey-Jones, said that the two major activities with which the president of a corporation should occupy himself are strategic planning and public relations (*The Economist*, 1989).

CSR0, CSR1, CSR2, CSR3, CSR4

Drucker argues that the essence of management defines responsibility not only for effectiveness and efficiency, but also as "social responsibility." The "enterprise is an organ of society and community" and management is "a social function" (1993).

It is interesting that Chandler, describing the DuPont corporation in 1921, said that executives, besides their "entrepreneurial or value-creating" and "administrative or loss preventive" role, "carried out an additional and most essential function, that of handling the enterprise's relations with legislatures and other governmental bodies concerning taxes, tariffs, and regulation" (1994: 327n). However, this role was only discussed in a footnote.

According to Chandler, until the 1970s most corporations had not two but three levels of autonomous planning and administration: business unit, division and the corporate HQ or office, and some even had five: profit center, business unit, division, group, and the corporate office. The increasing governmental regulation forced the corporate office to "sharply increase its role as mediator with government agencies and other public bodies"; Donaldson and Lorsch discovered that "of corporate office executives of 12 large American manufacturing companies, several CEOs said that they spend 30–40 per cent of their time in dealing with such matters" (Chandler 1994: 329). Other research in the UK showed that there are differences between different corporate offices. "Only in public, including government, relations were the numbers much the same" (1994: 331). "Like those of the US conglomerates these offices include a few general line officers and almost no functional staff executives except in finance and public relations" (1994: 336). Rayfield and Pincus (1992) say Drucker once estimated that managers spend up to 75 per cent of their time in public-relations-related activities.

From the beginning of the 1900s to the 1930s the concept of "public responsibility" of enterprises was developed: corporations are responsible not only for profits of their owners but also for the improvement of society (Frederick 1994b). The problem first emerged during the time of companies merging into bigger corporations nearly a century before. Managers of railway companies had to persuade the public that these mergers were in "the public interest" (Olasky 1987). The success of the first public relations campaigns is supposed to have given impetus for the development of public relations in the US (Olasky 1987). The term "public relations" was first used in its more or less contemporary meaning by Edward Bernays when he and his wife, Doris Fleischman, had to put a sign on the door of their office (Bernays 1965). Bernays, as the first to use the words public relations in similar contexts, mentions the works of Dorman B. Eaton (*The Public Relations and Duties of the Legal Profession*, 1882) and Hough Smith (*The Theory and Regulation of Public Sentiment*, 1842). "Public relations" deliberately evokes "public interest" and "public responsibility."

In a paper he wrote in 1978, and which was first published in that year, Frederick (1994b) named this concept CSR1 – corporate social responsibility. The idea is enlightening, normative and unclear. Critics claim that it is undesirable, unworkable, unlikely and impossible. And above all, it is related to the general public, which is a contradiction in terms (J. Grunig and Repper 1992).

Dilenschneider and Forrestal (1987) say that public relations gained nomentum in the 1940s and 1950s due to: increasing government regulation of economic life and some parts of private life that were previously considered to be private matters (e.g. programs for the poor and aged), increasing power of trade unions, a higher educational level of population that led to social movements (e.g. civil rights, environmentalism, consumerism) and an increasing awareness felt by all kinds of organizations that they depend on the support of their publics (similarly: Hoewig 1991). In 1954, the Effective Citizens Organization (now the Public Affairs Council) was created. The purpose of this organization was to educate and train executives to be active and efficient in politics. At the same time Ford, General Electric, and Johnson and Johnson established their own "political education" for their managers. In the first decade of the Effective Citizens Organization, approximately half a million managers went through its educational programs (Hoewig 1991: 64).

In the 1970s, a new approach to the question of the public responsibility of companies began to develop, one that was more managerial in its basic ideas and gave more emphasis to the concrete management of company relationships with society (Frederick 1994b) – corporate social responsiveness: CSR2. But, as CSR1 before it, CSR2 does not explain the substance of "social improvement." However, there is an important difference between the two concepts: while CSR1 still questions *whether* companies have any responsibilities, except those to owners, CSR2 works on the assumption that this question has been answered positively and works on the *how* (Frederick 1994b: 156).

CSR2 developed in the "Environmental Decade" (Blackman 1992: 2–30) in the US and is better known in the management theory (Ansoff 1987) and in the theory of public relations as "issues management" – furthermore the author of the term was a public relations consultant, Howard Chase (Grunig and Repper 1992). Grunig and Repper (1992) also say that public relations and issue management are the same thing (there are others that agree: e.g. Cutlip *et al.* 1985; Cheney and Vibbert 1987). Wittenberg and Lesly (1991) use the data according to which US companies are regulated by 116 governmental agencies and programs. In 1989, 500 corporations and 3,000 trade associations had their own government relations offices in Washington. Hoewig (1991) estimates that approximately 1,000–1,200 American companies have public affairs departments. The first chapter to the fifth edition of the casebook *The Corporate Social Challenge: Cases and Commentaries* (Stacey and Sturdivant 1994) is: "Managing social responsiveness." In 1992, the Public Relations Society of America adopted the "Official Statement on Public Relations" which underlined that the major purpose of public relations is problem solving (Cutlip *et al.* 1985). Ehling (1984; 1985) developed a theory of public relations as conflict management.

This transition from CSR1 to CSR2 also corresponds to the time of the clarification of the expression "public relations" which finally appeared to be ambiguous in original American English, too. So Jefkins (1977: 3) says: "Public relations is a constantly misunderstood expression. A simple explanation is offered by reversing the words to say 'relations with the public.'" Cole (1981: 4) says: "It is not 'public relations,' but 'publics relations.'" White (1991: ix): "Public relations is, quite literally, about the relationship between organization and various 'publics.'" George Cheney and George N. Dionispoulos (1989) entitled their article: "Public relations? No, relations with publics." And eventually, so did Bernays (1986: 35): "Public relations means exactly what it says, relations of an organization, individual, idea, whatever, with the publics on which it depends for its existence." Dozier and Grunig (1992) say that the identification of publics is the *strategic* decisions of a public relations manager.

But if we accept these notions of public relations we also have to accept Mackey's (1991: 157) proposal that every organization has at least "passive public relations" – *de facto* relations with its environment, no matter whether they are managed or not. The views of Jefkins are similar: "Every organization has PR whether it likes it or not" (1977: 3). This can be called unconscious relations with publics, which are not only important, but maybe even more important than planned public relations, "corporate social range," CSR0.

In the 1980s, Frederick (Wood and Jones 1994) added values and ethics to responsiveness and proposed a notion of "corporate social rectitude," CSR3. This would correspond to the concept of the "two-way symmetrical public relations" concept in public relations theory (J. Grunig 1989; 1992b; 1992c: 10; Grunig and White 1992).

In the afterword to the publication of his original 1978 text, Frederick (1994a) expressed his conviction that CSR3 would develop into CSR4, which he denotes without a name. Marx (1990), using different names, similarly identified phases of public relations development from reactive, proactive and interactive to the fourth phase: strategic. Verčič (1997) declared a need for fourth wave public relations. Arguably, CSR4 should be considered as "corporate social reason." Public relations not only has to efficiently and correctly manage relations of a company with its environment; it should include companies into the full creation of the same. As far as major social problems are concerned, corporations are practically alone with their necessary capabilities, in particular with know-how (Maynard and Mehrtens 1993).

In the first book on public relations, Bernays (1923) had written that public relations counsels succeeded press (or even worse: circus) agents and publicists. Following him, others accepted the three-phase development of public relations (e.g. Canfield 1968). In 1984, Grunig on that ground developed four models of public relations: first, the press agentry model, which had developed in the second half of the nineteenth century. This was followed by the public information model, starting at the beginning of the twentieth century and remaining popular into the 1920s when a two-way asymmetrical model emerged. In the 1960s and 1970s, a new, two-way symmetrical model developed (Grunig and Hunt 1984). The press agentry model is essentially a propagandistic model; the public information model disseminates truthful information, although not all of it; the two-way asymmetrical model is a scientific persuasion model based on the concept of engineering; and the two-way symmetrical model uses negotiation and strategic conflict resolution methods (Grunig 1989).

Later Grunig and Grunig (1992) replaced the four models with two continua. The first is a craft public relations continuum and has dimensions from propaganda to journalism. The second is a professional public relations continuum and has dimensions from the two-way asymmetrical model to the two-way symmetrical model.

If we translate the models into Frederick's denotation, then the press agentry and public information models become CSR1, the two-way asymmetrical model CSR2, and the two-way symmetrical model CSR3.

Summary

Efficiency, from Williamson's economic perspective, is an essential, but insufficient condition for successful management. The same applies to public relations, which emerged as an ambiguous concept of corporate social responsibility and became rational within a concept of social corporate responsiveness. Public relations will become successful when it passes through corporate social rectitude into corporate social reason.

Operationalizing strategy

As an academic field, strategic management is as young as public relations. Both disciplines have much in common, but until recently both have been oblivious to the other. Bowman (1990) said that business schools offered a capstone course in business policies in their MBA programs prior to the 1960s, courses in which students were expected to tie together the courses they had taken in different functional areas of management. In the 1960s, however, three books became available that helped strategic management to emerge as a field that was more than a composite of other management functions (Bowman 1990; Rumelt *et al.* 1994). These books were Chandler's (1962) historical study of how the strategic ideas of executives changed the direction of four major corporations, Ansoff's (1965) more normative book on the concept of strategy and the process of strategy formulation, and the Harvard textbook on business policy, *Business Policy: Text and Cases* (Learned *et al.* 1965).

Half of the Harvard book consisted of cases; but the other half, which was written largely by Kenneth Andrews, was devoted to discussing the formulation and implementation of strategy (Bowman 1990). According to Rumelt *et al.* (1994: 17), Andrews introduced "the notion of an uncertain environment to which management and the firm had to adapt":

> In Andrews's view, the environment, through constant change, gave rise to opportunities and threats, and the organization's strengths and weaknesses were adapted to avoid the threats and take advantage of the opportunities. An internal appraisal of strengths and weaknesses led to identification of distinctive competencies; an external appraisal of environmental threats and opportunities led to identification of potential success factors.
>
> (1994: 413)

Since Andrews introduced the concept of environment to strategy, the literature has been permeated by two words, "mission" and "environment." Together, they suggest that organizations must make long-term, strategic choices that are feasible in their environments. Higgins (1979: 1), for example, defined strategic management as "the process of managing the pursuit of the accomplishment of organizational mission coincident with managing the relationship of the organization to its environment." Greene *et al.* (1985: 536) similarly defined it as "a process of thinking through the current mission of the organization, thinking through the current environmental conditions, and then combining these elements by setting forth a guide for tomorrow's decisions and results."

According to Steiner *et al.* (1982: 6) "strategic management" can be distinguished from "operational management" by "the growing significance of environmental impacts on organizations and the need for top managers to react appropriately to them." Managers who manage strategically do so by balancing the mission of the organization – what it is, what it wants to be, and what it wants to do – with what the environment will allow or encourage it to do. Pearce and Robinson (1982: 65) described this internal–external balancing act as "interactive opportunity analysis."

Although the concept of environment pervades the literature on strategic management, until recently it has been conceptualized in "general, even rather vague" terms (Rumelt *et al.* 1994: 22). Pearce and Robinson (1982: 62), for example, defined environment as "the sum total of all conditions and forces that affect the strategic options of a business but that are typically beyond its ability to control." These writers mention many components of the environment, such as customers, suppliers, creditors and competitors. They also mention economic and cultural conditions. Most also mention the traditional stakeholders with whom public relations manages relationships: governments, communities, stockholders, employees, public and private interest groups, and constituents (e.g. Steiner *et al.* 1982; Holt 1987; Ring 1989). Pearce and Robinson (1982: 3) explained that executives must pay attention to "economic conditions, social change, political priorities, and technological developments." Wheelen and Hunger (1987) distinguished between the task environment and the societal environment. They explained that in accomplishing its mission an organization works in its task environment, but that the societal environment may divert its attention from the task environment.

In a comprehensive overview of theories of an organization's environment, Ring pointed out that researchers have paid more attention to the task environment than "to the categories and components of the external environment that do not fit within the scope of the task environment" (1989: 56). He added that

> historians, political scientists, and economists, among others, regularly chronicle changes in these [non-task] components of the external environment. Only rarely, however ... do they focus on

the impact that these changes have on the strategies of specific firms, or on how firms attempt to adapt to these changes.

(1989: 71)

Ring concluded:

> In summarizing this brief sketch of the environment–organization literature, a number of conclusions can be drawn. First, the external environment is now viewed as a critical determinant of organizational effectiveness. Second, the full extent of the role of the environment in determining organization–environment and environment–environment relationships is probably masked by a persistent focus on perceptions of the task environment. Third, while recognizing that environment–environment relationships exist, much of the research ignores these relationships and their implications for strategic choice. In combination, these conclusions lead one to question whether models of the environment that have guided explanations of environment–organization relationships are entirely satisfactory.
>
> (1989: 78)

To a public relations scholar, Ring's discussion of the inadequacies of strategic management theories in explaining how an organization should relate to the environment clearly suggests the role of public relations in strategic management. Although writers on strategic management discuss the environment and make lists of its components, only a few of these writers have recognized or described the role of public relations in helping the organization to identify the most important components of its environment, and in using communication to build relationships with them. The exceptions are Post *et al.* (1982), Gollner (1983) and Marx (1990). In general, management scholars seem largely to be unaware of how the work of public relations scholars can contribute to theories of strategic management.

The theory of sustainable international competitive advantages

Although scholars of strategic management originally conceptualized the environment as a constraint on an organization's mission and choices, Porter (1980; 1985; 1990; 1994) turned the relationship around and conceptualized the environment as a source of competitive advantage. Until Porter, the strategic management field had been concerned with the question of how firms adjust to a vaguely general environment.

Porter, in contrast, operationalized the environment in terms of five competitive forces: the threat of new entrants, the threat of substitute products or services, the bargaining power of suppliers, the bargaining power of buyers, and the rivalry among existing competitors (Porter 1990). The competitiveness of a firm's environment is determined by factor conditions (infrastructure, quality of labor force, etc.), demand conditions (the nature of domestic demand), related and supported industries (the presence or absence of internationally competitive suppliers), and the firm's strategy, structure and rivalry (conditions governing the creation, organization and management of companies and their rivalry) (Porter 1990; 1991).

Porter's (1990; 1991) study of competitive advantages of (and in) ten countries (Denmark, Germany, Italy, Japan, Korea, Singapore, Sweden, Switzerland, Great Britain and the USA) complements some and overthrows other ideas about public relations (although Porter does not mention it).

Porter uses national productivity as a comparative measure. The growth of productivity presupposes that the economy must upgrade itself. He found that competitive advantages are created and sustained as very localized processes which companies can influence. Or put differently: it is not a task for companies to maximize within given constraints, but to create advantages by changing those constraints (Porter 1990).

On the international market, firms compete, not countries (Porter 1990). In this process successful companies not only adjust to their environment, but also try to influence it in their favor because competitive "advantages may reside as much in the environment as in an individual firm" (Porter 1994: 451). Firms influence the environment with direct (unilateral) investment in factor creation, investing in factor creation in collaboration with other firms, and influencing and participating with government and the community in the processes of factor creation. For this reason, firms must influence governments.

Governments have a role to play, not only in the factor creation process, but also very importantly in the process of standards creation (health, the environment, etc.) and regulation, administration and enforcement (Porter 1990; 1991). Consumer pressures are also beneficial (Porter 1990). For example, Porter found that multinational corporations with strong competitors in their home country were better able to compete in other countries because of the pressure to excel at home (Porter 1994). Likewise, he found that government regulation, traditionally seen by corporate managers as an intrusion on their decision making, can stimulate changes in organizational behavior that provide a competitive advantage:

> Stringent standards for product performance, product safety, and environmental impact contribute to creating and upgrading competitive advantage. They pressure firms to improve quality, upgrade technology, and provide features in areas of important customer (and social) concern.
>
> (Porter 1990: 647)

Porter's idea that an organization can gain competitive advantage from successful relationships with competitors and governments in the environment can be extended to relationships with other stakeholder publics. For example, a corporation that successfully solves its environmental problems, usually when pressured by environmental activists, will gain an advantage from relationships with stockholders, consumers, employees, government, and communities that can support or constrain that corporation. Likewise, a government agency that responds well to pressures from its constituents will be more likely to gain support from those publics as it competes for limited public funding.

Porter's theory of sustainable international competitive advantages is the first theory of management that demonstrates the (economic) benefits of the effects of social pressures on firms, and the first that in economic terms explicates the need for corporate activism. Because of that we can consider it as sufficient guidance for corporate social reason (CSR4).

Theory of external effects

This concerns the consequences of decisions on people who were not part of decision making, but are suffering the effects economists term "externalities" (also: "external effects," "third-party effects," "neighborhood effects," "spillover effects," etc.). Externalities are the consequences of the absence of markets (Heller and Starrett 1976) or market failure (McCormick 1993) and are necessarily public in their nature (Heller and Starret 1976). Externalities can be negative or positive, but economists in general are more concerned with the negative.

It is true that in every society everybody has some effect on everybody else, but it is critical to discriminate between indirect influences which give a person a chance to decide pro or contra (as markets do via prices) and direct influences which deprive a person of decision-making possibilities (Mishan 1981). Economists also deal with externalities that are internal to industries (Mishan 1981), but here we consider only external externalities. It is also important to define exter-nalities to be by their origin accidental, unintentional and not essential to the original operation (Mishan 1981).

Economists are familiar with two basic classes of solutions for exter-nalities. The first was recommended by Arthur C. Pigou, who claimed that in the presence of externalities an economy cannot reach an optimal equilibrium. He recommended externalities to be repaid with subsidies or taxes (Groves 1976; Mishan 1981).

The alternative was proposed by Ronald Coase. In his explanation, in the absence of transaction costs rational agents would voluntarily find a way that was not originally offered by the market and reach an agreement that would lead to efficiency. If one agent is damaged due to a decision of the other, he can expect to be offered a settlement, usually called a "bribe," to repay the damage. If agents are artful enough in negotiations and leave no alternative unexplored, the final result will be an optimal one – the bribe and damage are symmetrical (Groves 1976).

The essence of both alternatives is the same: externalities must be internalized. There are several ways of achieving this result: externali-ties can be internalized with the creation of a new market (Mishan 1981), there is privatization (McCormick 1993), and the Pigouvian solution, which can take different forms of governmental intervention (regulation, licensing or rules).

Two points are important to understand. First, externality is depen-dent on the original property right assignment (externality has a meaning only as an intrusion into the property of others) – it concerns property rights (McCormick 1993). Second, externalities are recog-nized as such and the decision to reduce and internalize them depends on social norms (Mishan 1981); in the final analysis we see that they are a political problem (Mishan 1981). Environmental pollution had been a serious problem at least from the start of industrialization, but in general it was not considered "worth" solving as an externality until after World War II.

While economists are, in general, interested in eradicating or at least repaying externalities, Porter turned the whole problem on its head: in factors influencing the competitive advantages of firms he identified these very externalities. He did this in two ways: first, showing that unilateral reduction of negative externalities is in the self-interest of the competitiveness of firms (and he thus changed the so-called free rider problem), and second, showing that the conscious increase of positive externalities is in the self-interest of the competitiveness of firms.

The situational theory of publics

The basic problem of the economic theory of externalities is how to identify them, since they are socially and politically determined. This problem can be solved by the situational theory of publics that has been developed by James E. Grunig on the basis of Dewey's (1927) and Blumer's (1954) definitions of the public. The origin of this theory in microeconomic theory was described earlier in this chapter.

Dewey defined a public as a group of people who face a problem, recognize its existence, and organize to solve it. The latter defines the public as a group of people who face a problem, are divided on its solution and discuss it. People who are not involved in the problem constitute a nonpublic. Those who suffer the consequences but have not yet recognized the problem are a latent public. Those who recognize the problem are an aware public. Those who begin to discuss the solution become an active public (Grunig and Hunt 1984).

This situation Grunig operationalized with three independent and two dependent variables. The independent variables are problem recognition, constraint recognition, and the level of involvement. Dependent variables are information seeking and information processing (Grunig and Hunt 1984). The theory gives us four modes of (communication) behavior: problem-facing behavior, constrained behavior, routine behavior and fatalistic behavior (*ibid.*).

The situational theory of publics enables us to develop a strategic model of public relations management. This operationalizes the environment as groups who are unimportant for the firm, groups who are at the level of stakeholders (they have a relationship with the firm, but it is not brought to the level of consciousness yet), groups in the form of publics, and issue groups (activists) (Grunig and Repper 1992). The strategic public relations management model enables the explication of groups and possible strategies of communication with them: "Building relationships – maintaining interdependence – is the substance of public relations" (Grunig *et al.* 1992).

An important finding of the situational theory of publics is that organizations communicate easier with active publics than with passive, because the former are seeking information while the latter are only passively receiving it (Grunig and Childers 1988; Grunig and Repper 1992; J. Grunig 1997).

There are important connections between Porter's theory of sustainable competitive advantages, economic theory of externalities and Grunig's situational theory of publics. Dozier and Ehling (1992: 170) ‸aid: "Organizations *create* publics when organizational actions have ‸onsequences for other organizations or groupings of people." Larissa Grunig (1992a; 1992b) explains that publics, when they develop into activists, constrain the effectiveness of organizations. (A link between public relations and the economic theory of externalities has already been recognized by Culbertson *et al.* (1993); but they consider externalities to be external to public relations as a context – here we consider them to be on the same level of analysis.)

Strategic management of public relations

Out of this framework, the contribution of public relations to strategic management and, as a result, to organizational effectiveness, becomes clear. Public relations contributes to strategic management by building relationships with publics that it affects – or is affected by – publics that support the mission of the organization or that can divert it from its mission. Organizations plan public relations programs strategically, therefore, when they identify the publics that are most likely to limit or enhance their ability to pursue the mission of the organization, and to design communication programs that help the organization manage its interdependence with these strategic publics.

Public relations is most effective, in other words, when the publics with whom practitioners communicate are identified within the framework of organizational strategic management, and when the function is managed strategically at the level of the public relations department. These two levels of strategic management also are identified in the literature on strategic management. According to Pearce and Robinson (1982), strategic management takes place at three levels:

1 At the *corporate or organizational level*, where the board of directors, chief executive officer and chief administrative officers set grand strategies and reflect the interests of stockholders and society.
2 At *business or specialty levels*, which deal with market segments or provide specialized services.
3 At *functional levels*, composed of managers of products, geographic areas, or functions such as marketing or public relations.

In addition to these three levels, Bowman (1990: 30) added a fourth, *institutional level*, which involves "the issues of how a corporation fits itself into the social environment and the body politic." Of the four levels, Bowman said, scholars of strategic management have paid least attention to the institutional level and need to address that level much more: "For instance, problems of hazardous waste in the chemical industry are enormously important to that industry.... This is an institutional problem of the kind that strategy research typically ignores." What Bowman called the institutional level obviously is the substance of public relations, and a level at which theories of strategic management would benefit greatly from the work of public relations scholars and practitioners.

However, Brody (1987) has pointed out that public relations traditionally has been relegated to the functional level, where it has been assigned responsibility for implementing organizational objectives but not for helping scan the environment and to participate in the formulation of organizational objectives. Kotler and Andreasen (1987), for example, concluded that marketing is strategic for an organization but that public relations is not. However, a survey of public relations counselors reported in Nager and Truitt (1987) showed that respondents rated strategic planning and in-depth counseling of senior executives as the most important contributions that their firms make to clients. Only half as many counselors responding rated implementation of communication programs as their most important contribution.

In the IABC research project, researchers (J. Grunig 1992d) asked the CEO and the senior communication manager in 326 organizations in the United States, Canada and the United Kingdom the extent to which public relations is involved in organization-wide strategic management, and the extent to which they practice each step of the strategic process for public relations itself outlined in Figure 1.1. The results of that study strongly support the importance of strategic management for excellent public relations programs. Both involvement in overall strategic management and practising public relations strategically were among the strongest indicators of excellent departments.

It is crucial, therefore, for public relations to be involved in strategic management in all kinds of organizations; but in reality the two functions often have no connection. In contrast to the strategic approach to public relations described in Figure 1.1, most organizations carry out the same public relations programs year after year without stopping to determine whether they continue to communicate with the most important publics. Dozier and L. Grunig (1992) have pointed out that at some point in their history, most organizations probably develop their public relations programs strategically –

1 *Stakeholder stage.* An organization has a relationship with stakeholders when the behavior of the organization or of a stakeholder has consequences for the other. Public relations should do formative research to scan the environment and the behavior of the organization to identify these consequences. Ongoing communication with these stakeholders helps to build a stable, long-term relationship that manages conflict that may occur in the relationship.

2 *Public stage.* Publics form when stakeholders recognize one or more of the consequences as a problem and organize to do something about it or them. Public relations should do research to identify and segment these publics. At this stage focus groups are particularly helpful. Communication to involve publics in the decision process of the organization helps to manage conflict before communication campaigns become necessary.

3 *Issue stage.* Publics organize and create issues. Public relations should anticipate these issues and manage the organization's response to them. This is known as issues management. The media play a major role in the creation and expansion of issues. In particular, their coverage of issues may produce publics other than activist ones – especially "hot-issue" publics. At this stage, research is particularly useful to segment all of the publics. Communication programs at this stage usually use the mass media, but should also include interpersonal communication with activist publics to try to resolve the issue through negotiation.

Public relations should plan communication programs with different stakeholders or publics at each of the above three stages. In doing so, it should follow steps 4–7.

4 Public relations should develop formal objectives, such as communication, accuracy, understanding, agreement, and complementary behavior for its communication programs.

5 Public relations should plan formal programs and campaigns to accomplish the objectives.

6 Public relations, especially the technicians, should implement the programs and campaigns.

7 Public relations should evaluate the effectiveness of programs in meeting their objectives and in reducing the conflict produced by the problems and issues that brought about the programs.

Figure 1.1   Steps in the strategic management of public relations
Source: J. Grunig 1992d.

that is, the presence of a strategic public probably provides the motivation for initiating public relations programs. As time passes, however, organizations forget the initial reason for the programs and continue communication programs for publics that are no longer strategic. Public relations then becomes routine and ineffective because it does little to help organizations adapt to dynamic environments.

In explicating the role of public relations in overall strategic management and the strategic management of public relations itself, the model in Figure 1.1 also shows the relationship of public relations to issues management, and of issues management and public relations to strategic management. Although many writers on issues management have distinguished between public relations and issues management, this model makes clear – as Heath (1990) has also said – that public relations and issues management are synonymous when public relations is a part of strategic management.

The concept of issues management was developed by a public relations practitioner, Chase (1984). Since then it has been studied both by management scholars (for reviews, see Buchholz *et al.* 1989; Carroll 1989; Eadie 1989) and by public relations scholars. Heath has been the most consistent and active researcher of issues management among public relations scholars (Heath and Nelson 1986; Heath 1990).

Most of the literature on issues management conceptualizes the process as asymmetrical, i.e. as one of anticipating what issues publics or activists will create in the future and then taking positive action to defeat these potential opponents. The process in Figure 1.1, however, sees issues management as a more symmetrical process. Figure 1.1 states that issues arise because publics create them – i.e. publics make issues out of problems. Thus a public relations manager serves strategic management by identifying management decisions that have consequences for people not involved in the decision – i.e. that create problems for those people. Publics develop to address the problems and, if the organization does not involve them in the decision, make issues out of the problems. In symmetrical issues management, public relations managers attempt to communicate with publics before decisions are made so that problems are resolved collaboratively before publics are forced to make issues out of them.

Issues, then, are strategic to an organization because of what Eadie (1989: 172) called his "rough and ready" definition of a strategic issue: "It is a problem or opportunity that, if action is not taken on it *now*, it is likely to saddle the organization with unbearable future costs."

Public relations, as we will see next, helps the organization avoid these unbearable future costs.

Summary

Public relations has been concerned primarily with the question of how a firm can assure its autonomy of action under conditions of growing pressure from publics. While the economic theory of externalities lacks operationalization of those externalities (as socially and politically determined), the situational theory of publics offers it. And while the situational theory of publics lacked an economic operationalization of social interventions into the economy, Porter's theory of sustainable international competitive advantages offers that.

We suggest the three theories be merged into the following situational theory of double internalization of external effects:

1   In the interest of their sustainable international competitive advantages, firms must purposely cause positive external effects alone, in collaboration with other firms and with the government. Only in this way can they create the quality of factors. This is the factor creation theorem.
2   In the interest of their sustainable international competitive advantages, firms must purposely (physically) internalize negative externalities. These are defined by publics. Firms must seek their most active publics and use them to define the standards for their operations. This is the publics definition theorem.

Both theorems also lead us to the beginning of this whole discussion, to transaction costs, efficiency and effectiveness. We hypothesize that publics, through their influence of factor creation, determine both the efficiency (in the context of transaction costs) and effectiveness, as shown in Figure 1.2.

Active publics serve as guides and the creator of a firm's success (Porter 1990; 1991; 1994). Through this hypothesis we should also analyze the need (and success) of strong governments and of government/private sector collaboration in the late-comer economies (postwar Germany and Japan, what used to be called NICs, etc.) as a substitute for active publics, and also the limits of that mode of development under conditions of its own success (e.g. industrialized countries of Asia today). Active publics serve as a kind of positive feedback mechanism (while governments are negative feedback mechanisms) that encourages firms into a self-organizing, autopoietic (Maturana and Varela 1992) economic system.

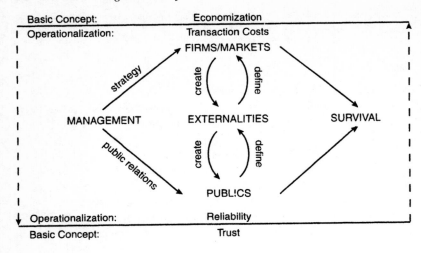

Figure 1.2   Business autopoiesis

This helps us redefine public relations. Until now, externalities were defined as causing public relations *problems* (Grunig and Hunt 1984). From now on, we should study externalities as public relations (and in general managerial, economic) *opportunities*.

Cultural differences and public relations

Public relations is the management of trust in conditions of opportunism and bounded rationality. As Williamson (1992) noted, firms (hierarchies) would be needless in conditions of perfect trustworthiness. It is this very identification of trust (usually treated as a problem of "matching" between private and public interests) as a special aspect of management and its analysis and operationalization (until now in phases from CSR1 to CSR3) that is the first cultural bias of American management in general and public relations in particular.

The present state of public relations can be summarized according to Grunig:

At the micro level of public relations programs practitioners should use the concepts of perception, cognition, attitude, schema, and behavior to derive objectives of communication programs and to develop measures to evaluate their effectiveness. Micro-level communication programs build symbolic relationships with publics, but symbolic relationships alone cannot solve public relations problems. At a more macro level, organizations need public relations because their behaviors affect publics and the behavior of publics affects them. Over the long term, therefore, organizations must evaluate the quality of their macro-level, behavioral relationships with publics if they are to determine the contribution that public relations makes to achieving organizational goals and missions.

(J. Grunig 1993: 136)

In literature dealing with relationships between different cultures and economic success it is often assumed that other cultural patterns which solve the problem of correspondence between private and public interests implicitly and articulate it at best in a broader framework, are better than American individualism and its analytic inclination (e.g. Hampden-Turner and Trompenaars 1993). We could say that the explicit concept of American public relations as a part of management is successfully substituted in other cultures with some implicit concepts of situational ethics: *tsukai-wake* in Japan, *lagom* in Sweden, *geuzen* and *aktie* in the Netherlands, to be a *gentleman* in Great Britain or *système-D* in France; or corporativist legal systems such as, for example, *Soziale Marktwirtschaft* in Germany (Hampden-Turner and Trompenaars 1993).

There are at least two kinds of evidence against such a position and in favor of explicit public relations: first, that public relations, as management before it, is vigorously spreading also in the aforementioned cultures. Meiden (1992) estimates that there are around a million and a half people working in the field of public relations worldwide. Budd Jr (1992) estimates that public relations is worth around eight billion dollars as a worldwide industry. Durić (1992) quotes from *Marketing Communications* review that the figure at the end of the 1980s was already around 14.5 billion US dollars.

The second kind of evidence is a more direct one. If we take Japan as an example, we see that their corporations are becoming more, not less American. That part of the Japanese economic miracle comes from the more systematic use of imported American methods of management than is employed in the US, is today no longer a secret (see Walton 1986). Even the most important Japanese management consultant, Kenichi Ohmae, who was trained in the US and is known at home as "Mr Strategy," advises Japanese corporations to place more emphasis on personal responsibility and even introduce "samurais" as "real strategists" and "staff analysts" (Ohmae 1982: 5). Above all, the present *risutura* (restructuring) of Japanese corporations follows

American logic. So, for example, Matsushita Electronic Co., the world's largest producer of consumer electronics, with sales of over sixty-six billion US dollars and owner of its own group – *keiretsu* in Japan (see Miyashita and Russell 1994) – and of the Hollywood giant MCA in the US, last year in a simple American way (not at all Japanese) dismissed the former president. The new president, Yoichi Morishita, who came to his present position bypassing the traditional seniority system, eliminated whole layers of middle management, decentralized decision making and introduced entrepreneurship with personal responsibility and the hiring of scientists for R&D with five-year contracts. Morishita calls his strategy "four S management" – simple, small, speedy and strategic: "I wanted to simplify management. I hate taking a long time to study things. I want to condense things, American style" (Neff 1994: 67).

Even if other cultures have built their economic success on cultural patterns which have not had such a need for explicit public relations as the US, this might have been only a temporary advantage, which is disappearing with the present Americanization of their management. With an explicit concept of management (which has been absent in those cultures) they will have to import an explicit concept of public relations.

The advantage of the fundamental bias is strengthened if we add the criteria of efficiency and strategy, which enable us to develop a productive definition of public relations that is not only preventive and cost saving, but also productive in the process of creation and development of production factors.

Such public relations (CSR4 – corporate social reason), based on the theory of sustainable international competitive advantages, the theory of externalities, and the situational theory of publics, may well become one of the essential competitive advantages of the US economy in the twenty-first century. Unless, of course, others again learn to use the American concept better.

A global and specific theory of public relations

Given the necessity of global public relations, both practitioners and scholars have begun to ask whether there are or can be global principles of public relations: can public relations programs in different countries be standardized, or must different, localized, programs be developed for each country – or indeed for different regions within a country with different cultures? The question is especially important for multinational organizations – those that work in more than one country or have publics in more than one country. The question is also important for public relations education and for the development of a global public relations profession: can the same principles be taught in different countries and included in a body of knowledge that can be used throughout the world?

Gavin Anderson, who heads the New York public relations firm that bears his name, used the terms "global" and "international" to distinguish between public relations practiced in the same way throughout the world and public relations customized for each:

> *International* public relations practitioners very often implement distinctive programs in multiple markets, with each program tailored to meet the often acute distinctions of the individual geographic market.
>
> *Global* public relations superimposes an overall perspective on a program executed in two or more national markets, recognizing the similarities among audiences while necessarily adapting to regional differences.
>
> (Anderson 1989: 413)

Anderson chose the global model over the international one, saying: "Global, as opposed to multinational, businesses demand that programs in distinctive markets be interrelated. While there will always be local differences and need for customization, the programs will probably share more than they differ" (1989: 413). Botan (1992) came to the opposite conclusion. He called the global approach the ethnocentric model, and concluded that practitioners from western countries often impose the assumptions of their culture on public relations practice in other countries. Under a polycentric model, in contrast, practitioners in each country in which a multinational organization works have considerable freedom to practise public relations in a way they believe is appropriate for that country.

Emerging out of this debate about the merits of two extreme positions seems to be a consensus that the ideal model for multicultural public relations lies somewhere in the middle – that public relations programs, in Ovaitt's (1988) words, can share strategic elements even if these strategies are implemented in different ways in different cultures. Two scholars of international management, Brinkerhoff and Ingle (1989), called this middle approach the use of "generic principles" and "specific applications."

To understand the concept of a generic theory, however, it is important to distinguish between a normative and positive theory. This global theory is a normative theory. It includes concepts that explain how public relations *should* be practiced throughout the world to be most effective. Public relations may be practiced in other ways – as those positive descriptions of the models of public relations practised in several countries provided by J. Grunig *et al.* (1995) showed.

We have only just begun to carry out scholarly research on a global theory of public relations. Verčič *et al.* (1995) and Wakefield (1994) have hypothesized that the fourteen characteristics of excellent public relations developed in the IABC Excellence Project will also be generic principles of global public relations. They have hypothesized further-more that five specific variables must be taken into account when the generic principles are applied in different settings:

1   the political-economic system
2   culture, including language
3   the extent of activism
4   the level of development and
5   the media system.

In essence, this global theory states that when public relations is managed strategically in a global context, these five variables must be taken into account when the public relations manager scans the envir-onment of an organization as part of the strategic management of public relations.

In the first research on the generic-specific propositions, Verčič *et al.* (1995) conducted a case study of Pristop, a Slovenian public relations firm in Slovenia that has made the fourteen principles of excellence the knowledge base for its practice – in essence, providing an experimental test of the normative principles. This case study analyzed, in particular, how the change in the political-economic system from communism to democracy affected public relations practice in Slovenia, and how the generic principles were affected by the cultural characteristics identi-fied by Hofstede (1980). In addition, Verčič *et al.* (1993) provided nine examples of specific applications of the generic principles used by the public relations firm; and they provided evidence that these principles have indeed been effective in Slovenia.

Conclusions

The critical elements of the theory of public relations management we have developed in this chapter did not arise in a linear effort to build such a theory. Middle-range theories such as the situational theory of publics, the models of public relations and their relationship to organizational and environmental conditions, strategic public relations and its role in organization-wide strategic management, corporate social reason, and the global-specific theory of global public relations were developed individually and on the basis of several bodies of knowledge in economics, management, sociology, political science and communication.

Nevertheless, the roots of all of these elements of a general theory of public relations can be traced to the simple concepts of neoclassical microeconomics, and to the adjustments made to those concepts to take account of the organizational, social and political factors that affect decisions made by managers, publics and markets. It is ironic, however, that public relations theories that arose from economic theory should add a social, ethical, and political dimension to management theory. By contributing the basic element of trust to the relationship between organizations and publics, the public relations function provides what is obviously the most important outcome of management decision making: public relations allows the organization to exist.

At the same time, excellent public relations provides an important competitive or strategic advantage for organizations, by internalizing the externalities that otherwise lead to activist opposition, consumer indifference, or government interference in organization behavior — thus resolving a key theoretical question in economic theory.

Notes

1   Kotler (1991) stated, for example,

> Hungry people can approach others and offer some resource in exchange, such as money, another good, or some service. Marketing arises from this last approach to acquiring products. Exchange is the act of obtaining a desired product from someone by offering something in return. Exchange is the defining concept underlying marketing.
>
>   (p.7)

2   The most commonly accepted answer to this question is that a dominant coalition of the most powerful individuals make key decisions. Cyert and March (1963) developed the concept, and the IABC Excellence team has popularized the concept in public relations circles (J. Grunig 1992d).

3   See also Ehling *et al.* (1992) and Grunig and Grunig (1991) for a discussion of the difference between publics and markets, and a broader discussion of the difference between public relations and marketing.

References

Anderson, G. (1989) 'A global look at public relations', in B. Cantor (ed.) *Experts in Action: Inside Public Relations*, 2nd edn, New York: Longman.

Ansoff, H. I. (1965) *Corporate Strategy: An Analytical Approach to Business Policy for Growth and Expansion*, New York: McGraw-Hill.

——(1987) *Corporate Strategy*, revised edn, London: Penguin.

Ansoff, H. I. and Hayes, R. L. (1976) 'Introduction', in H. l. Ansoff, R. P. Declerck and R. L. Hayes (eds) *From Strategic Planning to Strategic Management*, London: Wiley.

Ansoff, H. I., DeClerk, R. P. and Hayes, R. P. (1976) 'From strategic planning to strategic management', in H. I. Ansoff, R. P. Declerck and R. L. Hayes (eds) *From Strategic Planning to Strategic Management*, London: Wiley.

Assael, H. (1987) *Consumer Behavior and Marketing Action*, 3rd edn, Boston MA: Kent.

Avenarius, H. and Armbrecht, W. (eds) (1992) *Ist Public Relations eine Wissenschaft?*, Opladen: Westdeutsche Verlag.

Banta, M. (1993) *Taylored Lives: Narrative Production in the Age of Taylor, Veblen, and Ford*, Chicago IL: University of Chicago Press.

Barney, J. B. (1994) 'Beyond individual metaphors in understanding how firms behave: a comment on game theory and prospect theory models of firm behavior', in R. P. Rumelt, D. E. Schendel and D. J. Teece (eds) *Fundamental Issues in Strategy: A Research Agenda*, Boston MA: Harvard Business School Press.

Berle, A. A. (1968) [1932] in G. C. Means, *The Modern Corporation and Private Property*, revised edn, New York: Harcourt, Brace.

Bernays, E. L. (1923) *Crystallizing Public Opinion*, New York: Boni and Liveright.

——(1928a) 'Manipulating public opinion: the why and the how', *The American Journal of Sociology*, May, 958–71.

——(1928b) *Propaganda*, New York: Horace Liveright.

——(ed.) (1955a) *The Engineering of Consent*, Oklahoma: University of Oklahoma Press.

——(1955b) 'The theory and practice of public relations: a resume', in E. L. Bernays (ed.) *The Engineering of Consent*, Oklahoma: University of Oklahoma Press.

——(1965) *Biography of an Idea: Memoirs of Public Relations Counsel*, New York: Simon and Schuster.

——(1976) 'Public relations: past, present and future', *Public Relations Journal*, December, 24–6.

——(1986) *The Late Years: Public Relations Insights 1956–86*, Rhinebeck NY: H&M Publishers.

Blackman, W. C. Jr (1992) *Basic Hazardous Waste Management*, Boca Raton FL: CRC Press.

Blumer, H. (1954) 'Public opinion and public opinion polling', in D. Katz, D. Cartwright, S. Eldersveld and A. McClung Lee (eds) *Public Opinion and Propaganda*, New York: Holt, Rinehart and Winston.

Boiry, P. A. (1989) *Les Relations Publiques ou la Stratégie de la Confiance*, 2nd edn, Paris: Eyrolles.

Botan, C. (1992) 'International public relations: critique and reformulation', *Public Relations Review*, 18, 149–60.

Bowman, E. H. (1990) 'Strategy changes: possible worlds and actual minds', in J. W. Fredrickson (ed.) *Perspectives on Strategic Management*, New York: Harper Business.

Brinkerhoff, D. W. and Ingle, D. M. (1989) 'Integrating blueprint and process: a structured flexibility approach to development management', *Public Administration and Development*, 9, 487–503.

Brody, E. W. (1987) *The Business of Public Relations*, New York: Praeger.

Buchholz, A., Evans, W. D. and Wagley, R. A. (1989) *Management Response to Public Issues*, 2nd edn, Englewood Cliffs NJ: Prentice-Hall.

Budd, J. F. Jr (1992) *Street Smart Public Relations*, New York: Turtle.

Canfield, B. R. (1968) *Public Relations, Cases, and Problems*, 5th edn, Homewood IL: Richard D. Irwin.

Carroll, A. B. (1989) *Business and Society: Ethics and Stakeholder Management*, Cincinnati OH: Southwestern.

Chandler, A. D. Jr (1962) *Strategy and Structure: Chapters in the History of the Industrial Enterprise*, Cambridge MA: MIT Press.

——(1994) 'The functions of the HQ unit in the multibusiness firm', in R. P. Rumelt, D. E. Schendel and D. J. Teece (eds) *Fundamental Issues in Strategy: A Research Agenda*, Boston MA: Harvard Business School Press.

Chase, W. H. (1984) *Issues Management: Origins of the Future*, Stamford CT: Issue Action Press.

Cheney, G. and Dionisopoulos, G. N. (1989) 'Public relations? No, relations with publics: a rhetorical approach to contemporary corporate communications', in C. H. Botan and V. Hazleton Jr (eds) *Public Relations Theory*, Hillsdale NJ: Lawrence Erlbaum.

Cheney, G. and Vibbert, S. L. (1987) 'Corporate discourse', in F. M. Jablin, L. L. Putnam, K. H. Roberts and L. W. Porter (eds) *Handbook of Organizational Communication: An Interdisciplinary Perspective*, Newbury Park CA: Sage.

Chomsky, N. (1989) *Necessary Illusions: Thought Control in Democratic Societies*, London: Pluto Press.

Cole, R. S. (1981) *The Practical Handbook of Public Relations*, Englewood Cliffs NJ: Prentice-Hall.

Culbertson, H. M., Jeffers, D. W., Stone, D. B. and Terrell, M. (1993) *Social, Political, and Economic Contexts in Public Relations: Theory and Cases*, Hillsdale NJ: Lawrence Erlbaum.

Cutlip, S. M., Broom, G. M. and Center, A. H. (1985) *Effective Public Relations*, 6th edn, Englewood Cliffs NJ: Prentice-Hall.

Cyert, R. M. and March, J. G. (1963) *A Behavioural Theory of the Firm*, Englewood Cliffs NJ: Prentice-Hall

DeSerpa, A. C. (1988) *Microeconomic Theory: Issues and Applications*, 2nd edn, Boston MA: Allyn and Bacon.

Dewey, J. (1927) *The Public and its Problems*, Chicago IL: Swallow.

———(1938) *Logic: The Theory of Inquiry*, New York: Henry Holt.

Dilenschneider, R. L. and Forrestal, D. J. (1987) *The Dartnell Public Relations Handbook*, 3rd edn, Chicago IL: The Dartnell Corporation.

Doz, Y. L. and Prahalad, C. K. (1994) 'Managing DMNCs: a search for a new paradigm', in R. P. Rumelt, D. E. Schendel and D. J. Teece (eds) *Fundamental Issues in Strategy: A Research Agenda*, Boston MA: Harvard Business School Press.

Dozier, D. M. and Ehling, W. P. (1992) 'Evaluation of public relations programs: what the literature tells us about their effects', in J. Grunig (ed.) *Excellence in Public Relations and Communication Management*, Hillsdale NJ: Lawrence Erlbaum.

Dozier, D. M. and Grunig, L. A. (1992) 'The organization of the public relations function', in J. Grunig (ed.) *Excellence in Public Relations and Communication Management*, Hillsdale NJ: Lawrence Erlbaum.

Drucker, P. F. (1993) *Management: Tasks, Responsibilities, Practices*, New York: Harper.

Dunn, J. (1988) *Successful Public Relations: The Insider's Way to get Successful Media Coverage*, London: Longman.

Đurić, M. D. (1992) *Public Relations: Ključ uspešnog nastupa na tržištu*, Belgrade: Institut za tržišna istraživanja.

Eadie, D. C. (1989) 'Identifying and managing strategic issues: from design to action', in J. Rabin, G. J. Miller and W. Bartley Hildreth (eds) *Handbook of Strategic Management*, New York: Marcel Dekker.

Ehling, W. P. (1984) 'Applications of decision theory in the construction of a theory of public relations management, I', *Public Relations Research and Education*, 1, 15–38.

———(1985) 'Applications of decision theory in the construction of a theory of public relations management, II', *Public Relations Research and Education*, 2, 4–22.

Ehling, W. P., White, J. and Grunig, J. E. (1992) 'Public relations and marketing practices', in J. Grunig (ed.) *Excellence in Public Relations and Communication Management*, Hillsdale NJ: Lawrence Erlbaum.

Emmott, B. (1993) *Japan's Global Reach: The Influences, Strategies and Weaknesses of Japan's Multinational Companies*, London: Arrow.

Erikson, E. H. (1963) *Childhood and Society*, Harmondsworth: Penguin.

Frank, R. H. (1994) *Microeconomics and Behavior*, 2nd edn, New York: McGraw-Hill.

Frederick, W. C. (1994a) 'Coda: 1994', *Business and Society*, 33 (2) 165–6.

———(1994b) 'From CSR1 to CSR2: the maturing of business-and-society thought', *Business and Society*, 33 (2) 150–64.

Gandy, O. H. Jr (1992) 'Public relations and public policy: the structuration of dominance in the information age', in E. L. Toth and R. L. Heath (eds) *Rhetorical and Critical Approaches to Public Relations*, Hillsdale NJ: Lawrence Erlbaum.

Garfinkel, H. (1963) 'A conception of, and experiments with, "trust" as a condition of stable concerted actions', in O. J. Harvey (ed.) *Motivation and Social Interaction: Cognitive Determinants*, New York: The Ronald Press.

Giddens, A. (1986) *The Constitution of Society*, Oxford: Polity Press.

Gollner, A. B. (1983) *Social Change and Corporate Strategy: The Expanding Role of Public Affairs*, Stamford CT: Issue Action Press.

Greene, C. N., Adam, E. M. Jr and Ebert, R. J.(1985) *Management for Effective Performance*, Englewood Cliffs NJ: Prentice-Hall.

Groves, T. (1976) 'Information, incentives, and the internalization of production externalities', in S. A. Y. Lin (ed.) *Theory and Measurement of Economic Externalities*, New York: Academic Press.

Gruban, B., Maksimovič, M., Verčič, D. and Zavrl, F. (1990) *ABC PR: Odnosi z javnostmi na prvi pogled*, Ljubljana, Slovenia: Tiskovno sredisce Ljubljana.

Grunig, J. E. (1966) 'The role of information in economic decision making', *Journalism Monographs*, no. 3.

——(1968) 'Information, entrepreneurship, and economic development: a study of the decision making processes of Colombian *latifundistas*', unpublished doctoral dissertation, Madison WI: University of Wisconsin.

——(1969a) 'Economic decision making and entrepreneurship among Colombian *latifundistas*', *Inter-American Economic Affairs*, 23 (2) 21–46.

——(1969b) 'Information and decision making in economic development', *Journalism Quarterly*, 46, 565–75.

——(1969c) 'The minifundio problem in Colombia: development alternatives', *Inter-American Economic Affairs*, 23 (4) 2–23.

——(1971) 'Communication and the economic decision making processes of Colombian peasants', *Economic Development and Cultural Change*, 19, 580–97.

——(1976a) 'Communication behaviors occurring in decision and non-decision situations', *Journalism Quarterly*, 53, 252–63.

——(1976b) 'Organizations and publics relations: testing a communication theory', *Journalism Monographs*, no. 46.

——(1989) 'Symmetrical presuppositions as a framework for public relations theory', in C. H. Botan and V. Hazleton Jr (eds) *Public Relations Theory*, Hillsdale NJ: Lawrence Erlbaum.

——(1992a) 'The development of public relations research in the United States and its status in communication science', in H. Avenarius and W. Armbrecht (eds) *Ist Public Relations eine Wissenschaft?*, Opladen: Westdeutscher Verlag.

——(1992b) 'Communication, public relations, and effective organizations: an overview of the book', in J. E. Grunig (ed.) *Excellence in Public Relations and Communication Management*, Hillsdale NJ: Lawrence Erlbaum.

——(1992c) *Public Relations as a Two-Way Symmetrical Process*, The Hague: Phaedon.

——(ed.) (1992d) *Excellence in Public Relations and Communication Management*, Hillsdale NJ: Lawrence Erlbaum.

——(1993a) 'Image and substance: from symbolic to behavioral relation-ships', *Public Relations Review*, 19 (2) 121–39.

——(1993b) 'Implications of public relations research for other domains of communication', *Journal of Communication*, 43, 164–73.

——(1997) 'A situational theory of publics: conceptual history, recent challenges, and new research', in D. Moss, T. MacManus and D. Verčič (eds) *Public Relations Research: An International Perspective*, London: International Thompson Business Press.

Grunig, J. E. and Childers, L. (1988) 'Reconstruction of a situational theory of communication: internal and external concepts as identifiers of publics for AIDS', paper presented to the Association for Education in Journalism and Mass Communication, Portland OR.

Grunig, J. E. and Disbrow, J. B. (1977) 'Developing a probablistic model for communications decision making', *Communication Research*, 4, 145–68.

Grunig, J. E. and Grunig, L. A. (1989) 'Toward a theory of the public relations behavior of organizations: review of a program of research', *Public Relations Research Annual*, 1, 27–66.

——(1991) 'Conceptual differences in public relations and marketing: the case of health-care organizations', *Public Relations Review*, 17 (3) 257–78.

——(1992) 'Models of public relations and communication', in J. E. Grunig (ed.) *Excellence in Public Relations and Communication Management*, Hillsdale NJ: Lawrence Erlbaum.

Grunig, J. E., Grunig, L. A., Sriramesh, K., Huang, Yi-Hui and Lyra, A. (1995) 'Models of public relations in an international setting', *Journal of Public Relations Research*, 7(3), 163–86.

Grunig, J. E. and Hunt, T. (1984) *Managing Public Relations*, New York: Holt, Rinehart and Winston.

Grunig, J. E. and Repper, F. C. (1992) 'Strategic management, publics, and issues', in J. E. Grunig (ed.) *Excellence in Public Relations and Communication Management*, Hillsdale NJ: Lawrence Erlbaum.

Grunig, J. E. and White, J. (1992) 'The effect of worldviews on public relations theory and practice', in J. E. Grunig (ed.) *Excellence in Public Relations and Communication Management*, Hillsdale NJ: Lawrence Erlbaum.

Grunig, L. A. (1992a) 'Activism: how it limits the effectiveness of organizations and how excellent public relations departments respond', in J. E. Grunig (ed.) *Excellence in Public Relations and Communication Management*, Hillsdale NJ: Lawrence Erlbaum.

Grunig, L. A. (1992b) 'Power in public relations departments', in J. E. Grunig (ed.) *Excellence in Public Relations and Communication Management*, Hillsdale NJ: Lawrence Erlbaum.

Grunig, L. A., Grunig, J. E. and Ehling, W. P. (1992) 'What is an effective organization?', in J. E. Grunig (ed.) *Excellence in Public Relations and Communication Management*, Hillsdale NJ: Lawrence Erlbaum.

Hammond, T. H. (1994) 'Structure, strategy, and the agenda of the firm', in R. P. Rumelt, D. E. Schendel and D. J. Teece (eds) *Fundamental Issues in Strategy: A Research Agenda*, Boston MA: Harvard Business School Press.

Hampden-Turner, C. and Trompenaars, F. (1993) *The Seven Cultures of Capitalism: Value Systems for Creating Wealth in the United States, Britain, Japan, Germany, France, Sweden, and the Netherlands*, New York: Piatkus.

Hannan, M. T. and Freeman, J. (1989) *Organizational Ecology*, Cambridge MA: Harvard University Press.

Heath, R. L. (1990) 'Corporate issues management: theoretical underpinnings and research foundations', *Public Relations Research Annual*, 2, 29–65.

Heath, R. L. and Nelson, R. A. (1986) *Issues Management: Corporate Public Policymaking in an Information Society*, Newbury Park CA: Sage.

Heller, W. P. and Starrett, D. A. (1976) 'On the nature of externalities', in S. A. Y. Lin (ed.) *Theory and Measurement of Economic Externalities*, New York: Academic Press.

Hess, M. B., Kendall, R. and Terhune, J. L. (1986) *Where to Study Public Relations: A Student's Guide to Academic Programs in the United States and Canada*, New York: PRSA.

Higgins, J. M. (1979) *Organizational Policy and Strategic Management: Texts and Cases*, Hinsdale IL: Dryden.

Hoewig, R. L. (1991) 'Dynamics and role of public affairs', in Philip Lesly (ed.) *Lesly's Handbook of Public Relations and Communications*, 4th edn, Chicago IL: Probus.

Hofstede, G. (1980) *Culture's Consequences: International Differences in Work-Related Values*, Beverly Hills CA: Sage.

Holt, D. H. (1987) *Management: Principles and Practices*, Englewood Cliffs NJ: Prentice-Hall.

Jefkins, F. (1977) *Planned Press and Public Relations*, London: International Textbook Company.

Kahneman, D. and Lovallo, D. (1994) 'Timid choices and bold forecasts: a cognitive perspective on risk taking', in R. P. Rumelt, D. E. Schendel and D. J. Teece (eds) *Fundamental Issues in Strategy: A Research Agenda*, Boston MA: Harvard Business School Press.

Katona, G. (1951) *Psychological Analysis of Economic Behavior*, New York: McGraw-Hill.

——(1953) 'Rational behavior and economic behavior', *Psychological Review*, 60, 307–18.

Kay, N. M. (1994) 'Firm, theory of the (1)', in G. M. Hodgson, W. J. Samuels and M. R. Tool (eds) *The Elgar Companion to Institutional and Evolutionary Economics, A-K*, London: Edward Elgar.

Kennedy, P. (1993) *Preparing for the Twenty-First Century*, London: Fontana Press.

Knight, F. H. (1921) *Risk, Uncertainty and Profit*, New York: Augustus M. Kelley.

Kotler, P. (1991) *Marketing Management*, 7th edn, Englewood Cliffs NJ: Prentice-Hall.

Kotler, P. and Andreasen, A. R. (1987) *Strategic Marketing for Nonprofit Organizations*, 3rd edn, Englewood Cliffs NJ: Prentice-Hall.

56   PR and management theory

Krugman, H. E. (1965) 'The impact of television advertising: learning without involvement', *Public Opinion Quarterly*, 29, 349–56.

Lapinski, M. J. (1992) 'An exploration of the relationship between strategic management, public relations and organizational effectiveness in the federal government', unpublished master's thesis, College Park MD: University of Maryland.

Learned, E. P., Christensom, C. R., Andrews, K. R. and Guth, W. D. (1965) *Business Policy: Text and Cases*, Homewood IL: Irwin.

Linstead, S. (1993) 'Deconstruction in the study of organizations', in J. Hassard and M. Parker (eds) *Postmodernism and Organizations*, London: Sage.

Luhmann, N. (1979) [1975] *Trust and Power*, trans. H. Davis, J. Raffau and K. Rooney, Chichester: Wiley.

McCormick, R. E. (1993) *Managerial Economics*, Englewood Cliffs NJ: Prentice-Hall.

Mackey, S. (1991) 'The relationship of public relations to cultural studies and notions of ideology', in *Communications in the New Millennium: Selected Proceedings of the XII Public Relations World Congress*, Toronto: International Public Relations Association and Canadian Public Relations Society.

Marx, T. G. (1990) 'Strategic planning for public relations', *Long Range Planning*, 23 (1) 9–16.

Maturana, H. R. and Varela, F. J. (1992) *The Tree of Knowledge: The Biological Roots of Human Understanding*, Boston MA and London: Shambhala.

Maynard, H. B. Jr and Mehrtens, S. E. (1993) *The Fourth Wave: Business in the 21st Century*, San Francisco CA: Berrett-Koehler.

Meiden, A. van der (1992) 'Predgovor', in M. D. Đurić (ed.) *Public Relations: Ključ uspešnog nastupa na tržištu*, Belgrade: Institut za tržišna istraživanja, xi.

Mintzberg, H. (1983) *Power in and Around Organizations*, Englewood Cliffs NJ: Prentice-Hall.

Mishan, E. J. (1981) *Introduction to Normative Economics*, New York and Oxford: Oxford University Press.

Miyashita, K. and Russell, D. W. (1994) *Keiretsu: Inside the Hidden Japanese Conglomerates*, New York: McGraw-Hill.

Morgan, G. (1986) *Images of Organization*, Beverly Hills CA: Sage.

Nager, N. R. and Allen, T. H. (1984) *Public Relations Management by Objectives*, New York: Longman.

Nager, N. R. and Truitt, R. H. (1987) *Strategic Public Relations Counseling*, New York: Longman.

Neff, R. (1994) 'Tradition be damned: Matsushita's radical restructuring has it well on the way to a turnaround', *Business Week*, 31 October, 66–8.

Nelson, R. R. (1994) 'Why do firms differ, and how does it matter?', in R. P. Rumelt, D. E. Schendel and D. J. Teece (eds) *Fundamental Issues in Strategy: A Research Agenda*, Boston MA: Harvard Business School Press.

Nemec, P. (1993) *Public Relations: Zasady komunikace s verejnosti*, Prague: Management Press.

Ohmae, K. (1982) *The Mind of the Strategist: The Art of Japanese Business*, New York: McGraw-Hill.

Olasky, M. N. (1987) *Corporate Public Relations: A New Historical Perspective*, Hillsdale NJ: Lawrence Erlbaum.

Ovaitt, F. Jr (1988) 'PR without boundaries: is globalization an option?', *Public Relations Quarterly*, 33 (1) 5–9.

Pearce, J. A. II and Robinson, R. B. Jr (1982) *Strategic Management: Strategy Formulation and Implementation*, Homewood IL: Irwin.

Peters, T. J. and Waterman, R. H. Jr (1982) *In Search of Excellence: Lessons from America's Best-Run Companies*, London: Harper and Row.

Porter, M. E. (1980) *Competitive Strategy: Techniques for Analyzing Industries and Competitors*, New York: Free Press.

——(1985) *Competitive Advantage: Creating and Sustaining Superior Performance*, New York: Free Press.

——(1990) *The Competitive Advantage of Nations*, London: Macmillan.

——(1991) 'The competitive advantage of nations', in C. A. Montgomery and M. E. Porter (eds) *Strategy: Seeking and Securing Competitive Advantage*, Harvard MA: Harvard Business School Press.

——(1994) 'Toward a dynamic theory of strategy', in R. P. Rumelt, D. E. Schendel and D. J. Teece (eds) *Fundamental Issues in Strategy: A Research Agenda*, Boston MA: Harvard Business School Press, 423–61.

Post, J. E., Murray, E. E., Dickie, R. B. and Mahon, J. F. (1982) 'The public affairs function in American corporations: development and relations with corporate planning', *Long Range Planning*, 12 (2) 12–21.

Rayfield, R. E. and Pincus, J. D. (1992) 'The slowly changing face of business school communication education: a national study of MBA programs', paper presented to the Educator Academy of the International Association of Business Communicators, San Francisco CA.

Ring, P. S. (1989) 'The environment and strategic management', in J. Rabin, G. J. Miller and W. Bartley Hildreth (eds) *Handbook of Strategic Management*, New York: Marcel Dekker.

Robins, J. A. (1987) 'Organizational economics: notes on the use of transaction-cost theory in the study of organizations', *Administrative Science Quarterly*, 32, 68–86.

Roggero, G. A. (1993) *Le Relazioni Pubbliche: Enciclopedia di direzione e organizzazione aziendale*, 6th edn, Milan: Franco Angeli.

Rumelt, R. P., Schendel, D. E. and Teece, D. J. (1994a) 'Fundamental issues in strategy', in R. P. Rumelt, D. E. Schendel and D. J. Teece (eds) *Fundamental Issues in Strategy: A Research Agenda*, Boston MA: Harvard Business School Press.

——(1994b) 'Afterword', in R. P. Rumelt, D. E. Schendel and D. J. Teece (eds) *Fundamental Issues in Strategy: A Research Agenda*, Boston MA: Harvard Business School Press.

Samuelson, P. A. and Nordhaus, W. D. (1985) *Economics*, 12th edn, McGraw-Hill.

Schiller, H. I. (1989) *Culture, inc.: The Corporate Takeover of Public Expression*, New York: Oxford University Press.

Simon, H. A. (1948) *Administrative Behavior*, New York: Macmillan.

Sriramesh, K. and White, J. (1992) 'Societal culture and public relations', in J. E. Grunig (ed.) *Excellence in Public Relations and Communication Management*, Hillsdale NJ: Lawrence Erlbaum.

58 *PR and management theory*

Stacey, J. E. and Sturdivant, F. D. (1994) *The Corporate Social Challenge: Cases and Commentaries*, 5th edn, Burr Ridge IL: Irwin.

Steiner, G. A., Miner, J. B. and Gray, E. R. (1982) *Management Policy and Strategy*, 2nd edn, New York: Macmillan.

Thayer, L. (1968) *Communication and Communication Systems*, Homewood IL: Irwin.

Thurley, K. and Wirdenius, H. (1989) *Towards European Management*, London: Pitman.

Verčič, D. (1997) 'Towards fourth wave public relations: a case study', in D. Moss, T. MacManus and D. Verčič (eds) *Public Relations Research: An International Perspective*, London: International Thomson Business Press.

Verčič, D., Grunig, L. A. and Grunig, J. E. (1995) 'Global and specific principles of public relations: evidence from Slovenia', in H. M. Culbertson and N. Chen (eds) *International Public Relations: A Comparative Analysis*, Hillsdale NJ: Lawrence Erlbaum.

Vernon, R. (1968) 'Economic sovereignty at bay', *Foreign Affairs*, 47 (1) 110–22.

Wakefield, R. I. (1994) 'Excellence in international public relations: an exploratory Delphi study', unpublished dissertation prospectus, College Park MD: University of Maryland.

Wallace, C. D. (1982) *Legal Control of the Multinational Enterprise: National Regulatory Techniques and the Prospects for International Controls*, The Hague: Martinus Nijhoff.

Walton, M. (1986) *The Deming Management Method*, New York: Perigree.

White, J. (1991) *How to Understand and Manage Public Relations: A Jargon-Free Guide to Public Relations Management*, London: Business Books.

Wheelen, T. L. and Hunger, J. D. (1987) *Strategic Management*, 2nd edn, Reading MA: Addison-Wesley.

Williams, J. R. (1994) 'Strategy and the search for rents: the evolution of diversity among firms', in R. P. Rumelt, D. E. Schendel and D. J. Teece (eds) *Fundamental Issues in Strategy: A Research Agenda*, Boston MA: Harvard Business School Press.

Williamson, O. E. (1992) 'The modern corporation: origins, evolution, attributes', in D. Mercer (ed.) *Managing the External Environment: A Strategic Perspective*, London: Sage.

——(1994) 'Strategizing, economizing, and economic organization', in R. P. Rumelt, D. E. Schendel and D. J. Teece (eds) *Fundamental Issues in Strategy: A Research Agenda*, Boston MA: Harvard Business School Press.

Wittenberg, E. and Lesly, P. (1991) 'Working with federal government', in P. Lesly (ed.) *Lesly's Handbook of Public Relations and Communications*, 4th edn, Chicago IL: Probus.

Wood, D. J. and Jones, T. M. (1994) 'From the editors', *Business and Society*, 33 (2) 147–9.

Yoshihara, H. (1976) 'Towards a comprehensive concept of strategic adaptive behaviour of firms', in H. I. Ansoff, R. P. Declerck and R. L. Hayes (eds) *From Strategic Planning to Strategic Management*, London: Wiley.

2 Strategy and public relations

Danny Moss and Gary Warnaby

Background

One of the major themes that recurs throughout the strategy literature is that of the role of strategy as a continuous and adaptive
response to external opportunities and threats that may confront an
organisation (e.g. Argyris 1985; Mintzberg 1989; Steiner and Miner
1977). A broad consensus exists within the management literature,
that strategy is essentially concerned with a process of managing the
interaction between an organisation and its external environment so as
to ensure the best 'fit' between the two. From this perspective, it can
be argued that 'boundary-spanning' functions can play a key role in
the process of managing such environmental interaction (e.g. White
and Dozier 1992; Cutlip *et al.* 1994). As a boundary-spanning function, public relations operates at the interface between the
organisation and its environment; thus it is arguably in an ideal position both to help gather, relay and interpret information from the
environment as well as representing the organisation to the outside
world. For example, White and Dozier argue that 'when organisations
make decisions, they do so based on a representation of both the
organisation itself and its environment', and they go on to suggest
that public relations practitioners play an important role in shaping
perceptions of the environment and the organisation itself among
decision-makers (1992: 92).

However, for the vast majority of organisations, the strategic
potential of this boundary-spanning role appears to go largely unrealised. This, Dozier (1990) argues, is because management tends to
treat public relations largely as a tactical communications function,
concerned primarily with the technical gathering of information and
external representation, and thus, public relations practitioners are
often cast in the role of 'communications technicians' rather than

managers, and are rarely included in the dominant coalition responsible for the formulation of organisational strategies.

This chapter sets out to explore to what extent public relations can contribute to the strategic management of organisations, setting this discussion of the role of public relations in the context of recent developments in thinking about the concept and process of strategy-making. Drawing on the strategic management literature, we suggest a conceptual framework which may help to explain the potential role which public relations can play in the development of both corporate and competitive strategies, and the implications for public relations practice.

Perspectives on strategy

Despite the emergence over the past thirty years of a growing volume of literature devoted to the subject of strategy, a comprehensive, consensus definition of strategy has remained elusive. However, some broad areas of agreement about what constitutes the basic dimensions of strategy have emerged, particularly in terms of recognising the role of strategy as a means of handling changing environments; in recognising the need to explore issues relating to both content and process of strategy formulation; in acknowledging that strategy exists at different levels (at the corporate, competitive and operational levels) and in terms of recognising that strategy-making comprises both conceptual as well as analytical exercises.

Beyond these areas of broad consensus, Chaffee (1985) argues, agreement tends to break down amongst strategy scholars. Indeed, in recent years some aspects of these so-called 'areas of agreement' have come under increasingly critical scrutiny themselves. For example, Pettigrew (1992) has challenged whether the separation of content of strategy from the process of strategy formulation implicit in most traditional conceptualisations of strategy does, in fact, reflect the reality of strategy-making practices in most organisations. Recognising the fluid nature of the debate about strategy and the strategy process, Chaffee goes on to identify three distinct 'clusters' of strategy definitions and approaches to strategy – 'linear strategy', 'adaptive strategy' and 'interpretive strategy' – each of which, when reviewed individually and collectively, reveals something of the contested nature of our current understanding of the concept of strategy. The emphasis, and fundamental assumptions underpinning each of these three strategy models are summarised in Figure 2.1.

STRATEGY MODEL

	Linear	Adaptive	Interpretive
EMPHASIS			
	Methodical, directed, sequential, rational planning process	Importance of link between company and environment	Open systems perspective emphasises role of strategy in shaping the attitudes of stakeholders towards the organisation and its outputs
	Overall aim is the achievement of pre-stated goals	Firms seek to 'match' existing strengths and capabilities to opportunities and risks	Emphasises the idea of managers holding a 'cognitive map' or 'world-view' which influences their interpretation of environmental changes
		Continuous, iterative, strategy-making process	Corresponds to stakeholder perspective of strategy
ASSUMPTIONS			
	The company is formally structured to facilitate implementation of strategic plans	The environment is more dynamic and less susceptible to prediction	Strategy strongly influenced by 'politics' and prevailing socio-cultural characteristics of company
	The environment is relatively predictable, or company is well insulated from environmental forces	The company must adapt to environment rather than attempt to impose its will on it	The company's success/survival depends on balancing conflicting stakeholder interests
	Managers act in a more or less rational manner	Managers must take into account more external variables	Seeks legitimacy for the company's policies
PROCESSES			
	Rational planning	Logical incrementalism, or emergent strategy	Seeks to deal with the environment through symbolic actions and communications; emphasises negotiation and bargaining to achieve consensus

Figure 2.1 Three models of strategy: emphases, assumptions and processes
Source: Chaffee 1985.

As this summary of the main characteristics of these models clearly reveals, each represents a fundamentally different view of how organisations approach the task of strategy formulation. Moreover, given the multi-faceted nature of strategy, it can be argued that no one model in isolation is capable of explaining adequately all the nuances of strategy formulation that might be found within different industry sectors and organisations.

Integrating the different approaches

Chaffee (1985) recognises the need to consider these various approaches or models not simply as distinct alternatives, but as a set of hierarchically related approaches representing differing levels of complexity and sophistication in organisational strategy-making. Thus Chaffee suggests that some organisations might initially rely largely on linear planning approaches, but might then move on to adopt adaptive and then interpretive approaches to strategy-making as circumstances dictate and as they become more sophisticated and adept at strategic management. However, as Chaffee emphasises, even very strategically sophisticated organisations may still rely, in part, on less complex strategy approaches. In fact, she argues that more complex levels of strategy that ignore less complex strategy models ignore the foundations on which they must be built if they are to reflect organisational reality. In short, these three models of strategy may be best thought of in terms of a 'menu' of options, from which strategists can select and/or combine those approaches that appear to offer the best means of responding to the particular opportunities and challenges that the organisation faces.

Building on Chaffee's work, Johnson (1988) suggests that these three strategy models can be seen to represent two main thrusts in thinking about the *process* of strategy formulation. On one hand, Johnson argues that strategy formulation can be seen to involve logical, rational processes conducted either through the planning mode or through the adaptive, logical incremental mode. In both cases, the role of the strategist is seen as one of consciously seeking to understand and analyse the environment in which the organisation operates, so as to configure organisational resources to best meet environmental needs. On the other hand, strategy formulation can involve what Johnson terms an 'organisational action' approach, in which strategy is seen as 'the product of the political, programmatic, cognitive, or symbolic aspects of management within the organisation' (1988: 80). Thus the first of these broad themes can be seen to correspond broadly to the linear or adaptive models of strategy, whereas the latter theme can be seen to correspond broadly to the interpretive model of strategy.

One could argue, therefore, that there is a growing consensus among strategy scholars that strategy-making in organisations may be best explained in terms of an integrated set of models or approaches, rather than in terms of one dominant approach. However, as Chaffee admits, there is still little understanding of how and to what extent such integration may take place in operational terms. Here, a useful starting point in conceptualising how organisations may in practice combine different strategy-making approaches may be to consider the process of strategy-making in terms of the notion of a continuum of strategy approaches. From this perspective, strategy formulation is seen to embrace, as Chaffee has suggested, not one dominant approach, but may take place through a combination of strategy approaches, ranging from formalised planning approaches at one extreme, through adaptive, incremental approaches, towards, at the other extreme, approaches that embrace a strongly interpretive orientation. Here, strategists are seen to select and perhaps combine different strategy approaches from along this continuum, according to which they perceive to offer the best means of tackling the complexity of the problems/situation facing the organisation, as well as based on the experience and sophistication of the strategic management team itself.

Of course, any attempt to explain organisational strategy-making practices must take account of the many factors within inner and outer contexts of the organisation if it is to reflect the reality of strategic decision making in organisations today. Here, for example, it is recognised that differences in organisational characteristics in terms of size, structure, political make-up and cultural values, as well as in the political, cultural and cognitive biases that may exist among the strategy-making team, are likely exert a strong influence on the strategic decision-making process (e.g. Johnson 1988; Pettigrew 1992). Equally, an organisation's freedom to manoeuvre with respect to its choice of strategy is likely to be strongly influenced by the nature of the industry or market structure (Porter 1980), as well as by management perceptions of the broader macro-environmental conditions facing the organisation, particularly in terms of the level of complexity and dynamism within its environment (Duncan 1972).

Competitive strategy

Having examined some of the major themes in what can be seen as the debate about the generic nature of strategy and strategy formulation, we must now turn to examine what many scholars (e.g. Day 1994; Porter 1980; 1985) see as the central question at the heart of the strategy development process, namely that of how organisations achieve and maintain a superior competitive position. Here, an equally contested debate can be found among scholars about the basis on which firms should seek to formulate successful competitive strategies – i.e. strategies that are designed to deliver sustainable competitive advantage. Day (1994) identifies two broad schools of thought on this subject. First, and until recently, the dominant paradigm in the competitive strategy field has been the competitive forces or competitive positioning approach championed most notably by Porter (1980; 1985). This approach places the emphasis on analysing the intensity of competition in industries and market segments so as to enable the firm to develop a position in an attractive market that it can defend against competitors. Here Porter (1980) argues that the route to sustainable competitive advantage lies in the pursuit of one or other of what he defines as two main 'generic strategies' open to firms – cost leadership or differentiation. Day points to a second and more recent school of thought – the capabilities or resource-based theories of competitive advantage – which locate the sources of a defensible competitive position in the distinctive and hard-to-imitate resources that the firm has developed. Here Day distinguishes between the firm's assets – the resource endowments it has accumulated – and the firm's capabilities – the glue that brings these assets together and enables them to be deployed advantageously (1994: 38). Moreover, since all organisations possess capabilities – complex bundles of skills and accumulated knowledge that are exercised through organisational processes – it is only those capabilities that enable an organisation to outperform its competitors that are treated as 'distinctive capabilities', since they support the organisation's competitive position. Not only are distinctive capabilities hard to imitate, but they are also normally robust enough to be used in different ways to speed up an organisation's adaptation to environmental change (Prahalad and Hamel 1990). Those capabilities that support multiple lines of business, and enable each business unit to develop the distinctive capabilities that it needs to attain a superior competitive position in the markets it serves, are commonly termed 'core competencies'.

Day distinguishes between three categories of capabilities, based on their orientation and the focus of their defining processes: those focusing on internal processes which are deployed from the 'inside-out' in response to market forces, competitor activity, etc.; those which focus on 'outside-in' processes that connect the organisation's capabilities to the external environment and enable it to compete successfully by anticipating market needs ahead of competitors; and 'spanning capabilities' which help integrate the inside-out and outside-in capabilities. Examples of 'inside-out' capabilities include manufacturing apabilities, logistics, human resource management, etc. Outside-in capabilities include market sensing, customer linking and channel bonding activities. Spanning capabilities include strategy development, new product development, and customer service delivery – critical activities that must be informed by both inside-out and outside-in analysis (Day 1994: 41).

The way in which distinctive capabilities can provide the basis for competitive success is exemplified in the work of John Kay (1993), who argues that companies develop successful strategies by understanding and matching their distinctive capabilities to the external environment in which they operate. Here Kay questions the underlying logic of Porter's arguments about the effectiveness of generic strategies, arguing instead that each firm's source of competitive success must be, by definition, unique, otherwise it would not be sustainable. Thus Kay argues that the foundations of each firm's competitive success will tend to be built around the unique distinctive capabilities it possesses, and which it is able to exploit in the industries and markets in which it operates. Kay identifies three types of 'distinctive capabilities' which he suggests, either individually, or more often, in combination, have formed the basis on which many firms have been able to build and sustain successful competitive positions. These Kay identifies as 'corporate architecture', 'reputation' and 'innovation'. The characteristics of each of these three types of distinctive capabilities are summarised in Figure 2.2. We have also indicated the possible roles which public relations can play in supporting each of these distinctive capabilities. When compared with Day's (1994) classification of capabilities, it can be argued that the three dominant types of capability identified by Kay embrace elements of both outside-in, inside-out and spanning capabilities.

While the question of how firms can best achieve competitive advantage within their industries or markets has continued to be the dominant theme within much of the competitive strategy literature, little attention has been paid to what role, if any, public relations might play in the competitive strategy context. For example, Kay (1993) makes no reference to a role for public relations either in helping to build, maintain or spread an organisation's reputation or in helping to create or sustain corporate architecture. Yet public relations scholars would argue that the management of reputation, in particular,

DISTINCTIVE CAPABILITIES	DESCRIPTIVE CHARACTERISTICS	SOURCE OF COMPETITIVE ADVANTAGE	IMPLICATIONS FOR PUBLIC RELATIONS
Architecture	Comprises the 'network of relational contracts within or around a firm'. These may be: • Internal – e.g. with employees • External – e.g. with customers or suppliers and distributors • Networks – e.g. among a group of firms engaged in related activities	The value of architecture lies in its capacity to create organisational knowledge and routines which can result in more flexible responses to changing circumstances, and the rapid and open exchange of information. To be an effective source of advantage, such knowledge must be distinctive to the individual firm. As all firms possess forms of internal and external architecture, it is the unique way in which firms create and use their relationships and network of contacts to enhance their position that gives rise to competitive advantage. Equally, it is the inability of competitors to replicate such architecture that allows the advantage derived to be sustained.	The creation and maintenance of internal and external architecture relies to a large degree on effective communications between the parties involved. Communications can be seen as the essential 'glue' which holds such relationships and networks together. Public relations is the obvious function to handle such communications on both an internal and external basis.
Reputation	The most important commercial mechanism for conveying information to customers and other stakeholders. Can be regarded as a more extensive form of architecture applied on a nationwide or even international scale. Reputation is influenced by: people's experiences of a firm and its products; how the firm presents itself; how employees, others and the media talk about it – the sum of the stories that people tell.	The value of reputation lies in its influence on customer and other stakeholder groups' behaviour towards the firm. Specifically in allowing a firm to differentiate itself and its offering from its competitors and to charge premium prices *vis-à-vis* competitors' products or services. Reputations are not immutable nor are they created easily, and once established must be carefully preserved.	The management of reputation is generally recognised as the core responsibility of public relations. Here the role of public relations includes: spreading knowledge of an organisation widely; promoting its attributes; and defending its reputation, where necessary, from misrepresentation and attack.
Innovation	Comprises the ability of firms to generate unique products or services that cannot be easily replicated by other firms and to sustain this innovative ability over time.	Undoubtedly the most difficult source of competitive advantage to sustain, and can be both expensive and the outcomes uncertain. Success relies on the inability of other firms to replicate or imitate the new products or services introduced by the firm. Thus innovation tends to be used in conjunction with another distinctive capability – either reputation and/or architecture.	While public relations may have no obvious role in the process of innovation, it can play an important part in supporting this capability, by helping to promote awareness of new innovations, and in supporting other distinctive capabilities that may be deployed in conjunction with that of innovation.

Figure 2.2   Kay's three distinctive capabilities of successful organisations and the implications for the role of public relations

Source: Kay 1993.

is one of the primary responsibilities of any public relations function. Similarly, while Day (1994) emphasises the importance of the free flow of information within organisations to facilitate organisational learning and the adjustment of processes to external change, as well as the importance of creating and managing close relationships with customers, he, like Kay, makes no explicit mention of a role for public relations in supporting these processes. This failure to acknowledge any explicit role for public relations in supporting the development of capability-based strategies is mirrored throughout the strategy literature, in which any potential role for public relations remains effectively 'hidden from view'.

The strategic potential of public relations

While management scholars have failed to acknowledge that public relations may have a significant role to play in the strategic management of organisations, public relations scholars have continued to argue that public relations should be treated as a strategically important function (e.g. Grunig and Repper 1992; Cutlip *et al.* 1994). Here their principal arguments have focused around the boundary-spanning capability of public relations practitioners in terms of helping organisations to manage exchanges between environmental actors and forces, and the capabilities and competencies of the organisation – i.e. in helping organisations to adapt, or match themselves to their environments.

In what is perhaps the most comprehensive examination of the strategic role of public relations to date, Grunig and Repper (1992) suggest that management theories often fail to explain how organisations actually go about diagnosing the environment, or who within the organisation should be responsible for this task. Drawing on Weick's (1969; 1979) work, they go on to suggest that public relations can play an important part 'in helping the organisation to identify – to "enact" – the most important components of its environment' (1992: 122–3). Thus they suggest that public relations, when managed strategically, can fill the 'environmental void' in theories of strategic management.

Here Grunig and Repper go on to define the strategic role of public relations in terms of building long-term relationships with an organisation's strategic constituencies – those stakeholder groups who may limit the autonomy of an organisation to pursue and realise its strategic goals. Thus maintaining such relationships is seen as a strategically important task. However, as we have suggested, this view

PRACTITIONER ROLE		IMPLIED STRATEGIC ROLE
Communication technician	Production of communication 'products' for organisations and dealing with the media.	Little, if any, involvement in the process of defining organisational problems and solutions. Practitioners produce communications products and implement programmes, sometimes without full knowledge of original motivation or intended results.
Expert prescriber	Regarded as the authority on PR problems and solutions. Practitioners define PR problems, and develop and implement the programme. Senior management usually take a largely passive role.	PR may become compartmentalised, often apart from the mainstream of the organisation. PR practitioners may only work periodically with senior management (e.g. in crisis situations).
Communication facilitator	Practitioners act as liaisons, interpreters and mediators between the organisation and its publics, communication and maintaining two-way facilitating exchanges.	Emphasis on providing management and stakeholders with the information they need to make decisions of mutual interest. PR practitioners occupy a boundary-spanning role – linking organisations and publics and thereby improving the quality of decisions by facilitating communication.
Problem-solving process facilitator	Practitioners collaborate with other managers to define and solve organisational problems.	Practitioners recognised as part of the strategic management team, engaged in the formulation of strategies. Incorporates the boundary-spanning role of public relations.

Figure 2.3 Practitioners' roles and their strategic implications
Source: Broom and Smith 1979.

of the strategic role of public relations is not reflected in most management theories of strategy. From a management perspective, public relations has been viewed as a largely 'functionary' activity in which practitioners are seen as 'communications technicians' oncerned primarily with projecting a favourable image for an organisation, with little, if any, involvement in more strategically important activities such as environmental scanning, analysis, or management counselling.

In examining the role that individual practitioners may play in strategic management processes, the pioneering research of Broom (1982) and Broom and Smith (1979) in defining the various roles which practitioners may play in organisations, offers a potentially useful conceptual framework for considering how and where practitioners may contribute to both the formulation and implementation of strategy. Here Broom and Smith identified four types of roles which practitioners may fulfil in organisations: 'communication technician', 'expert prescriber', 'communication facilitator' and 'problem-solving process facilitator'. The characteristics of each of these practitioners' roles, together with their implications in terms of public relations participation in strategic decision making, are summarised in Figure 2.3.

Building on this earlier role research, Dozier (1984) went on to distinguish between two dominant role forms – a 'public relations manager' role which embraced attributes of problem-solving process facilitation, expert prescription, and communication facilitation; and a 'public relations technician' role which closely matches Broom and Smith's 'communication technician' role in that practitioners do not participate in management decision making and are involved only in generating communication products that implement policy decisions made by others.

In examining the reasons behind the particular configuration of roles occupied by practitioners, Cutlip *et al.* (1994) suggest that practitioner roles may be strongly related to the type of environment in which organisations operate. They suggest that the communication technician role is more likely to be found in organisations operating in relatively stable, non-threatening environments, whereas communication facilitators tend to predominate in relatively turbulent, but low-threat environments. Practitioners are more likely to occupy the roles of problem-solving facilitators and expert prescribers where organisations are perceived as facing more threatening environments. Here problem-solving facilitators are more likely to predominate in environments that, while threatening, are relatively stable, whereas expert prescribers are more likely to predominate in conditions that are both threatening and relatively turbulent. Thus, by combining these two environmental dimensions (relative dynamism/stability and low/high threat), Cutlip *et al.* suggest that it is possible to predict the type of practitioner roles that one might expect to find in organisations operating under different environmental conditions. Moreover, drawing on Dozier's (1984) refinement of this practitioner roles paradigm, it follows that the extent to which public relations practitioners are allowed to enact a 'public relations manager' role, rather than simply serving as 'public relations/communication technicians' is likely to depend to a large degree on the environment in which the organisation operates, or more precisely, management perceptions of this environment. This distinction between these two dominant role forms is important, since it will largely determine the extent to which practitioners are likely to participate in the strategic decision-making process within organisations, and thus contribute directly to the formulation of organisational strategies.

Towards a broad strategy-making framework

While this practitioner roles paradigm offers a potentially useful starting point in conceptualising the conditions under which public relations is most likely to participate in the strategic management process, and suggests some of the important ways in which practitioners can contribute to this process, this framework is insufficient on its own to explain fully the input that public relations can make to strategic decision-making at both the corporate and competitive levels; nor does it help explain how public relations strategy is itself formulated. For this purpose, we need to construct a new conceptual framework/model to explain the interrelationship between corporate, competitive and public relations strategy-making practices.

Of course, since all models are, by definition, a simplification of reality, it is recognised that no one model could hope to capture fully the potentially rich texture of corporate and competitive activity found within any one, let alone all organisations, and hence, by implication, the interaction of public relations with such activity. However, as Grunig and Grunig (1992) point out, without a model to work with, it would be impossible to begin to construct an understanding of strategic phenomena. Thus, while the model which will be advanced in this chapter might be seen to represent a largely normative view of the strategic role of public relations, it can at least help to extend our understanding of how public relations can contribute to the strategic management function, particularly within many of the larger more strategically sophisticated organisations today. In this sense, we believe this model does offer a useful basis from which it may be possible to construct a more comprehensive positive (descriptive) theory to explain ⸀he role which public relations can play within the overall strategic ṉanagement function, as well as how the public relations function ıtself can be managed strategically.

Because very few empirical studies have been conducted into the strategic role of public relations, and because of the contested nature of debate surrounding the subject of strategy itself, it has been necessary to make certain assumptions about the fundamental purpose and approach to strategy-making that is represented within the model that has been advanced. First, it has been assumed that, for most organisations, the central purpose of strategy revolves around attempts to 'match' the organisation to its environment, either through corporate positioning or through attempts to influence and shape the environment through the exploitation of the organisation's superior resources and distinctive capabilities – what are generally recognised as the two dominant approaches to strategy development (e.g. Day 1994). Here it is recognised that for some organisations, strategy formulation may be conducted predominantly through a combination of planning as well as logical incremental processes. However, it is also acknowledged that in many larger and more strategically sophisticated organisations, strategy will often reflect what may be a complex interplay between the cognitive, political and social processes inherent within such organisations. Equally, for many organisations, the question of how particular strategies may affect key stakeholder relationships has become an increasingly important consideration shaping the thinking of strategy-makers. In this sense, it is recognised that strategy formulation may often take on a far more prominent stakeholder orientation akin to that suggested by the interpretive model.

At the competitive strategy level, the model is based around the belief that the way in which organisations seek to secure competitive advantage is perhaps best explained in terms of the successful exploitation of an organisation's distinctive capabilities and/or strategic assets (Prahalad and Hamel 1990; Kay 1993; Day 1994), rather than in terms of competitive positioning based on the type of generic competitive strategies suggested by Porter (1980). However, this is not to suggest that differentiation or the pursuit of low-cost leadership cannot prove to be effective sources of competitive advantage – rather it is to recognise that not all firms can be successful cost leaders, nor can they always expect to rely on sustaining a differentiated position for their products or services over the longer term.

When considering strategy and strategy-making at the public relations level, the model recognises that public relations strategy cannot be understood in isolation from the corporate and competitive strategies to which it should contribute, and from which it derives its essential purpose. Thus we suggest that the way in which public relations practitioners approach the task of formulating and managing public relations strategies is likely to reflect the prevailing dominant approach to corporate and competitive strategy formulation adopted elsewhere within the organisation. And so, in organisations where formal strategic planning systems predominate, one would expect to find a similar emphasis on formalised planning within the public relations function. Whereas in organisations which favour a more flexible incremental approach to strategy-making (adaptive model), one would expect to find that public relations strategy-making would also exhibit similar adaptive or incremental characteristics. In fact, it can be argued that it would be illogical, if not impossible, for practitioners not to follow a similar pattern of strategy-making to that found elsewhere within their organisation. While there appears to be a reasonably strong logic underpinning these assumptions, it must be recognised that rules are there to be broken, and each organisation will tend to have its own unique way of dealing with the strategic problems it faces (Stacey 1993).

A nested model of strategy and strategy formulation

As we have acknowledged earlier, the lack of empirical evidence about how, and to what extent, public relations does, in fact, contribute to the strategic management function in organisations makes it impossible, at this stage, to construct a definitive model to explain how public relations, corporate and competitive strategies may interact in all cases. Equally, because strategy can exist at different levels within an organisation, as well as at the industry or sector level, it is also necessary to consider how strategy-making at any one level relates to, and is influenced by, strategic decisions and actions taken at other levels.

In order to try to capture a sense of the potential strategic complexity within organisations and the potential interplay between different levels of strategy-making, a 'nested model' of strategy and strategy formulation has been proposed, in which corporate, competitive and public relations strategies are seen as interrelated layers in the total strategy-making structure of the organisation (see Figure 2.4). Conventionally, the development of strategies at these different levels is normally seen to cascade down from the corporate to the competitive

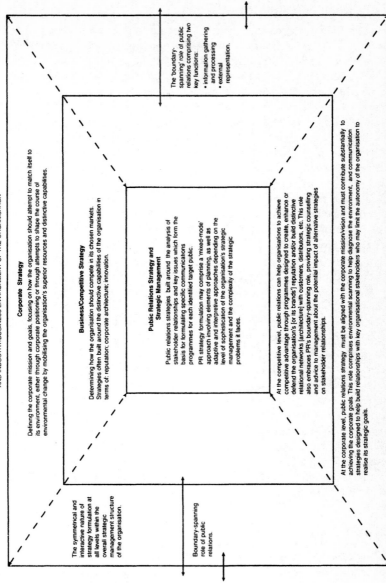

EXTERNAL SOCIAL, POLITICAL, ECONOMIC, TECHNOLOGICAL
AND INDUSTRY/BUSINESS ENVIRONMENT OF THE ORGANISATION

Corporate Strategy

Defining the corporate mission and goals, focusing on how the organisation should attempt to match itself to its environment, either through corporate positioning or through attempts to shape the course of environmental change by mobilising the organisation's superior resources and distinctive capabilities.

Business/Competitive Strategy

Determining how the organisation should compete in its chosen markets. Strategies often built around the distinctive capabilities of the organisation in terms of: reputation; corporate architecture; innovation.

Public Relations Strategy and Strategic Management

Public relations strategies built around the analysis of stakeholder relationships and key issues which form the basis for formulating specific communications programmes for each identified target public.

PR strategy formulation may comprise a 'mixed-mode' approach involving elements of planning, as well as adaptive and interpretive approaches depending on the level of sophistication of the organisation's strategic management and the complexity of the strategic problems it faces.

At the competitive level, public relations can help organisations to achieve competitive advantage through programmes designed to create, enhance or defend the organisation's [or its brands'] reputation and/or build distinctive relational networks [architecture] with customers, distributors, etc. This role also embraces PR's boundary-spanning role, providing strategic counselling and advice to management about the potential impact of alternative strategies on stakeholder relationships.

At the corporate level, public relations strategy must be aligned with the corporate mission/vision and must contribute substantially to achieving the corporate goals. This role comprises environmental scanning to help diagnose the environment, and communication strategies designed to help build relationships with key organisational stakeholders who may limit the autonomy of the organisation to realise its strategic goals.

The 'boundary-spanning' role of public relations comprising two key functions:
• information gathering and processing
• external representation.

The symmetrical and interactive nature of strategy formulation at all levels within the overall strategic management structure of the organisation.

Boundary-spanning role of public relations.

Figure 2.4 The role of public relations in the strategic management of organisations

level and then ultimately to the functional (e.g. public relations) level, with each level of strategy providing the immediate context for the next 'lower' level of strategy-making. However, as a number of scholars have suggested (Mintzberg 1989; Johnson and Scholes 1993; Whittington 1993), strategy-making need not always follow such a rigid, hierarchical top-down pattern. For example, Whittington (1993) argues that the emphasis on formal top-down planning systems has been a characteristic of strategic management in Anglo-Saxon corporations in particular, and that this approach is by no means universal. Even here, Whittington suggests, there has been a move away from a reliance on the type of centralised system of formal planning favoured during the 1970s, towards a more flexible and often decentralised approach to strategic management in which divisional or business unit management teams are encouraged to initiate ideas that are then passed upward for approval at the appropriate senior management level.

From this perspective, business unit and functional management teams may be responsible not only for developing strategic responses to the problems or opportunities encountered at their own level, but may sometimes initiate ideas that then become the catalyst for changes in strategy throughout the organisation. For example, it is not impossible to conceive of situations where problems with key stakeholder relationships which are identified at communications/public relations function level may trigger a review and change in both the organisation's competitive and corporate strategies. For example, the widespread criticisms of the way in which many UK financial services providers have attempted to market financial products such as personal pension plans and other investment products in recent years, has caused many firms in this sector to undertake a radical review not only of their marketing and sales strategies, but also their overall positioning within the industry.

Deconstructing the model

While acknowledging that the different levels of strategy-making within an organisation should be recognised as interrelated layers of the organisation's total strategy-making structure, nevertheless it may be useful to deconstruct this nested model of organisational strategy-making, in order to examine in more detail how public relations can contribute to strategy-making at the corporate and competitive levels, as well as to explore how public relations strategies are themselves formulated.

As we have shown, at the corporate level, strategy is usually seen to be concerned with providing direction and determining how the organisation should manage its interaction with its environment. Thus, by implication, corporate strategy is concerned with understanding and responding to the forces driving environmental change. Here, it has been suggested that public relations can help support strategic decision making through its boundary-spanning capability in terms of managing exchanges across organisational-environment boundaries. In this boundary-spanning role, practitioners can contribute to corporate strategy-making in a number of important ways. First, because boundary-spanning practitioners operate at the interface between an organisation and its environment, they are ideally placed to assist management to keep abreast of, and alert to, the implications of changes taking place within the organisation's environment, particularly in terms of identifying how such changes may impact on key stakeholder relationships. In this sense, public relations can be seen to function as the 'antenna' of the organisation, providing an early warning system to detect the emergence of issues which may have significant implications for the organisation's current or future strategies. Boundary-spanning practitioners can also help to bring a stakeholder perspective into the strategic decision-making process, representing the likely reaction of stakeholders to alternative strategy options, and thereby assisting management to give a more balanced consideration to the attractiveness and feasibility of the strategy options open to them. Boundary-spanning practitioners can also play an important part in the implementation of corporate strategies by helping to communicate the organisation's strategic intentions to both internal and external stakeholders, which may help avoid misunderstandings that might otherwise frustrate the smooth implementation of the organisation's strategy.

Thus, at the corporate strategy level, public relations practitioners can be seen to play two important roles: 'environmental scanning' (in terms of information gathering and processing) to assist corporate strategy-makers in analysing the organisation's position and identifying emerging issues which may have significant implications for future strategy development; and 'external representation' to help build and maintain relationships with those organisational stakeholders who may have the power to influence the successful realisation of the organisation's goals (Aldrich and Herker 1977). Through these two roles, public relations practitioners can assist strategy-makers to anticipate and adapt to environmental change, or to (re)deploy organisational resources so as to help shape environmental change to the organisation's advantage. Public relations can also help organisations to attract and maintain the support of key stakeholders both within the organisation as well as within its environment, whose support or opposition may be crucial to the successful realisation of the organisation's goals.

Of course, public relations practitioners can only realise the full potential of this boundary-spanning role insofar as they are allowed to collaborate with senior managers to define and solve problems – i.e. insofar as their role as 'problem-solving process facilitators' is recognised within the organisation. However, as White and Dozier (1992) suggest, all too often, practitioners only operate on the periphery of the dominant coalition, functioning largely as communication facilitators, communication technicians or, in some cases, expert prescribers. Clearly, where this is the case, practitioners are likely to have only a limited influence on the decision-making process.

The role of public relations at the competitive strategy level

If, as we have assumed, successful competitive strategies tend to be built around the distinctive capabilities that organisations either possess or are able to create (Kay 1993; Day 1994), then it follows that the public relations role in supporting competitive strategy development will tend to revolve around activities that help to create, sustain or enhance those distinctive capabilities by which each organisation seeks to derive its competitive advantage. In this sense, public relations may help to support 'outside-in', 'inside-out' and 'spanning'-related capabilities (Day 1994). Here, public relations' environmental scanning and representational roles are likely to be particularly important, as well as its role in helping to keep effective lines of communication open between members of an organisation. The latter role can be particularly important during periods of significant organisational or environmental change, where the acquisition, processing and interpretation of information often play a vital part in facilitating organisational learning (Slater and Narver 1995).

If we look, for example, at ways in which public relations can support each of the three main types of distinctive capabilities identified by Kay (1993), at least theoretically, it can be argued that public relations can play a potentially powerful role in supporting competitive strategies based around these types of distinctive capabilities (see Figure 2.2). Here, the role of public relations is perhaps most easily discerned where an organisation's competitive position is based around either its reputation (or that of its brands), and/or the exploitation of distinctive corporate architecture (e.g. in terms of exclusive distributor networks or supplier relationships). In fact, as Kay suggests, reputation and corporate architecture are more often than not used to support one another, and both are distinctive capabilities whose successful application, arguably, depends to a large degree on maintaining effective communications between the organisation and its customers, suppliers, distributors, opinion formers and, of course, its employees. Moreover, it is generally recognised that reputation, and particularly architecture, cannot be built or sustained simply through the use of corporate or brand advertising or other traditional promotional tools, but requires that organisations establish two-way communications in the form of an ongoing 'dialogue' with all key stakeholders. Arguably, developing mechanisms that facilitate this type of two-way communication is a task which is widely acknowledged to be one of the key responsibilities of the public relations function. In fact, public relations is frequently defined in terms of its role in 'managing communication between an organisation and its publics' (Grunig and Hunt 1984) as well as in terms of the 'management of reputation' (Institute of Public Relations, UK).

Here again, from a practitioner roles perspective, if public relations is to contribute significantly to competitive strategy development, one would expect to find practitioners operating as 'public relations managers' rather than simply as 'public relations technicians' – i.e. their role might be expected to involve elements of expert prescription, problem-solving facilitation and communication facilitation. Yet, as we have shown, Kay makes no explicit reference to a role for public relations, either in the creation or the sustaining of an organisation's distinctive capabilities, despite acknowledging the importance of communications as a means of sharing knowledge and sustaining organisational relationships. Thus in Kay's work we again find the same lack of recognition of any strategic role for public relations that is common throughout the management literature.

Public relations strategy

In considering the nature of strategy-making within public relations itself, it is generally recognised that public relations strategy cannot be divorced from the organisation's corporate and/or competitive strategies, to which it must contribute if it is to be seen to have a genuine strategic role. As Webster maintains:

> To be strategic, public relations must pass one basic test: At minimum everything done must be aligned with the corporate vision or mission ... and must substantially contribute to achieving the organisation's objectives.
>
> (1990: 18)

From this perspective, one would again expect to find public relations practitioners operating primarily as problem-solving facilitators, actively collaborating with senior management in the formulation and implementation of organisational strategies. However, whether this is, in fact, generally the case remains open to question. As Cutlip *et al.* (1994) have pointed out, many practitioners tend to fantasise about their roles in strategic planning, but few are really involved in a meaningful fashion. Here Cutlip *et al.* suggest the main obstacle to greater public relations participation in strategic decision making is that practitioners often fail to understand and meet management expectations in terms of understanding and responding to the needs and concerns of the organisation's operating units – i.e. in terms of demonstrating how public relations can contribute to the bottom line.

While acknowledging these doubts about the extent to which public relations does, in practice, contribute to strategic decision making, it is important not to accept them at face value without first examining the type of strategy-making practices that are generally employed within public relations, and considering to what degree they are normally aligned with the corporate and competitive strategy-making practices found elsewhere within organisations. Here, for example, Grunig and Repper (1992), while arguing that public relations should be treated as an integral part of the overall strategic management function in organisations, recognise the need to separate public relations strategy-making from corporate and competitive strategy-making practices, at least for the purposes of analysis. Grunig and Repper (1992) go on to suggest a seven-stage model for the strategic management of public relations, which they argue incorporates the dual role of public relations in the overall strategic management of the organisation, as well as in the strategic management of public relations itself (see Figure 2.5). Here they argue that the term 'strategic' should be defined as an essentially symmetrical concept, and thus the strategic aim of an organisation should be seen as that of achieving a balanced relationship with its environment, rather than one in which the organisation seeks to manipulate the environment in its favour. Of course, whether this symmetrical orientation is widely recognised as a desirable goal by management strategists is open to question.

When compared with conventional strategic management models such as that advanced by Johnson and Scholes (1993), broad parallels can be drawn between the initial three stages in Grunig and Repper's model and what is generally defined as the 'strategic analysis' stage in many conventional strategy models. Thus, while there may be little

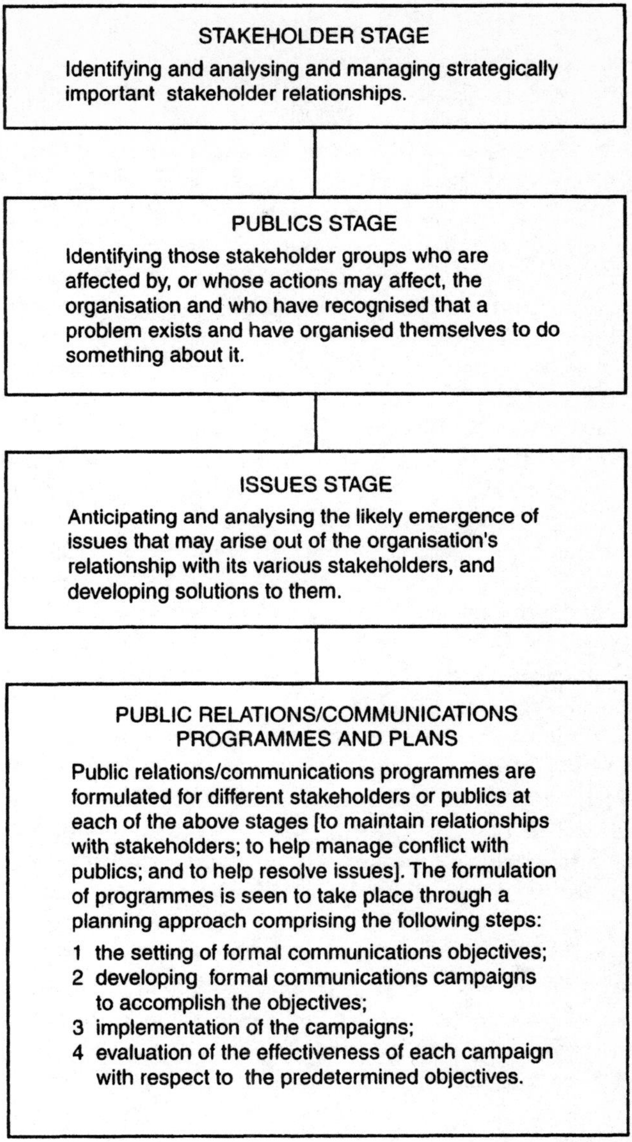

STAKEHOLDER STAGE

Identifying and analysing and managing strategically important stakeholder relationships.

PUBLICS STAGE

Identifying those stakeholder groups who are affected by, or whose actions may affect, the organisation and who have recognised that a problem exists and have organised themselves to do something about it.

ISSUES STAGE

Anticipating and analysing the likely emergence of issues that may arise out of the organisation's relationship with its various stakeholders, and developing solutions to them.

PUBLIC RELATIONS/COMMUNICATIONS PROGRAMMES AND PLANS

Public relations/communications programmes are formulated for different stakeholders or publics at each of the above stages [to maintain relationships with stakeholders; to help manage conflict with publics; and to help resolve issues]. The formulation of programmes is seen to take place through a planning approach comprising the following steps:

1 the setting of formal communications objectives;
2 developing formal communications campaigns to accomplish the objectives;
3 implementation of the campaigns;
4 evaluation of the effectiveness of each campaign with respect to the predetermined objectives.

Figure 2.5 Grunig and Repper's model of the strategic management of public relations

Source: Adapted from Grunig and Repper 1992.

reason to contest this conceptualisation of what can be seen as the analytical steps involved in defining the parameters of organisational/public relations problems and establishing the priorities for action, there are some obvious weaknesses in Grunig and Repper's conceptualisation of the subsequent stages in their model – i.e. in their conceptualisation of the process through which public relations programmes are formulated and put into action. Here their model displays a strong linear orientation, assuming that strategy is normally formulated through a rational, sequential planning process which, as we have shown, may not always be the case. Moreover, even in the initial three analytical stages in their model, there is an underlying assumption that the decision-making process will normally follow a logical, rational path. Thus Grunig and Repper appear to ignore the possibility that the strategy-making process, whether at the corporate, competitive or public relations level, may display a more incremental, adaptive, or perhaps interpretive orientation. Here, for example, there is little reason to believe that public relations practitioners are any less likely than management strategists to experience the type of internal political pressures and cognitive and socio-cultural biases that often militate against the use of the type of rational planning approach which Grunig and Repper seem to suggest characterises the formulation of public relations strategies.

Thus, while the model of strategic management for public relations that has been advanced in this chapter incorporates elements of Grunig and Repper's model, it attempts to address some of the chief weaknesses identified in their model, particularly in terms of recognising that the formulation of public relations strategies and programmes may involve a combination of approaches other than planning. However, it is recognised that further empirical research is needed before it will be possible to say whether this model represents a largely normative view of how public relations should contribute to strategic management process, or whether it does, in fact, capture the essential characteristics of the way in which public relations is managed and interacts with the corporate and competitive strategy-making functions, in at least some of today's more strategically sophisticated organisations.

As we have already shown, a number of scholars have expressed doubts about the extent to which public relations practitioners are generally accepted as part of the dominant management coalition in organisations, and hence are able to participate directly in strategic decision making. On balance, it would appear that in the majority of UK organisations, practitioners may well be asked to provide advice to the strategic decision-making team, but will rarely participate directly in the formulation of corporate or competitive strategies. However, anecdotal evidence appears to suggest that, in at least some cases, public relations practitioners do, in fact, contribute directly to strategy formulation and are actively involved in its implementation. This is most likely to be the case in those organisations which operate in particularly high profile or politically sensitive industries (e.g. nuclear energy and the privatised utility companies), or in organisations whose operating environment may be undergoing rapid and perhaps unpredictable change. However, further research is clearly needed to substantiate what must remain, at this stage, rather tentative conclusions about the factors that may influence the extent to which public relations is able to participate directly in the strategic decision-making function within organisations.

Implications for strategic management and future research

Although the strategic management model that has been advanced in this chapter must, of necessity, be treated as a largely normative model at this stage, we believe it does offer a useful framework from which to build a more comprehensive and positive model of strategic management in public relations. Moreover, despite the lack of empirical data to underpin the constructs represented within this conceptual model, we believe that the model does help focus attention on a number of important questions concerning the strategic management of organisations as a whole, as well as the strategic management of public relations itself.

First, this chapter has highlighted the need for a clearer understanding of how organisations go about diagnosing and defining the environment in which they operate. Here scholars such as Weick (1969; 1979), Duncan (1972), Starbuck (1976) and Leifer and Delbecq (1978) have argued that the borders between an organisation and its environment are often an arbitrary invention of the organisation itself, and, as Weick suggests, organisations may create their environment by paying attention to only some parts of the total information flow from outside the organisation – a process he terms 'enactment'. Understanding how, in practice, organisations go about defining and interpreting their environment may hold the key to understanding how far public relations is able to realise the full potential of its boundary-spanning role, in particular. Second, given the increasing emphasis on the importance of 'organisational learning' as perhaps the key source of longer-term competitive advantage (e.g. Day 1994; Slater and Narver 1995), the question of how organisations can create an appropriate culture and climate to promote organisational learning comes to the fore. Here, arguably, communications has a vital role to play in fostering a receptive climate in which organisational learning can take place, and public relations may be the most appropriate function to help manage this communication process.

Another important question that must be addressed concerns the arguments about the significance of the boundary-spanning role of public relations. While public relations scholars have emphasised the importance of the boundary-spanning role of public relations, clearly, public relations is not the only boundary-spanning function within organisations. In fact, Achrol (1991: 81) argues that, increasingly, successful organisations will be those that demonstrate 'functional ambidexterity' in which people will have multiple roles, constantly forming and participating in new and different organisational groups around new and different problems/solutions. Here Achrol argues that successful organisations will need to be very efficient at processing knowledge and information by integrating expertise, technology, decision authority and implementation at almost the individual level, but he also recognises that there will still be a need for some specialised expertise in coping with the vast amount of information available to organisations. Here it can be argued that boundary-spanning functions may have an important role to play in buffering organisations from information overload (Huber 1984), while ensuring that relevant information is disseminated throughout the organisation. However, the advent of ever more powerful and sophisticated information technologies may arguably reduce an organisation's dependence on specialist boundary-spanning personnel as a source of environmental and market intelligence. Thus one of the key issues which advocates of a more prominent and strategic role for public relations must address is that of redefining the nature of the boundary-spanning role of practitioners against the background of changes in organisational structure and task roles coupled with the availability of increasingly powerful information technologies.

An equally important question concerns the extent to which the different practitioner roles identified by Broom and Smith (1979) can be found to exist in organisations today and, more significantly, whether, in practice, the *problem-solving facilitator* role is widely recognised and accepted by senior management at least in some of today's larger, more strategically sophisticated organisations. The advent of the post-industrial era, characterised by increasing diversity, the increasing availability of knowledge and increasing turbulence (Huber 1984), poses new challenges for organisations in terms of adapting their strategies to cope with an increasingly knowledge-rich environment. Here the predicted move towards more flexible, multi-role functional teams (Achrol 1991) has important implications regarding where public relations practitioners may fit into such new structures, as well as what specific roles they may play.

A further set of important questions that needs to be addressed relates to the way in which different approaches to strategy-making may co-exist and be integrated within the strategic management function. In addition, from a public relations perspective, it is necessary to explore how, and to what extent, the role of public relations may change as an organisation's approach to strategy-making evolves and changes over time. Here, for example, it is necessary to explore whether the existence of a dominant model of corporate and/or competitive strategy-making – i.e. in terms of the linear, adaptive or interpretive models – will, in turn, be reflected in the way in which public relations strategies are formulated and managed.

Clearly, some of these questions relate not only to the strategic role of public relations, but are of more general concern to scholars interested in strategic management at both corporate and competitive levels. Further empirical research, perhaps involving a cross-section of organisational types, is needed in order to address the issues raised here. Such research may also help to confirm whether the model of strategic management for public relations that has been advanced in this chapter represents a largely normative view of the strategic role of public relations and of the strategy-making process in public relations, or whether it does, in fact, provide a reasonably sound basis for explaining the strategic role and the strategy-making process in public relations in at least some of today's larger and more strategically sophisticated organisations.

References

Achrol, R. S. (1991) 'Evolution of the marketing organisation: new forms for turbulent environments', *Journal of Marketing*, 55, 77–91.

Adlrich, H. and Herker, D. (1977) 'Boundary spanning roles and organisational structures', *Academy of Management Review*, 2, 217–30.

Argyris, C. (1985) *Strategy Change and Defensive Routines*, Marshfield MA: Pitman.

Broom, G. M. (1982) 'A comparison of sex roles in public relations', *Public Relations Review*, 8 (3) 17–22.

Broom, G. M. and Smith, G. G. (1979) 'Testing the practitioner's impact on clients', *Public Relations Review*, 5 (3) 47–59.

Chaffee, E. E. (1985) 'Three models of strategy', *Academy of Management Review*, 10 (1) 89–98.

Cutlip, S., Center, A. and Broom, G. (1994) *Effective Public Relations*, 7th edn, Englewood Cliffs NJ: Prentice Hall.

Day, G. S. (1994) 'The capabilities of market-driven organisations', *Journal of Marketing*, 59, 37–52.

Dozier, D. M. (1984) 'Program evaluation and the roles of practitioners', *Public Relations Review*, 10 (2), 13–21.

——(1990) 'The innovation of research in public relations practice: review of a programme of studies', in L. A. Grunig and J. E. Grunig (eds) *Public Relations Research Annual, Vol. 2*, Hillsdale NJ: Lawrence Erlbaum.

Duncan, R. B. (1972) 'Characteristics of organisational environment and perceived environmental uncertainty', *Administrative Science Quarterly*, 17, 313–27.

Eisenhardt, K. M. and Zbaracki, M. J. (1992) 'Strategic decision-making', *Strategic Management Journal*, 13, 17–37.

Granovetter, M. (1985) 'Economic action and social structure: the problem of embeddedness', *American Journal of Sociology*, 91 (3) 481–510.

Grant, R. M. (1991) 'The resource-based theory of competitive advantage: implications for strategy formulation', *California Management Review*, 114–35.

Grunig, J. E. and Grunig, L. A. (1992) 'Models of public relations and communications', in J. E. Grunig (ed.) *Excellence in Public Relations and Communications Management*, Hillsdale NJ: Lawrence Erlbaum.

Grunig, J. E. and Hunt, T. (1984) *Managing Public Relations*, New York: Holt, Rhinehart and Winston.

Grunig, J. E. and Repper, F. C. (1992) 'Strategic management, publics and issues', in J. E. Grunig (ed.) *Excellence in Public Relations and Communications Management*, Hillsdale NJ: Lawrence Erlbaum.

Huber, G. P. (1984) 'The nature and design of postindustrial organisations', *Management Science*, 30, 928–51.

Johnson, G. (1988) 'Rethinking incrementalism', *Strategic Management Journal*, 75–91.

Johnson, G. and Scholes, K. (1993) *Exploring Corporate Strategy: Text and Cases*, 3rd edn, Hemel Hempstead: Prentice Hall.

Kay, J. (1993) *Foundations of Corporate Success: How Business Strategies Add Value*, Oxford: Oxford University Press.

Leavy, B. and Wilson, D. (1994) *Strategy and Leadership*, London: Routledge.

Leifer, R. P. and Delbecq, A. (1978) 'Organisational/environmental interchange: a model of boundary spanning activity', *Academy of Management Review*, 3, 40–50.

Lindblom, C. E. (1959) 'The science of muddling through', *Public Administration Review*, 19, 79–88.

Mintzberg, H. (1989) 'Strategy formation: schools of thought', in J. Frederickson (ed.) *Perspectives on Strategic Management*, San Francisco CA: Ballinger.

——(1994) *The Rise and Fall of Strategic Planning*, Englewood Cliffs NJ: Prentice Hall.

Pettigrew, A. M. (1992) 'The character and significance of strategy process research', *Strategic Management Journal*, 13, 5–16.

Porter, M. E. (1980) *Competitive Strategy: Techniques for Analysing Industries and Competitors*, New York: The Free Press.

——(1985) *Competitive Advantage: Creating and Sustaining Superior Performance*, New York: The Free Press.

Prahalad, C. K. and Hamel, G. (1990) 'The core competence of the corporation', *Harvard Business Review*, May/June, 71–91.

Slater, S. F. and Narver, J. C. (1995) 'Market orientation and the learning organisation', *Journal of Marketing*, 59, 63–74.

Stacey, R. (ed.) (1993) *Strategic Thinking and the Management of Change*, London: Kogan Page.

Starbuck, W. H. (1976) 'Organisations and their environments', in M. D. Dunnette (ed.) *Handbook of Industrial and Organisational Psychology*, Chicago IL: Rand McNally.

Steiner, G. A. and Miner, J. B. (1977) *Management Policy and Strategy*, New York: Macmillan.

Webster, P. J. (1990) 'Strategic corporate public relations: what's the bottom line?', *Public Relations Journal*, 46 (2) 18–21.

Weick, K. E. (1969) *The Social Psychology of Organising*, Reading MA: Addison-Wesley.

——(1979) 'Cognitive processes in organisations', *Research in Organisational Behavior*, 1, 41–74.

White, J. and Dozier, D. M. (1992) 'Public relations and mangement decision-making', in J. E. Grunig (ed.) *Excellence in Public Relations and Communications Management*, Hillsdale NJ: Lawrence Erlbaum.

Whittington, R. (1993) *What is Strategy – and Does it Matter?*, London: Routledge.

Part II

Contemporary perspectives of public relations

3 A feminist phase analysis of research on women in postmodern public relations

Larissa A. Grunig

Introduction

Understanding gender[1] and changing relations between the sexes is a necessary foundation for understanding this postmodern era. Philosopher Patricia S. Mann (1994) contended that our most socially significant transformations are occurring in the area of gender relations. This chapter explores selected literature of public relations over the last two decades from the basis of feminist phase theory to describe and to analyse that transformation. Looking at the role of women in traditionally patriarchal relationships should provide a solid basis for assessing the role of postmodern women into the next century.

This study applies feminist phase theory to the literature of public relations for the first time. Thus this classification system, dating from the work of Mary Kay Tetreault (1976)[2] in higher education, offers a new approach for feminist scholarship in our field. Campbell defined feminist scholarship in communication as follows:

> Feminist scholarship is distinguished by the systematic inclusion of women, by an absence of language and/or perspective that degrades women or minorities, by rigorous testing of assumptions that hark back to stereotypes and social mythology, and by a concern to rectify the omissions, the degradation, and the errors of the past.
>
> (Campbell 1989: 4)

As I pointed out in an earlier paper on transforming public relations education and practice (L. Grunig 1989), men may find feminist research "boring, dull, unimportant." However, feminism is a basic movement for human liberty. For any of us, male or female, to consider it less seriously is, in my view, to ignore the history and achievements of half the human race. But as Howe explained about some people's disinterest:

> It is not about them and hence not interesting. If it is critical of them, they find it painful. In any event, they look to one another for professional recognition, and mastery of the products of female scholarship will not win that recognition.
>
> (Howe 1984: 281)

Langland and Gove (1983) established this resistance to incorporating feminist research into any body of knowledge – attributing it largely to its challenge of deeply held, almost sacred beliefs. However, inclusivity in research offers the promise of developing a community of scholars whose work validates women and men alike rather than perpetuating any ahistorical or imperialistic generalisations.

Conceptualisation

Feminist phase theory defines five stages of such research: male scholarship, compensatory, bifocal, feminist and multifocal. Each will be explained in some detail below. First, however, I make this disclaimer: assessing the impact of postmodernity on women in public relations is beyond the scope of this study. In other words, I cannot determine how the ultimate or multifocal phase of writing about women may affect our thinking about women – much less how it may affect women's careers or their daily life at work. However, as Dozier said, the "fate of women in public relations – particularly their participation in management decision-making – is inexorably linked to the survival and growth of public relations" (1988: 6). So, in my analysis of the fifth phase identified by Tetreault (1976), I will superimpose Mann's (1994) postmodern cyborgean analysis and her revised conceptualisation of agency in particular.

Agency

The concept of agency has been central to feminist research at least since the mid-1960s, the beginning of the most recent women's liberation movement in the United States. At that time Bakan (1966) developed his personality theory to help explain gender effects. He proposed that throughout their development, individuals move toward the integration of what he considered two fundamental modalities, agency and communion. Agency is associated with individualism – self-assertion, self-protection and self-expansion. Communion describes the individual in relationship with a larger whole. Bakan found that socialisation interferes with what he considered to be the natural integration of these dual aspects in the mature personality. Socialisation leads to the preferencing of one modality over the other – whether it be in life at home or at work. Subsequently, Block (1973) found cross-cultural support for this theory (especially that women are socialised to emphasise communion over agency). Later still, Marshall (1984) used Bakan's theory to explain managerial differences between women and men.[3]

By exploring contemporary notions of pregnancy, motherhood and abortion, Mann (1994) showed that contraception has made organic motherhood passé. Her research furthered Haraway's (1991) argument that late twentieth-century women can be considered cyborgean – simultaneously animal and machine. The machine aspect derives from the authority women often have for their procreative decisions and their dependency on technology for control over procreation. So, I focus on agency and how a politicised, interpersonal agency in particular should figure prominently in the final, postfeminist phase.

Agency is at the core of Mann's (1994) theorising about what she has termed the "postfeminist era." She called, first, for a more complex social analysis of agency in appreciating women's actions than historically has been accomplished. Thus she suggested a new category of agency, interpersonal agency, as fundamental to any postmodern theory of social transformation. Interpersonal agency encompasses actions in which people seek to create and maintain affirmative psychic connections to others. We can see such interpersonal agency in Gaye's (1994) case study of a woman-owned public relations firm in the Pacific Northwest of the United States. From her case-comparison analysis, Gaye concluded that such all-female organisations use the assumptions of bounded emotionality as their mode of organising.

Bounded emotionality represents Mumby and Putnam's (1992) deconstruction of bounded rationality. It distinguishes between a system of organising based on nurturance, caring, communality, supportiveness and interrelatedness (fused with individual responsibility) and the more traditional notion of management that lacks any conceptualisation of the role of emotions in the workplace (e.g. Simon 1976; Weber 1981; Weick 1979). Bounded emotionality, consistent with Brush's argument that female entrepreneurs consider their business "a co-operative network of relationships rather than primarily as a separate profit-making entity" (1992: 17), is also consistent with interpersonal agency.

Mann (1994) went beyond the interpersonal to call for a more politicised theory of agency for analysing gender (and other social relationships) today as well. In public relations, we can see at least a micro-political struggle. It is similar to the struggle that characterised women's infusion into the military and their determination to participate in combat during the Persian Gulf War. Women in public relations not only determine to "get in" to the field; they want to "get on."

A word about postmodernism

This postmodern approach should reveal the gendered identities that result from the stories research tells about women and men in public relations. Readers must keep in mind, however, that depictions of women may not reflect the reality of their experiences. Likewise, voids in the literature may not mean that women were passive or absent in the situation being depicted.

Before I review this research, brief definitions are in order. "Post" in both "postfeminism" and "postmodernism" alludes to the "afterness" resulting from both resistance to and historical reliance on patriarchal antecedents (Denzin 1991; Jones *et al.* 1993; Smith and Turner 1995). This prefix suggests rejection of such modern concepts as truth, enlightenment, linear progress, certainty and universal laws. In particular, it rejects the notion of society's inexorably moving from the dim past toward a brighter future (Agger 1992). Through deconstructive processes, it may delegitimise or demystify any such seemingly cohesive or totalised visions. Thus postmodern or postfeminist theories often explore "marginal" phenomena ignored by classical theory. In the process, they valorise the differences and heterogeneities that modern science tended to suppress (Best and Kellner 1991).

Feminist phase analysis

Both the interpersonal and the political nature of women's agency in public relations figures prominently in my phase analysis of gender research in the field. Phase analysis, undertaken from a postfeminist perspective, is an important means of identifying how women have been conceptualised in public relations.

In this analysis, I embrace the deconstructionists' approach to reading the text (in this case, the scholarly literature of public relations). Deconstruction, as Smith and Turner (1995) said, is more a general orientation toward texts than a method. This contemporary philosophical and critical movement considers texts (or events) to be constructs of linguistic systems. Since the 1960s, deconstructionists have considered language a changing system based on differences and absences (Capek 1987). Derrida (1976) may be the best known of the deconstructionists. He believed that the binary oppositions governing western culture and philosophy construct a far-from-innocent hierarchy of values. These constructions, played out in such differences as subject/object and man/woman, keep us from arriving at a solid foundation for knowledge. Thus Derrida argued for a deconstruction or dismantling of the binary thought that prevailed in the modern era. The danger of what he considered "binary metaphysics" was well explained by Best and Kellner: "This binary metaphysics thus works to positively position reality over appearance, speech over writing, men over women, or reason over nature, thus positioning negatively the supposedly inferior term" (1991: 21). Smith and Turner reminded us, however, that even with this radical critique of modern philosophy, "There remains a need for particular analytical methods" (1995: 155). Feminist phase analysis is one such method.[4]

Tetreault's (1976) classification system is designed to reflect the evolution of thought about women's inclusion into a field. Beginning by adding women to the literature, it progresses through more fundamental reconstructions (if any exist) of key concepts as follows.

The first phase, *male scholarship*, assumes the male experience to be universal. The absence of women is ignored. This essentially womanless phase can be considered hostile and patronising toward women. Research conducted forty years or more ago frequently made assertions about women, but at the same time failed to include women in the population studied (Caplan 1985; Carlson 1985). Thus men served as the reference group (Minnich 1990) – despite actual contributions women may have been making to the field all along. Because gender may be less relevant to some research, I will consider male scholarship as that which fails to address gender issues when such issues are central.

In the second phase, *compensatory*, the previously unquestioned absence of women is overcome by searching for profiles of important women. Thus it offers an alternative history of the field. Whether called "women in" (McIntosh 1983), the "search for missing women" (Schuster and VanDyne 1985) or "women worthies" (Lerner 1990), the standards used to determine which women are worthy are those of the so-called "great men." There are two main kinds of compensatory scholarship: descriptions of "women who have made it" and counting, or census-taking. Such demographic studies have value because they help track women's progress in the field.

In the third, *bifocal* phase, men and women are conceptualised as separate, equal sexes. Neither is better; they are different. This phase represents the start of a "sensitivity to difference" model. An understanding of inherent, complementary difference helps explain the oppression of women depicted in this phase. This scholarship often includes suggestions for helping women overcome sexism. In fact, the goal of bifocal research is to overcome the previous notion that women are deficient by valuing alternative models equally (even though new stereotypes may replace the old because this scholarship often treats women as a homogeneous group). The unfortunate result is that women end up being seen, once again, as less than or deviant from the (male) norm.

With the fourth phase, *feminist*, women are conceptualised on their own terms. Women's experiences are valued in and of themselves. Their activities become central. Stereotypes are set aside, largely because the methodology of choice gives women voice. Researchers are not privileged over the researched. In this sense, then, the feminist phase also could be considered "postfeminist." It not only focuses on women, but it explores differences among women – refusing to assume any universal traits automatically associated with one gender or another.

Because postmodern and postfeminist theorising deals with this kind of plurality, it may result in fragmentation – what Harvey called "the cacophony of voices through which the dilemmas of the modern world are understood" (1989: 116). The challenge for postmodern or postfeminist scholars is to avoid privileging the fragmentary over the systematic. The challenge is important to accept, however. Through the multiplicity of voices characteristic of what Tetreault (1976) called the fourth phase, feminist, we can come to understand the multiple ways in which practitioners approach or make sense of their work in public relations.

The fifth and final phase, *multifocal*, is most difficult to describe because it remains largely unrealised. However, we do know that its defining characteristics include an exploration of the relationship between men and women and a reconceptualisation of the human experience as a continuum (rather than dichotomy) between the masculine and feminine. Multifocal research has the potential to redefine a field. Its more immediate goal is to develop an understanding of both women's and men's experiences to achieve knowledge and practice that truly are inclusive.

Methodological approach

Data for this study come from the US academic literature of public relations published between 1976, marked by Tetreault's (1976) ovarian treatise,[5] and the present. I concentrate my analysis on the two JS scholarly journals of the field, *Public Relations Review* and the *Journal of Public Relations Research* (formerly the *Public Relations Research Annual* and before that, *Public Relations Research and Education*).

Delimitations of the study are many. I exclude unpublished research by graduate students and proprietary research commissioned, say, by the professional associations of our field. I also omit the professional or trade press. Such publications may report on research, but they typically abbreviate the data for their non-academic subscribers. Likewise, I do not analyse the treatment of gender in public relations textbooks, because at best these sources typically report on previously published research.

Also absent from my phase analysis is research published as chapters in books or articles in journals that are broader than public relations (such as *Journalism and Mass Communication Quarterly*). No comprehensive list of such books or journals could be imagined. I further omit conference papers, which may present cutting-edge research in public relations, but for which no comprehensive database exists.

No books on women in public relations have been published, so none could be included in this analysis. Because a feminist phase analysis of any one of the publications that *is* included in this study would represent a major undertaking, this overview is meant to be suggestive rather than definitive.[6]

I served as the equivalent to a "coder" for the data.[7] Within each publication, I considered the following kinds of information: date, authorship and topic. In some cases, length was an important factor as well; length may be an indicator of significance. I often determined "male scholarship" by the absence of consideration of gender issues where I thought such attention was warranted. This added to the complexity of the analysis, of course, because it meant analysing what was not there.

Most important to my study, however, was treatment of the topic that would place it in one or more of the five phases. Here I had to rely on my own understanding of Tetreault's classification system, because this effort appears to be the only feminist phase analysis of the literature of public relations to date. Other potential coders could not be expected to be so familiar with the taxonomy.

My determination of which phase a study fits into was inherently subjective but born of more than twenty years of study, teaching and research in the field. I did remain aware of the partiality resulting from my having written or edited much of the research reviewed here. I also acknowledge that as a white American woman, my gender helps explain why I consider this feminist analysis so important. At the same time, I grant that through my nescience of other races and cultures, I may inadvertently distort or even omit issues of equal concern to other ethnicities.

However, accepting a postmodern philosophy of multiple ways to approach and deconstruct any text gave me confidence in making sense of the literature I was attempting to analyse with credibility. Thus categorising the explicit text was not difficult. Recognising potentially important subtexts and especially critical omissions was trickier. Here it was especially helpful to have conducted feminist research myself.

Results

Rather than reporting on findings by phase, as Twombly (1993) did, I have chosen to explore two research publications for their treatment of feminist scholarship. In this way, I shift the focus from any false assumption of linearity. Also, in some cases research is conducted many years before it is published.[8] To emphasise timing above all else may distort any patterns that emerge from the data.

I begin with the *Public Relations Review*, the only journal in this field published continuously since my starting point, the issuance of Tetreault's classification system in 1976. I continue with the *Journal of Public Relations Research*, the only journal in the field directed primarily at an audience of researchers and educators.[9] As the founding co-editor of this quarterly (which began as an annual), I am eminently familiar with what it has published over time.[10] Also, because that time period encompasses only six of the twenty years included in this analysis, I can devote greater attention to each article than was possible with the longer-running *Public Relations Review*. My analysis encompasses a total of 606 articles in these two scholarly journals, each important in its own way.

Public Relations Review (1976–95)

The *Public Relations Review* is the only publication included in this analysis that is represented in each of the years this study encompasses, 1976–95. Thus this exploration of the literature may provide the best overview, making it a fitting entry point into the analysis. Altogether I assessed 531 articles from *PRR* in the twenty-year period under review.

In 1976, the first year included in this analysis, a total of eighteen articles appeared.[11] All of these are consistent with male scholarship; women are conspicuously absent. Biographies dealt only with famous men, such as presidential advisers Amos Kendall (to Andrew Jackson) and Sherman Adams (to Dwight Eisenhower). A survey of education described enrolment trends yet ignored any mention of gender in demographics. A projection about the future of public relations included in an article on the functional or functionary aspects of the field misses feminisation. In one article, Knodell (1976) used the feminine pronoun "she" when referring to food writers. I mention this because twenty years ago, the male "generic" pronoun "he" was used more typically. Even in this co-orientational study in which women obviously were central, however, there was no mention of gender.

In 1977, *PRR* published twenty-two articles. Once again, only male scholarship was done. As an example of the kind of article that could have (and should have) gone beyond this exclusion, consider the study of the qualifications and attitudes of public relations faculty. It looked at factors deemed "general background": faculty rank, age, salary, tenure status and educational achievements – but not gender.

In 1978, seventeen articles were published. The third issue of this year deserves special attention. It is devoted to public relations in American history. In all seven articles, however, there is no mention of women. All were authored by men. Similarly, in an historical article in the second issue, a public relations pioneer is profiled. Here we find one of the few mentions of a woman's name: "James Drummond Ellsworth, son of Alfred A. and Angelina Ellsworth, was born in Milford, Massachusetts, on 14 October 1863. His father was a preacher" (Griese 1978: 22). Apparently women in the literature of public relations in 1978 were credited with agency only insofar as they were involved in childbirth.

The next year, 1979, thirteen articles appeared – including one of the earliest studies of public relations roles. Even in Broom and Smith (1979), however, there is no mention of what became an established relationship between gender and roles in subsequent research. And a suggestive title, "The missing link in public relations research," turned out to be a disappointment. However, 1979 marked the publication of the first article in *Public Relations Review* that goes beyond purely male scholarship. Wilcox, studying the hiring criteria of employers, questioned whether "a woman or a member of an ethnic minority is more likely to be hired" (1979: 35).

In 1980, fourteen articles were published. Few went significantly beyond male scholarship. I find the first line of the first article appearing in the fall issue indicative of the prevailing worldview of authors in this volume:

> By the turn of the twentieth century a few *men* of courage and vision, some the heads of large enterprises, others newspaper and advertising *men*, realised that the needs of the United States called for development of a clearer understanding of human relations.
>
> (Harlow 1980: 3, emphasis added)

Perhaps most important, with this retrospective look I can say that a "clearer understanding of human relations" requires an understanding of the dynamics between men and women – a dimension left unexplored in Harlow's (1980) trend piece and in almost every other article published in *PRR* that year.[12] One exception is an intriguing essay aimed at improving practitioners' and educators' understanding of what Hutchison (1980) called "micro-relations." He advocated students examining themselves and their professional goals so as to learn the difference between subservience and rendering service. To illustrate this conundrum, he offered the following scenario:

> How should a young woman entering a PR firm respond to the advances of a married man? What should she say to an invitation to a mother–daughter or a father–daughter relationship with those two older members of the firm? Will she know the danger inherent in such role playing?
>
> (Hutchinson 1980: 29)

The following year, 1981, fifteen articles were published. A new tone characterised this research. It suggests a movement away from totally male scholarship. For example, a compensatory survey of professionalism of Army public affairs personnel included gender (the typical PAO was male).

Twenty-four articles were published in 1982. Only one of these two dozen was authored by a woman. One issue focused on information strategies for preventing violence in America and another on education for public relations. Perhaps because of the preponderance of male authors, or perhaps because neither of these lengthy special issues lent itself to feminist issues,[13] few of these articles depart from male scholarship. In 1982, though, for the first time gender became central to an article in the *Public Relations Review*. Broom's (1982) bifocal investigation compared women's and men's perceptions of their roles in public relations.

In 1983, for the first time, *PRR* included fourteen brief research reports along with twenty full-length articles. Of the half-page reports published in vol. 9, no. 3, one dealt specifically with gender issues. Cline and Masel-Walters (1983) studied the use of non-sexist language n employee publications. Findings of gender-free communication encouraged them, although they also found two remaining problem areas: grammatical errors resulting from avoiding the "generic" "he", and "pervasive chaos" in the use of titles (Cline and Masel-Walters 1983: 51). Other than this four-paragraph article, nothing in 1983 goes beyond male scholarship. (Even this article was too brief to characterise in any of Tetreault's five phases.)

Volume 10 included twenty-six full-length articles and twenty research briefs. That year, 1984, seems to represent a reversion to all-male scholarship. The roles study (Rayfield 1984) ignored gender differences that had been established two years earlier.

In 1985, *PRR* included twenty-one articles and twelve brief research reports. This volume contained three significant articles that go beyond male scholarship, including the first article to focus on the gender shift from a male to female majority.

In her compensatory study of perceptions of sexism in the workplace, Theus (1985) queried students of the University of Maryland, former students and their employers. She found that male alumni were twice as likely as females to report high levels of job satisfaction, salary and chances for advancement. Both students and alumni reported instances of sexism as well. The proportion of women studying public relations at Maryland had reached 80 per cent at the time of this research.

PRR also dedicated an issue in 1985 to roles research. Of the four articles included in that winter issue, one bifocal study (Selnow and Wilson 1985) focused on gender and job satisfaction.[14]

The third article to explore women's issues this year was a profile of female Canadian practitioners. Scrimger (1985) reported statistics showing a trend toward an increasing number of women among members of IABC Canada and the Canadian Public Relations Society. Her study approaches the feminist phase because it valued women's experiences in and of themselves.

One other article published in 1985 at least alluded to women. Hiebert and Devine (1985) found that women in government public relations were considerably more enthusiastic about the benefits of research in changing their agencies' policies than were men in their sample. Women conducted more research, both formal and informal. However, the authors failed to report why they had included gender as a demographic variable, and also to explain or discuss the implications of this significant divergence in their bifocal findings.

Of the twenty-one articles and ten research-in-briefs published in 1986, only one deals specifically with gender concerns. Broom and Dozier's (1986) update of their roles study cannot be considered a feminist phase, because it retained the male/female comparison or bifocalism central to this program of research. However, it certainly advances our understanding of women and the bias they face in public relations.

Only one other article published in the *Review* in 1986 mentions women. A description of professionalism in Nigerian public relations alluded to the fact that 97 per cent of all practitioners there are male, and suggested that the exclusion of women results from the perception that women do not make good managers. This two-sentence reference in Pratt (1986), however, is more than one reads about women even in articles about future trends in public relations, education for the 1980s or the content of public relations textbooks.

In 1987, there were twenty-one articles and twenty-six research briefs in the *PRR*. None focused on feminist issues. One of the only mentions of women came in a study of the campaign for abortion rights: both the public information officer and the journalist whose work was central to the campaign were women. However, even in this case analysis, Olasky (1987) made no attempt to consider the role that gender might have played in communicating about this issue of reproductive rights – which, again, is central in the lives of many feminists. Other obvious omissions of gender-based research occurred in historical articles, reports of roles research and trend pieces.

It was in this year, however, that the *Review* abstracted a conference paper aimed at reversing the sex gap in undergraduate education. Hunt and Thompson (1987) explored options for recruiting male students back to the public relations classroom. Their solution to feminisation of the field included changing application procedures, providing male role models and mentors and selecting clients with "masculine appeal." This only can be considered anti-feminist research – not one of Tetreault's categories and, fortunately, not typical of the literature of public relations as a whole.

In 1988, twenty-one articles were published in the *PRR*, including a special issue on women in public relations. As issue editor, I solicited the eight articles (including my own) from the presentations made at annual conventions of the International Communication Association and the Association for Education in Journalism and Mass Communication. Authors were a mix of scholars and practitioners; one was a graduate student. One of the authors was male. In addition to this diversity, the scholarship goes beyond gender issues to also embrace race, age, class and ethnicity.

Despite these strengths, the journal's editor, Ray E. Hiebert, told ne (personal communication, 1989) that of all *PRR*'s special issues, this "women's issue" sold the fewest extra copies. And, like the Theus (1985) study of female students three years earlier, this issue prompted one of a handful of letters to the editor ever printed in the *Review*. British Professor Sam Black (1988) expressed his sorrow at receiving "such a biased set of papers" on a concept – the glass ceiling – he considered out of date. Why? He wrote that "rampant feminism was in full retreat," and expressed the "hope that the USA would catch up with Britain in this regard" (Black 1988: 102). I continue to believe that Black's contention ("it is true that women have to work very hard to succeed in our profession but there are no artificial barriers to success" [1988: 102]) is belied by much empirical and anecdotal evidence from both sides of the Atlantic.

Topics in the issue to which Black (1988) objected included breaking the glass ceiling, the depiction of women in annual reports, issues surrounding the feminisation of the field, women in foundation and corporate public relations, an analysis of whether women had made progress in public relations, women in graduate study, and a feminist research agenda. Most of these articles subsequently were critiqued by Hon (1995), who found most of them lacking the feminist perspective that characterises her own research.

Along with Hon (1995), Toth (1988), in her article in the same issue, also seemed to question the viability of Dozier's, Stewart's and Mathew's arguments. She surveyed literature primarily from sociology that established, for example, that women are unlikely to gain individual power even when they contribute to the organisation's maintaining power. As Hon put it, "As long as the standard continues to be defined by men, many women will always come up short no matter what they do or avoid doing" (1995: 34).

An alternative, of course, is not to blame women but to urge institutions to value the diversity and the other strengths that women can bring to communication management. I (L. Grunig 1988) suggested this feminist alternative in my proposal for a research agenda that would, first, explore whether the study and practice of public relations can be characterised as masculine and, second, produce better, more comprehensive knowledge by including a feminist perspective. I emphasised that this new knowledge would go beyond the feminist, however, because it would be inclusive rather than simply different and gender-based. Thus in 1988 I was advocating the multifocal phase of Tetreault's classification system without recognising it as such.

Another article in the special issue took an intensively personal approach. Miller began and ended her piece with revelations along this line: "When Lauri Grunig asked me to write about the female experience, I had mixed feelings. I was excited at the possibility of appearing in print with such noted and well respected women, but then I panicked" (1988: 29). The bulk of her study reported on interviews with ten women, four of whom were black, two white, two Hispanic and two Asian. Each of these participants was enrolled in a graduate program or had completed a graduate degree. They recounted an incredibly stressful set of barriers to success in graduate studies (although Miller did not quote them extensively). Miller termed the situation for female graduate students "a national emergency" and urged universities to support and encourage female and minority faculty, in particular, to be mentors to their female students.

Taken together, the articles published in the *Review's* special issue on women are a mixed bag. None is male scholarship. However, my critique and Hon's (1995) confirm that some (Mathews 1988; Stewart 1988) of the research is compensatory because it speaks to "women in" public relations who have achieved great success – and what it takes to emulate the male model. Some, such as Dozier's (1988) strategic direction for lifting women from the technical to the managerial role, is bifocal. It contrasts women's and men's career paths, suggesting that women change to achieve power and control. Still other articles, such as Miller's (1988), are feminist because they validate women's experiences alone. At least one of the articles (L. Grunig 1988) approaches the multifocal.

A second issue of the *PRR* published in the same year adds to our understanding of feminist research by focusing on the body of knowledge in public relations. The PRSA Task Force (1988) included a category titled "Effects of gender on roles," which listed eight articles published or conference papers presented since 1975. Gratifying as the inclusion of this subsection under the larger section of "Public relations roles" is, it is also discouraging in its limited number of studies.

In 1989, two dozen full-length articles and thirteen brief research reports were published. There were two special issues, one on education and the other on ethics. This year is characterised by a sprinkling of articles that mention gender issues; only one (DeRosa and Wilcox 1989) focused on women. Only one other article in *PRR's* special issue on education even mentioned women. Turk (1989) pointed out that the omission of gender was a significant gap in her survey of management skills that should be taught.

A third issue published in 1989 contains a significant article about ⁻he status and roles of minority practitioners. Kern-Foxworth (1989) lid not focus on gender in her profile of minorities in public relations. However, she found that the typical practitioner of color in the United States is an African American female.[15]

The fourth issue of 1989 also mentioned gender, albeit it peripherally and in a single article. This bifocal research on job satisfaction (Olson 1989) attempted to reject stereotypes but, because women were not central, it cannot be considered feminist.

In 1990, the *PRR* published twenty-nine articles. Special issues focused on issues management (which failed to mention women or gender concerns at all), on publicity and American culture, and on using research to plan and evaluate public relations. The latter included an inventory of the gaps apparent in PRSA's body of knowledge project (VanLeuven 1990). As a member of the BOK board, I was quoted as pointing out one such omission in the category I was responsible for (the managerial and organisational context):

> In assessing the organisational section, L. Grunig believes that it reflects fairly well on past and present writing, but also that it points to some of the kinds of research that will be found in tomorrow's BOK including the *impact of gender on roles*, problems of encroachment of other organisational units on public relations, organisational and societal culture, and to the increasingly global practice of public relations.
>
> (VanLeuven 1990: 23, emphasis added)

My own article (L. Grunig 1990b) on focus group research mentioned the desirability of conducting at least one group of women alone to help guard against an over-representation of male viewpoints in a given study. I had found in my investigation of the stigma associated with mental illness that conversation among the participants of the group of all women was remarkably more balanced than among participants in the three groups of men and women. (Observers and facilitators agreed that all but one participant in the female-only group contributed almost equally to the discussion.)

The remaining special issue in 1990, which dealt with popular culture, contained two articles – both compensatory scholarship – with references to women. Badaracco (1990) described Harriet Monroe's publicity work in promoting the arts. Kern-Foxworth (1990) established Aunt Jemima as the first US trademark to be personified.

In 1991, thirty articles appeared. *PRR* continued its tradition of special issues. This year featured, first, the relationship between public relations and marketing, second, crisis management, and third, Scott M. Cutlip's contributions to education. None emphasised feminist concerns. One tribute to Cutlip's legacy of research published in this last special issue did acknowledge Cutlip's views of women dating back forty years – views J. Grunig considered "ahead of [his] time" (1991: 373).

In an issue containing a variety of topics, however, Toth and Cline (1991) presented their benchmark survey of practitioners' attitudes toward gender issues. Pratt (1991) explored (as one aspect of a larger study) the influence of gender on ethical differences among public relations practitioners.

Most other articles published in 1991 consisted of male scholarship – without even the historical or futuristic studies that by this new decade reasonably could include information about women's contributions or growing feminisation of the field. So, too, did an article on marketing imperialism fail to mention gender directly as a factor we know to influence such encroachment. Lauzen (1991) merely alluded to this dimension in a footnote that cited her own unpublished works.

A second article in the issue focusing on marketing and public relations also contained at least an acknowledgement of the effect that an increasing proportion of women in the field may have. My co-author and I (J. Grunig and L. Grunig 1991) cautioned that feminisation may limit the potential of the public relations department if the organisation discriminates against women and thus keeps them out of the managerial role. We further theorised that "excellent public relations departments have women in management roles and have mechanisms to help women gain the power they need to advance from the technician to the management role" (Grunig and Grunig 1991: 272). To feminists such as Creedon, this would seem to devalue both the technician's role and the women who (through their own agency rather than subjugation) choose to remain in that role. Because the mention of women in this and in Lauzen's (1991) article is peripheral rather than central to the research, I do not place these studies in any of Tetreault's five feminist phases.

A third article in this issue included a demographic analysis that incorporated gender of survey respondents. Spicer (1991) studied how practitioners in marketing and public relations differ in their reliance on communication skills.

Finally, in 1991 Lesly reiterated his doomsday appraisal of public relations in what he called "the turbulent new human climate" (1991: 1). New, perhaps, but he repeated his description of the role women play in degradation of the function word-for-word from his 1988 treatise.

In 1992, *PRR* published thirty-three articles. None goes significantly beyond male scholarship since most are entirely "womanless." There were two special issues. One, on public relations and religion, contained nothing about women. The other, on international practice, included one article that at least mentioned women. Sriramesh (1992), in one of the *PRR*'s few ethnographies, contrasted the roles that women and men occupy in southern Indian public relations.

As in the previous year, 1993 offered readers two special issues of the *PRR* – one on ethics and the other on public relations paradigms. There was a total of thirty articles. The male scholarship that predominated belies the importance of the two studies that *did* focus on women.

One (Zerbinos and Clanton 1993) surveyed the career influences and job satisfaction of minority practitioners – nearly two-thirds of whom were women (close to the same percentage in the field of public relations itself). This study is particularly important to my phase analysis because, despite its descriptive and largely atheoretical nature, it speaks to the inclusiveness that marks multifocal research.

One of the most significant feminist studies ever published in the *PRR* came in the same year. Creedon (1993), in an example of the multifocal phase of feminist research, exposed the absence of a critical feminist perspective in any discussion of the systems paradigm in public relations.

In 1994, twenty-seven articles appeared in the *Review*. Given the absence of women as focal points in these articles, perhaps my feminist phase analysis should have ended with the strengths of the previous year. However, at least one study contained a small subsection that considered gender. Kinnick and Cameron (1994), in their bifocal analysis of the status of teaching about public relations management, said that lack of managerial skills has particularly critical implications for women.

Of the ten articles published at the time of the analysis in 1995, one focused on women. This ambitious study of women in public relations education and practice in the United Arab Emirates (Creedon *et al.* 1995) explored women's experiences alone, qualifying it as feminist-phase research. Such analyses were conspicuously missing from a report of public relations in Europe (Nessmann 1995), published in the same year in *PRR*.

Summary from the Public Relations Review

So what would subscribers to the *Public Relations Review* learn about feminism in the field after two decades of reading? Not until 1979, the fourth year of publication, would they read anything at all about women. That compensatory scholarship was followed by fewer than two dozen articles that mentioned gender issues, from a total of 531 articles printed. Of these, most were bifocal, comparing women and men primarily in terms of the roles they played. One fitted the feminist phase and two, the multifocal. The remaining half-dozen of the twenty-three articles mentioning women or gender concerns combined bifocal and feminist phases (two articles); compensatory, bifocal and feminist phases; compensatory and bifocal phases; compensatory and feminist phases; and compensatory, bifocal and multifocal phases.

Public Relations Research Annual *(1989–91)*

Altogether I examined seven reviews and twenty-four research reports from the *Public Relations Research Annual*. Findings that follow for this journal are somewhat more detailed than for the other journals because the *Annual* encompassed significantly fewer years and thus fewer articles.

Volume 1   No research review nor report of original work in Volume 1, 1989, focused on gender. In hindsight, this is an obvious omission in a lengthy review I co-authored: "Toward a theory of the public relations behavior of organisations: review of a program of research" (J. Grunig and L. Grunig 1989). Other literature has shown that gender is a factor in several key aspects of the models of public relations. For example, gender correlates with public relations roles, with choice of or preference for the models, with organisational power and values and with approaches to conflict resolution. However, sex is never mentioned in our meta-analysis of this significant program of research on models.

A second article in this first *Annual* is also surprising in its failure to even touch on gender issues: "The gap between professional and research agendas in public relations journals" (Broom *et al.* 1989). In fact, only two of the ten articles in the first volume of the *Annual* even mentioned women or gender.

Perhaps the greatest insight into gender research as exemplified in this first volume comes from its subject index. There is no listing for such topics as diversity, gender, sex, feminisation or feminist theory, women or females. For Volume 1, then, one would have to conclude that male scholarship is the norm – even among authors such as L. Grunig and Broom, who had developed a reputation for feminist research, and with topics such as roles and models where gender would seem eminently relevant.

Volume 2   As in the first *Annual*, we find nothing written specifically about women in the second volume. However, in one of the three major research reviews, Dozier (1990) provided the *Annual*'s first look at women in public relations. In "The innovation of research in public relations practice: review of a program of studies," he cited a number of studies on women, research and decision making. Surprisingly, a Canadian study dedicated to roles and conducted by two female scholars, Piekos and Einsiedel (1990) failed to mention gender – despite the significant correlation of women with the technician role, in particular.

My own study of power in the public relations department (L. Grunig 1990a) at least alluded to gender as a determinant of the inclusion of public relations in the dominant coalition. (Marginalisation of the function, as Hon [1992] would go on to establish, is a more powerful explanation of the exclusion.) Sexism emerged as an explanation for the lack of autonomy typical of public relations practitioners. However, I did not pursue this finding in the implications of the study.

The subject index of Volume 2 alludes to glass ceiling, women in public relations, and women and programs of research. Taken together, the index and the content of this volume suggest the predominance of male scholarship, with only a sprinkling of the bifocal research that compares women with men.

Volume 3   By 1991, the *Annual* shifted from almost totally male scholarship to greater gender balance. The index to the two research reviews and eight reports of original research in Volume 3 alludes to women as communicators and in the foreign service, a feminist look at research, diversity, and feminism and roles. However, all of these citations encompass only two articles. Thus the majority of research published in this volume can still be considered male scholarship.[16]

However, the first two research reports in Volume 3 both deal with the feminisation of the field. Creedon (1991), building on the line of inquiry about public relations roles, questioned the assumptions underlying some reactions to the gender switch. I explored (1991) the implications of a legal victory for women working in communication for the US Foreign Service. Even the titles of these articles suggest

108 *Contemporary perspectives*

where they fit in a phase analysis. Creedon characterised her study as "Toward a feminist analysis of public relations roles." This suggests the fourth, or feminist phase. I alluded to "Court-ordered relief from sex discrimination," pointing to one aspect of the third, or bifocal phase (suggesting strategies for women to overcome sexism). Taking a closer look at each article should establish the legitimacy of this kind of assumption based on title.

Having thus applauded Creedon (1991) for her attempts to move the field forward, I find my own work (1991) in Volume 3 of the *Annual* all the more disappointing. I cannot conclude that it is "feminist," much less "multifocal." Instead, this case study of sexism in the US Department of State took an historical (compensatory) and comparative (bifocal) look at women's and men's roles and opportunities in the Foreign Service.

However, my focus in "Court-ordered relief from sex discrimination in the foreign service" clearly was on women and on their potential for superior work in diplomatic communication. I attributed their success in the courts to their own agency – 600 female Foreign Service officers filing the class-action lawsuit that took thirteen years to resolve. Also, I did not fall prey to the contribution history that would ignore the efforts of less-than-notable women in achieving equity or in serving as communicators in posts overseas. And I did not assume the male model as the norm. Instead, I speculated that when women manage to transcend their typically routine tasks, "male FSOs [Foreign Service Officers] will be affected positively by the model of their female counterparts" (1991: 110). Because of this perspective and the concentration on women, I conclude that this study approaches the fourth or feminist phase as well as the obviously compensatory and bifocal.

From the preceding analysis, I also conclude that titles tell part – but not all – of the story of where a given article fits within Tetreault's classification system. Thus I cannot proceed by analysing titles alone. At the same time, having laid this analytical groundwork, I go on to report more skeletally on the large quantity of research that follows.

Journal of Public Relations Research *(1992–5)*

In 1992, the *Annual* became the quarterly *Journal of Public Relations Research*.

The four issues of Volume 4, 1992, encompassed a total of thirteen articles. Of these, not one title would suggest any focus beyond male scholarship. Because the quarterly did not include the subject index, as its predecessor the *Annual* had, this approach to initial phase analysis was mute as well. Closer exploration of each of the articles, however, shows that male scholarship remains the norm.

Thirteen articles were also published in the fifth volume of the *ournal of Public Relations Research*. The second issue in 1993 evolved from an international conference on image, held in Munich. Thus vol. 5, no. 2 takes on special importance. However, none of the articles addressed gender issues. The same is true for the three articles in no. 1 and the two articles in no. 4.

Only the third issue in 1993 features an article that goes beyond male scholarship. Its title, "The missing story of women in public relations" (Toth and L. Grunig 1993), suggests that it fits into Tetreault's second or compensatory phase – making up for a previous exclusion of women. This assumption would be erroneous. The study offered a distinctly feminist analysis of roles women perform in public relations. As the abstract stated, "Although management and technician roles have been useful as parsimonious tools to educate future public relations practitioners about public relations, these labels have begun to develop values of hierarchy and power not found when they were operationalised" (*ibid.*: 154). Thus we see an important dimension to this research: It is one of the few studies reviewed here that is programmatic. It built both on the extensive program of roles research and on Creedon's (1991) feminist critique of that research.

Further, we (Toth and L. Grunig 1993) explicitly questioned the assumptions of both compensatory and bifocal research, as follows:

> As feminist scholars, we felt responsible to explain why we have considered male as well as female practitioners in our factor analysis of roles. Our first thought when producing this report was to consider only the roles of women in public relations. However, we concluded that the first question asked would be, "How do the role activities of the women compare to those of the men?" We did not report the roles of both women and men as a means of determining how the women are somehow deficient in relation to the men in the sample. Rather, we provided both to reveal in what ways women may have different roles than do men in public relations, as a first step toward resolving the underlying causes that create any such differences.
>
> (158)

Through our analysis of a large data set (which included qualitative and quantitative data), we both reaffirmed and reconceptualised the two-role set of technician and manager. Although this dichotomous construct emerged, we also found that men's activities within the managerial role were more exclusively managerial than were women's. Women blurred the distinction — "doing it all" (including many so-called technical tasks) in the managerial role. In other words, we found dual-role fulfilment among the women in our sample.

Thirteen articles were published in 1994, the sixth volume of the *Journal of Public Relations Research*. Of these, only one went beyond male scholarship to focus on women. Weaver-Lariscy *et al.* surveyed women and men in higher education public relations "to examine environmental constraints, styles of research, and certain personal characteristics to determine if they differentiate female and male practitioners" (1994: 125). Their study clearly was bifocal, juxtaposing men and women in terms of the roles (dominant insider or conscience of the organisation, respectively) they fulfilled. In addition, it encompassed elements of the fourth or feminist phase as well, in large part because of its rich grounding in feminist theory.

Two issues of the seventh volume of the *JPRR* were available at the time of this analysis. One, the second issue of 1995, carried my study of "The consequences of culture for public relations: the case of women in the Foreign Service." This research exemplifies one of the few instances of multifocal scholarship in the published literature of public relations to that date. Its combined methodology relied on primary and secondary sources to look at the subcultures within the larger organisational context. It focused on female Foreign Service Officers and, most significantly, their relationship with the men who continued to disadvantage them despite legal admonishments to the contrary. It drew heavily on feminist theory, especially the work of Rakow (1987) and my own previous theorising along these lines (L. Grunig 1988; 1991). I concluded, in a statement (unknowingly, at the time it was written) consistent with the multifocal phase:

> Feminist scholarship such as this, then, must go beyond the study of gender as a cause of any particular communication process. It needs to do more than compare the way men and women may practice communication — based on any a priori notions about their polarity. Instead, it must elucidate the relation between the dominant and the subordinate that characterises our social, political, economic, and cultural system. In so doing, the study speaks to any group that may find itself outside of the dominant norms.
>
> (L. Grunig 1988; 1991: 158)

More significantly for this analysis, one issue of the *JPRR*'s seventh volume goes beyond male scholarship in its entirety. Both long articles acknowledge the impact of gender on public relations. Dozier and Broom (1995), in their longitudinal research on roles, teased out the implications of gender primarily on the managerial dimension.

The single article most central to this feminist phase analysis is Hon's (1995) development of a feminist theory of public relations. It approaches the multifocal phase by suggesting societal transformation as a necessary solution to sexism and by placing women's issues in public relations in that larger context. Hon also pioneered a combined methodological approach that empowered her participants to an extent that little previous research had done.

The remaining two articles published so far in 1995 represent a return to male scholarship, or the bifocal phase at best. One (Twombly 1993) analysed the literature of community colleges – questioning why scholars included a measure of gender or why they would have expected a difference in the fund-raising efforts of women and men. Kelly reported in her exploratory study of fund-raising in US charitable organisations that "female fund-raisers prefer the press agentry model for annual giving programs, whereas male fund-raisers tend to practice the more sophisticated two-way asymmetrical model when raising major gifts" (1995: 129).

Summary of the Annual/Journal of Public Relations Research

Of the total of seventy-five articles published in six and a half years since the *Journal* began as the *Annual*, I found a predominance of male scholarship. Only a handful of research reviews or research reports focused on women. There was an obvious lack of attention to gender issues where such issues should have been relevant (especially in studies of power, the dominant coalition, culture, roles, job satisfaction, professionalism and so forth).

Omissions became more apparent in the *Journal* than in the *Public Relations Review*, perhaps because the former publishes research exclusively whereas the *PRR* includes texts of speeches and other commentary as well. Also, the work of scholars accepted in the *Journal* exemplifies the programmatic nature of research that becomes, over time, the most sophisticated and most complex. This research is most capable of contributing to the theoretical body of knowledge rather than remaining at the anecdotal or descriptive level, more characteristic of even the most adroit practitioners or the academics who engage in one-shot studies.

More of these studies, all published since 1989, are also qualitative compared to research typically published in the *Review*. Qualitative study, or a combination of methods, lends itself to feminist research.

Interestingly, of the nine major studies about women (three of which were published under the editorship of Elizabeth Toth), only one was even somewhat compensatory. It combined elements of "adding women" with comparisons between women and men and feminist theorising as well. Feminist phase research was obvious in six of the articles. Although only one was truly multifocal, this analysis makes clear that time matters. The *Journal*, begun as the *Annual* in 1989, did not go through the early fits and starts evident in writing about women in the *Public Relations Review*.

Discussion

Any research biased by partiality or stereotypes is flawed because it violates general principles of good science – regardless of the topic under investigation. Stereotyping women, typically accomplished through the compensatory or bifocal scholarship described here, brands them as second-class citizens in the world of work outside the home in public relations. Given women's agency, a result of both their own determination and new technologies of reproduction and birth control, the postmodern era suggests we go beyond the "add women and stir" approach or the limits of one-on-one comparisons with men alone.

As the prescient social psychologist Jessie Bernard explained decades ago, "In the industrial age, the traits associated with maleness were called for; but in the post-industrial or cybernetic age, the traits associated with femaleness as we know it today will be" (1976: 12). At the very least, I hope readers will agree that women are not unqualified nor underqualified to excel in the management of public relations by virtue of their biological sex or gendered socialisation. They have been shown not only to be nurturing but highly motivated, ethically conscious, research-oriented, hard-working, well educated and able (and often expected) to balance competing responsibilities.

Unlike Twombly (1993), I did not find much of the seemingly gratuitous inclusion of gender as an independent variable absent; nor did I find any adequate theorising about why sex should be expected to affect the dependent variable. However, our literature too seems to be based on the bedrock of women's silence. As a result of this analysis, then, I am forced to conclude that a research agenda proposed years ago is relevant today (L. Grunig 1988). The purpose of that treatise was to empower all women educators, researchers and practitioners of public relations by legitimising a feminist research agenda that would include the following:

1   research and teaching about women in public relations that would bring together all people in the field, not just white males;
2   feminist scholarship that would show what a conceptual democracy might really be like; and
3   feminist research that would serve as a laboratory for thinking through the complexities of community.

These purposes all could be coalesced into the theoretical framework of the postmodern feminist movement in public relations, as Hon (1995) suggested.

Even now, however, women will not give up – any more than they did when Doris E. Fleischman fought to retain her maiden name on her passport (and became the first American woman to do so). The odds are against a major turnaround even in a postmodern era. But there are signs that we may have seen the worst. Postfeminist scholars and, perhaps especially, female practitioners of public relations, are full of hope that we will succeed in overcoming the pay gap and our exclusion from the highest decision-making levels of the organisation. Many want to transcend the technician's role. Some aspire to management, whereas others want to be paid fairly and credited for perfecting their craft and for the contributions that technical work provides – whether it is done by men or women.

Our understanding of public relations must be reconstructed by bringing gender (and also race, class and ethnicity) fully to the center of our research and our teaching. Much preliminary theorising has been done along these lines, and some empirical work also. The transformed perspective that should result when feminist research is established in our field (beyond the bifocal scholarship I found to be most prevalent) may lead to more comprehensive choices for our students, the future of the field. Both young women and men may come to reject the notion that the public relations department where they hope to work is a meritocracy. They may develop instead a critical view of their profession – informed by the literature establishing problems women encounter on the job and the potential they bring to their work as technicians and as managers (or both at the same time).

Postfeminism is an inevitable force in public relations theory and practice. Its counter-forces may accuse feminist scholars of unnecessary shrillness in their critique of the existing body of knowledge, marked as it is with the partiality I have established here. To those critics, I reiterate the words of Mary Wollstonecraft (in Schneir 1972: xxi) two centuries ago: "I might have expressed this conviction in a lower key, but I am afraid it would have been the whine of affectation, and not the faithful expression of my feelings."

Notes

1   I use "gender" and "sex" interchangeably in this chapter, in part to minimise redundancy but also because scholars disagree about whether "gender" or "sex" should refer to biological attributes and to socially and culturally created differences between men and women. Many, such as Twombly (1993) and Epstein (1988), simply decide which term will refer to which and inform readers of their decision.

2   For later approaches to feminist phase theory, see McIntosh (1983), Schuster and VanDyne (1985) and Warren (1989).

3   Perhaps the best explanation of agency was provided not by a privileged female manager but by a black domestic worker. Sojourner Truth, a woman born into slavery in 1795, has been identified with the feminist and abolitionist causes since the beginning of the women's and anti-slavery movements in America. Speaking to a woman's convention in the mid-1880s, she said: "If the first woman God ever made was strong enough to turn the world upside down all alone, these women together ought to be able to turn it back, and get it right side up again! And now they is asking to do it, the men better let them" (Sojourner Truth, in Schneir 1972: 95).

4   By contrast with feminist phase analysis, Smith and Turner (1995) chose metaphor analysis for their theorising about organisational socialisation.

5   I also chose to begin this analysis with 1976 because that was the year I began my graduate education in public relations. Thus I am particularly familiar with the literature from that point forward.

6   For a somewhat more comprehensive feminist phase analysis of the US literature of public relations – encompassing major proprietary research projects, selected graduate student theses and dissertations and the writings of Edward L. Bernays – see L. Grunig (1995b).

7   Twombly (1993) termed her feminist phase research on the literature of community colleges a "content analysis." My own study (and I would argue hers, as well) does not fit the traditional description of content analysis. Instead, I consider my research more of a "content inventory," along the lines of Broom *et al.* (1989).

8   The most extreme example I encountered was Hatfield's 1994 study of public relations education in the United Kingdom. The editor of *Public Relations Review* noted that the article had been submitted in 1987, seven years earlier. He added, "No attempt has been made to update the information" (1994: 189).

9   This is not to say that the editors failed to emphasise the research's relevance to practitioners. In our editors' introduction to Volume 4, the first issue of the *Journal*, we (Grunig and Grunig 1992) pointed out that each article begins with "an abstract that places the article into the context of public relations practice as well as theory" (2).

10 After my six years as co-editor, the feminist scholar of public relations Elizabeth Toth became editor of the *JPPR* in 1995.

11 Even a cursory look at its first year establishes that *Public Relations Review* published nothing directly related to women or gender issues in 1975. Thus I feel justified in omitting this one year from my feminist phase analysis.

12 One article did explore sex stereotyping. O'Brien (1980) analysed TV commercials and found, as predicted, that little had changed in the tele-vised portrayal of women and men over the years. She explained the link with public relations as follows: "It is expected that public relations professionals will continue to have greater influence in selected aspects of ad campaigns" (O'Brien 1980: 20). Despite her assertion, I do not include this article about television spots as an integral part of my feminist phase analysis because I do not believe it contributes to the body of knowledge in public relations.

13 One could argue, as I would, that missing the growing proportion of female students in the typical public relations classroom is an egregious gap in the issue focusing on educational trends.

14 One research report, the abstract of a conference paper by Wright and Hantz (1985), hinted at a study with important gender implications. This comparison of social responsibility among members of Canadian and US IABC members found "there are greater differences in terms of sex and age than nationality" (Wright and Hantz 1985: 51).

15 This first systematic study of people of color in the field has inspired several graduate students at the University of Maryland to design their own thesis research along similar lines. Two (Smith, forthcoming; Wise, forthcoming) are looking specifically at African-American *women* in public relations – one emphasising entrepreneurship and the other, socialisation. When completed, these theses should add substantially to our under-standing of both gender and race in American public relations.

16 As with the previous two volumes, this one shows obvious omissions. For example, the first lengthy review of research (Pincus *et al.* 1991) reported that the typical CEO is a man, without commenting on the absence of women at high levels. Thus the authors used the male pronoun "he" throughout their discussion of the role of top communicators. In the subsection dealing with demographics, only age and years of experience were reported. To continue to analyse what is missing from Volume 3 would constitute a book-length treatise.

References

Agger, B. (1992) *Cultural Studies as Critical Theory*, London: Falmer Press.

Badaracco, C. (1990) 'Publicity and modern influence', *Public Relations Review*, 16 (3) 5–18.

Bakan, D. (1966) *Isolation and Communion in Western Man: The Duality of Human Existence*, Boston MA: Beacon Press.

Bernard, J. (1976) 'Sex differences: an overview', in A. G. Kaplan and J. P. Bean (eds) *Beyond Sex-Role Stereotypes: Readings Toward a Psychology of Androgyny*, Boston MA: Little, Brown.

Best, S. and Kellner, D. (1991) *Postmodern Theory: Critical Interrogations*, New York: Guilford Press.

Black, S. (1988) 'Letters to the editor: on women in public relations', *Public Relations Review*, 15 (1) 102.

Block, J. H. (1973) 'Conceptions of sex role: some cross-cultural and longitudinal perspectives', *American Psychologist*, 28, 512–26.

Broom, G. M. (1982) 'A comparison of sex roles in public relations', *Public Relations Review*, 8 (3) 17–22.

Broom, G. M. and Dozier, D. M. (1986) 'Advancement for public relations role models', *Public Relations Review*, 12 (1) 37–56.

Broom, G. M. and Smith, G. D. (1979) 'Testing the practitioner's impact on clients', *Public Relations Review*, 5 (3) 47–59.

Broom, G. M., Cox, M. S., Krueger, E. A. and Liebler, C. M. (1989) 'The gap between professional and research agendas in public relations journals', *Public Relations Research Annual*, 1, 141–54.

Brush, C. G. (1992) 'Research on women owned business owners: past trends, a new perspective, and future directions', *Entrepreneurship Theory and Practice*, 16, 5–30.

Campbell, K. K. (1989) 'What really distinguishes and/or ought to distinguish feminist scholarship in communication studies', *Women's Studies in Communication*, 11, 4–5.

Capek, M. E. S. (ed.) (1987) *A Women's Thesaurus: An Index of Language used to Describe and Locate Information by and about Women*, New York: Harper and Row.

Caplan, P. J. (1985) 'Introduction to special issue on sex roles and sex differences and androgyny', *International Journal of Women's Studies*, 8 (5) 437–40.

Carlson, R. (1985) 'Masculine/feminine: a personalogical perspective', *Journal of Personality*, 53 (2) 384–99.

Cline, C. G. and Masel-Walters, L. (1983) 'We're getting better: a pilot study to evaluate sexism in employee publications', *Public Relations Review*, 9 (3) 51.

Creedon, P. J. (1991) 'Public relations and "women's work": toward a feminist analysis of public relations roles', *Public Relations Research Annual*, 3, 67–84.

——(1993) 'Acknowledging the infrasystem: a critical feminist analysis of systems theory', *Public Relations Review*, 19 (2) 157–66.

Creedon, P. J., Al-Khaja, M. A. W. and Kruckeberg, D. (1995) 'Women and public relations education and practice in the United Arab Emirates', *Public Relations Review*, 21 (1) 59–76.

Denzin, N. K. (1991) *Images of Postmodern Society: Social Theory and Contemporary Cinema*, London: Sage.

Derrida, J. (1976) *Of Grammatology*, Baltimore MD: Johns Hopkins University Press.

DeRosa, D. and Wilcox, D. L. (1989) 'Gaps are narrowing between female and male students', *Public Relations Review*, 15 (1) 80–90.

Dozier, D. M. (1988) 'Breaking public relations' glass ceiling', *Public Relations Review*, 14 (3) 6–14.

——(1990) 'The innovation of research in public relations practice: review of a program of studies', *Public Relations Research Annual*, 2, 3–28.

Dozier, D. M. and Broom, G. M. (1995) 'Evolution of the manager role in public relations practice', *Journal of Public Relations Research*, 7 (1) 3–26.

Gaye, B. M. (1994) 'Bounded emotionality in two all-female organizations: a feminist analysis', *Women's Studies in Communication*, 17 (2) 1–19.

Griese, N. L. (1978) 'James D. Ellsworth, 1863–1940', *Public Relations Review*, 4, (2) 22–31.

Grunig, J. E. (1991) 'Public relations research: a legacy of Scott Cutlip', *Public Relations Review*, 17 (4) 357–76.

Grunig, J. E. and Grunig, L. A. (1989) 'Toward a theory of the public relations behavior of organizations: review of a program of research', *Public Relations Research Annual*, 1, 27–63.

——(1991) 'Conceptual differences in public relations and marketing: the case of health-care organizations', *Public Relations Review*, 17 (3) 257–78.

——(1992) 'From the editors: an annual becomes a quarterly', *Journal of Public Relations Research*, 4 (1) 1–2.

Grunig, L. A. (1988) 'A research agenda for women in public relations', *Public Relations Review*, 14 (3) 48–57.

——(1989) 'Toward a feminist transformation of public relations education and practice', paper presented to the Seminar on Gender Issues and Public Relations, Public Relations Division, Association for Education in Journalism and Mass Communication, Washington DC, August.

——(1990a) 'Power in the public relations department', *Public Relations Research Annual*, 2, 115–56.

——(1990b) 'Using focus group research in public relations', *Public Relations Review*, 16 (2) 36–49.

——(1991) 'Court-ordered relief from sex discrimination in the Foreign Service: implications for women working in development communication', *Public Relations Research Annual*, 3, 85–114.

——(1995a) 'The consequences of culture for public relations: the case of women in the Foreign Service', *Journal of Public Relations Research*, 7 (2) 139–61.

(1995b) 'A feminist phase analysis of research on women in postmodern public relations', paper presented to the Second International Public Relations Research Symposium, Bled, Slovenia, July.

Haraway, D. J. (1991) *Simians, Cyborgs, and Women: The Reinvention of Nature*, New York: Routledge.

Harlow, R. (1980) 'A timeline of public relations development', *Public Relations Review*, 6 (3) 3–13.

Harvey, D. (1989) *The Condition of Postmodernity*, Oxford: Blackwell.

Hatfield, C. R. (1994) 'Public relations education in the United Kingdom', *Public Relations Review*, 20 (2) 189–99.

118   *Contemporary perspectives*

Henry, S. (1988) 'In her own name? Public relations pioneer Doris Fleischman Bernays', paper presented to the Public Relations Division, Association for Education in Journalism and Mass Communication, Portland OR, July.

Hiebert, R. E. and Devine, C. M. (1985) 'Government's research and evaluation gap', *Public Relations Review*, 11 (3) 47–56.

Hon, L. C. (1992) 'Toward a feminist theory of public relations', unpublished doctoral dissertation, College Park MD: University of Maryland.

——(1995) 'Toward a feminist theory of public relations', *Journal of Public Relations Research*, 7 (1) 27–88.

Howe, F. (1984) *Myths of Coeducation: Selected Essays, 1964–83*, Bloomington IN: Indiana University Press.

Hunt, T. and Thompson, D. W. (1987) 'Making PR macho: reversing the sex gap in undergraduate public relations programs', paper presented to the Public Relations Division, Association for Education in Journalism and Mass Communication, San Antonio TX. (Also abstracted in *Public Relations Review* (1987) 13 (3) 62.)

Hutchinson, E. (1980) 'Micro-relations for students and practitioners', *Public Relations Review*, 6 (3) 23–32.

Jones, J. P., Natter, W. and Schatzki, T. R. (1993) *Postmodern Contentions*, New York: Guilford Press.

Kelly, K. S. (1995) 'The fund-raising behavior of US charitable organizations: an explanatory study', *Journal of Public Relations Research*, 7 (2) 111–37.

Kern-Foxworth, M. (1989) 'Status and roles of minority public relations practitioners', *Public Relations Review*, 15 (3) 39–47.

——(1990) 'Plantation kitchen to American icon: Aunt Jemima', *Public Relations Review*, 16 (3) 55–67.

Kinnick, K. N. and Cameron, G. T. (1994) 'Teaching public relations management: the current state of the art', *Public Relations Review*, 20 (1) 69–84.

Knodell, J. E. (1976) 'Matching perceptions of food editors, writers, and readers', *Public Relations Review*, 2 (3) 37–56.

Langland, E. and Gove, E. (1983 *A Feminist Perspective in the Academy: The Difference It Makes*, Chicago IL: University of Chicago Press.

Lauzen, M. M. (1991) 'Imperialism and encroachment in public relations', *Public Relations Review*, 7 (3) 245–55.

Lerner, G. (1990) 'To think ourselves free: review of *Transforming Knowledge* by E. Minnich', *Women's Review of Books*, 3, 10–11.

Lesly, P. (1988) 'Public relations numbers are up but stature down', *Public Relations Review*, 14 (4) 3–7.

——(1991) 'Public relations in the turbulent new human climate', *Public Relations Review*, 17 (1) 1–8.

McIntosh, P. (1983) 'Interactive phases of curricular revision: a feminist perspective', Working Paper Series no. 124, Wellesley MA: Wellesley College Center for Research on Women.

Mann, P. S. (1994) *Micro-Politics: Agency in a Postfeminist Era*, Minneapolis MN: University of Minnesota Press.

Marshall, J. (1984) *Women Managers: Travelers in a Male World*, New York: Wiley.

Mathews, W. (1988) 'Women in public relations: progression or retrogression?', *Public Relations Review*, 14 (3) 24–8.

Miller, D. A. (1988) 'Women in public relations graduate study', *Public Relations Review*, 14 (3) 29–35.

Minnich, E. K. (1990) *Transforming Knowledge*, Philadelphia PA: Temple University Press.

Mumby, D. K. and Putnam, L. L. (1992) 'The politics of emotion: a feminist reading of bounded rationality', *Academy of Management Review*, 17, 465–86.

Nessmann, K. (1995) 'Public relations in Europe: a comparison with the United States', *Public Relations Review*, 21 (2) 151–60.

Newsom, D. (1988) 'How women are depicted in annual reports', *Public Relations Review*, 14 (3) 15–19.

O'Brien, A. (1980) 'Public relations of anti-stereotype TV spots', *Public Relations Review*, 6 (3) 14–22.

Olasky, M. N. (1987) 'Abortion rights: anatomy of a negative campaign', *Public Relations Review*, 13 (3) 12–23.

Olson, L. D. (1989) 'Job satisfaction of journalists and PR personnel', *Public Relations Review*, 15 (4) 37–45.

Piekos, J. M. and Einsiedel, E. F. (1990) 'Roles and program evaluation techniques among Canadian public relations practitioners', *Public Relations Research Annual*, 2, 95–113.

Pincus, J. D., Rayfield, R. E. and Cozzens, M. D. (1991) 'The chief executive officer's internal communication role: a benchmark program of research', *Public Relations Research Annual*, 3, 1–36.

Pratt, C. (1986) 'Professionalism in Nigerian public relations', *Public Relations Review*, 12 (4) 27–40.

Pratt, C. B. (1991) 'PRSA members' perceptions of public relations ethics', *Public Relations Review*, 17 (2) 145–59.

PRSA Task Force (1988) 'Public relations body of knowledge task force report', *Public Relations Review*, 14 (1) 3–39.

Rakow, L. F. (1987) 'Looking to the future: five questions for gender research', *Women's Studies in Communication*, 10, 79–86.

Rayfield, R. E. (1984) 'Setting goals: the public relations outreach program', *Public Relations Review*, 10 (1) 59–67.

Schneir, M. (ed.) (1972) 'Declaration of sentiments and resolutions, Seneca Falls', in M. Schneir (ed.) *Feminism: The Essential Historical Writings*, New York: Vintage Books.

Schuster, M. and VanDyne, S. (eds) (1985) *Women's Place in the Academy: Transforming the Liberal Arts Curriculum*, Totowa NJ: Rowman and Allanheld.

Scrimger, J. (1985) 'Profile: women in Canadian public relations', *Public Relations Review*, 15 (3) 40–46.

Selnow, G. W. and Wilson, S. (1985) 'Sex roles and job satisfaction in public relations', *Public Relations Review*, 11 (4) 38–47.

Simon, H. (1976) *Administrative Behavior*, New York: Free Press.

Smith, R. C. and Turner, P. K. (1995) 'A social constructionist reconfiguration of metaphor analysis: an application of "SCMA" to organizational socialization theorizing', *Communication Monographs*, 62, 152–81.

Spicer, C. H. (1991) 'Communication functions performed by public relations and marketing practitioners', *Public Relations Review*, 17 (3) 293–305.

Sriramesh, K. (1992) 'Societal culture and public relations: ethnographic evidence from India', *Public Relations Review*, 18 (2) 201–11.

Stewart, L. J. (1988) 'Women in foundation and corporate public relations', *Public Relations Review*, 14 (3) 20–3.

Tetreault, M. K. (1976) 'Feminist phase theory', *Journal of Higher Education*, 56 (4) 363–84.

Theus, K. T. (1985) 'Gender shifts in journalism and public relations', *Public Relations Review*, 11 (1) 42–50.

Toth, E. L. (1988) 'Making peace with gender issues in public relations', *Public Relations Review*, 14 (3) 36–47.

Toth, E. L. and Cline, C. G. (1991) 'Public relations practitioner attitudes toward gender issues: a benchmark study', *Public Relations Review*, 17 (2) 161–74.

Toth, E. L. and Grunig, L. A. (1993) 'The missing story of women in public relations', *Journal of Public Relations Research*, 5, 153–76.

Truth, S. (aka Isabella). (1972) 'Ain't I a woman?', in M. Schneir (ed.) *Feminism: The Essential Historical Writings*, New York: Vintage Books.

Turk, J. V. (1989) 'Management skills need to be taught in public relations', *Public Relations Review*, 15 (1) 38–52.

Twombly, S. B. (1993) 'What we know about women in community colleges: an examination of the literature using feminist phase theory', *Journal of Higher Education*, 64 (2) 186–210.

VanLeuven, J. K. (1990) 'Body of knowledge: tomorrow's research agenda', *Public Relations Review*, 16 (2) 17–24.

Weaver-Lariscy, R. A., Cameron, G. T. and Sweep, D. D. (1994) 'Women in higher education public relations: an inkling of change?', *Journal of Public Relations Research*, 6 (2) 125–40.

Weber, M. (1981) 'Bureaucracy', in O. Grusky and G. A. Miller (eds) *The Sociology of Organizations: Basic Studies*, New York: Free Press.

Weick, K. (1979) *The Social Psychology of Organizing*, 2nd edn, Reading MA: Addison-Wesley.

Wilcox, D. L. (1979) 'Hiring criteria of public relations employers', *Public Relations Review*, 5 (2) 35–42.

Wright, D. K. and Hantz, A. (1985) 'Examination of social responsibility differences between Canadian and American IABC members', *Public Relations Review*, 11 (4) 51.

Zerbinos, E. and Clanton, G. A. (1993) 'Minority practitioners: career influences, job satisfaction, and discrimination', *Public Relations Review*, 19 (1) 75–91.

4 Public relations and rhetoric

History, concepts, future

Elizabeth L. Toth

United States communication scholars began less than fifteen years ago to explore public relations from a rhetorical mode. Since 1979, communication scholars have published two lines of rhetorical research related to public relations. One line reflected the fundamentals of rhetoric. The second line considered organisational communication as rhetoric.

Fundamental rhetorical researchers assumed that the meanings and channels of today's rhetors are an influence in some way on our society. While they qualified their examinations of corporate rhetoric's impact on society, they referred to its effects as well as its intentions. These fundamentals focused on the speech act or text and its meanings. Such fundamentals included institutions, ideologies, rhetors, media and audiences (Sproule 1988: 477). Some of the fundamentals that Crable proposed for his model of the modern rhetorical transaction were: organisational self-concept; audiences; support as the organisational goal; stage managers; script writers; set; media delivery systems; message intermediaries; spokespersons; perceptions and evidence of impact. He noted that while the "rhetor" is featured, the real rhetor is an organisation (Crable 1990: 122).

Organisational rhetorical scholars posited a rhetorical view of organisations as symbolic contexts in which organisational members and outsiders used different language strategies. Cheney and Vibbert (1987) proposed that such language strategies were used to manage organisational values, issues, image and identities. Organisational rhetoricians did not consider the effect of rhetorical strategies on society. Instead, they examined the impact of rhetorical strategies on employees inside the organisation.

While these two approaches have showed convergence over time in publications that include co-mingled references, their authors have contributed distinct perspectives that developed and contributed to the public relations body of knowledge. This chapter describes these two rhetorical approaches to public relations and examines the kinds of theories these approaches have produced. This chapter looks at the kinds of public relations problems these communication scholars have matched with their rhetorical theories. By matching public relations practices to the rhetorical theories proposed, I suggest what rhetorical theories can and cannot do, and what the future of rhetorical research on public relations may be.

A description of rhetoric

In attempting to define rhetoric and identify the historical roots of rhetorical theory and public relations, Blair's (1992) criticism of rhetorical histories provided specific cautions. First, one should seek to avoid tracing influences as a means of discovery. Not only may one run the risk of seeing patterns where none exist, the past becomes admired to an extent that unless ancients are quoted and related to contemporary theories, these theories are devalued. Blair cautioned us to beware of historians' "fervent admiration for and privilege of classical sources because that which is 'new' is suspect, or it is itself rendered as a marker of decline, reduced to a flawed or inadequate version of the traditional" (Blair 1992: 410).

Found in the works of rhetorical scholars studying public relations and communication management was a wide regard for the works of Kenneth Burke (1969a; 1969b). Scholars such as Heath, Tompkins, and Cheney have turned to Burke's collective writings to extend Burkean theory into the domains of public relations and organisational communication. Tompkins and Cheney (1993) even took up the task of responding to an article critical of Burke's expansive use by rhetorical scholars who proposed limits on the Burkean system. Tompkins and Cheney (1993) believed that their extended interpretations of Burke were more representative of his intentions.

Second, Blair cautioned against the notion of historical "systems" of rhetorical theory. The systems view, by Ehninger (1968), proposed three distinct groups of theories unique to various eras. His purpose in grouping several rhetorical theories was to capture the discreteness of rhetoric's history. For Ehninger, there were three crucial eras in the development of western rhetorical thought – a "grammatical ancient rhetoric, a psychological rhetoric of the late eighteenth century, and a sociological contemporary rhetoric" (1968). This criticism was important to my analysis of the history and concepts of rhetorical theory applied to public relations, because there has been extended an argument for a fourth system of rhetoric that focused on the rhetorical nature of organisations.

Crable proposed this fourth great system of rhetoric that "portrays ~he rhetor, not as someone we see and hear, but as an organisation we ieither see nor hear" (1990: 124). Rhetors were viewed as inseparable from their organisations. They used a variety of media for their messages (often mass media). Their audiences were multiple, "but they may be a curious combination of mass media and self-selected (albeit electronic) audiences" (Crable 1990: 118). Any one audience member may have several organisational identifications, which would often overlap or conflict with one another. "The goal of rhetoric within the organisational system concerns securing support, instead of praise or blame, persuasion in its isolated sense, or understanding" (Crable 1990: 118).

Blair cautioned that any systemisation of rhetoric represented abstract categories whose legitimacy as descriptive categories has never been established or defended (1992: 412). While the systems view assumed pluralistic advantages, Blair argued that systems may well be arbitrary in that pluralism. We may get dominant theories, but not particular theories of any given period. Blair believed that Ehninger's systems assumed that the eras of rhetoric were progressive. She posited also that Ehninger's systems took an optimistic view of rhetoric as more and more of a contribution to society.

These two concepts of rhetorical histories, the influence and systems perspectives, resulted in, according to Blair, "the influence seekers privileging classical authors, while the systematisers valorising contemporary thinkers" (1992: 417).

I have tried in my analysis to follow Blair's four-part proposal to provide a critical history of rhetorical theory and public relations. First, my analysis is intended to regard the rhetorical theories of public relations published over time as texts or instances of discourse, rather than as monuments or relics. I focus on the concepts and propositions of the authors rather than on the author's uses of earlier rhetorical theorists to support their points of view. Second, I attempt to expose more than just the predominant rhetorical theories, but particular views of rhetoric and public relations. I intend to separate and make distinct the contributions that seem to overlap, because individual authors have taken over each other's ideas and arguments. Third, I have sought to avoid the problems of preservative or progressive views. I intend to identify positions that are idealistic but as yet little tested or untested in our academic forums. Fourth, I am seeking to criticise rather than hold sacred or find optimism in past research, so that there is instead a look at formulations in terms of their ability to explain and make more understandable the practice of public relations.

The concept of rhetoric

The writings on rhetorical theory and public relations seem curiously lacking in much discussion of what the concept of rhetoric means. Defining rhetoric would appear to be central in importance to any discussions of its application. One has to conclude that communication scholars assume that their audiences are already well aware of what was meant by rhetoric. As an example of an abstract definition of rhetoric, Crable and Vibbert defined corporate rhetoric as "the art of adjusting organisations to environments and environments to organisations" (1986: 394).

There are present in the works of Heath references to the concept of rhetoric; however, the discussions of the concept stated are abstract and philosophical. In his earliest work on rhetoric and public relations, Heath referred to Kenneth Burke's definition of rhetoric: "For him, rhetoric is the study of the 'competitive use of the co-operative' and 'is designed to help us take delight in the Human Barnyard, with its addiction to the Scramble'" (Heath 1980: 371). Heath (1992a), in a more expansive work on rhetorical approaches to public relations, gave us Aristotle's view of rhetoric: "the ability to observe in any given case the available means of persuasion – what needs to be said and how it should be said to achieve desired outcomes" (Heath 1992a: 21). However, Heath subsequently favored Donald Bryant's 1953 definition of rhetoric: "the function of adjusting ideas to people and of people to ideas" (Heath 1992a: 24). Heath concluded that this definition of rhetoric "makes a commitment to discover truth and acknowledges the organic interaction between people and ideas" (1992a: 24).

There are very few definitions of rhetoric provided in the works of organisational communication scholars writing about rhetoric in organisations. Tompkins and Redding (1988), who represent the earliest advocates for rhetoric and organisational communication, prefer the more sweeping view from Charles Conrad (1985) that "in essence, communication in organisations is rhetorical communication" (Tompkins and Redding 1988: 172). More specifically, this rhetoric of organisations was defined as symbolic action "that creates organisational realities and environments as well as the motives of those who act" (Tompkins 1987: 83).

Four perspectives of rhetoric: humanistic, dialogue, symbolic, critical

Rather than select from among the definitions of rhetoric used when discussing public relations, I shall describe rhetoric through four perspectives: humanistic, dialogical, symbolic and critical (Toth 1994). Each aspect provides some distinct characteristics of the concept of rhetoric, "particularities" according to Blair (1992), that should give us a wider understanding of the meaning of rhetoric and clarify our assumptions about the concept of rhetoric.

First, rhetorical scholars have argued that rhetoric is humanistic in the sense that one's self is a valued part of any analysis of human inter-action. Several scholars have referred to rhetoric as in the humanistic rather than the scientific tradition (Bitzer 1971; Arnold and Frandsen 1984; Redding 1989; J. Grunig and White 1992), "although rhetoric is guided by theories and produces theories in the same way as the social sciences" (J. Grunig 1992: 546).

Rhetoricians were humanists who believed that their personal judgements were a valuable contribution to knowledge. Arnold and Frandsen described the humanistic tradition as a search: "behind every premise, discovery must occur, which is 'to find' the point of compar-ison and similarity between reality and ourselves as human beings" (1984: 21). Arnold and Frandsen broadly defined the self as "an organ-isation of perceptions that enable or perhaps disable communicative interactions among distinctly separated but interacting individuals" (1984: 3). They emphasised the "self" in the making of communica-tion by implying individual choice and decision making, as opposed to social scientists, "who have concerned themselves chiefly with perceivers' responses to perceptions of others" (1984: 12). In other words, rhetoricians have made judgements based on their self-perceptions of events and texts rather than asking others for their interpretations of what the events or texts mean.

Because of the humanistic tradition, rhetorical studies of public relations have not considered whether communication reaches or affects audiences in ways that can be scientifically measured. Instead, rhetorical scholars themselves established criteria by which to judge messages, communicators and audiences. For example, Goldzwig and Cheney (1984) established four criteria by which to analyse the rhetor-ical actions of the US Catholic bishops' public stances on nuclear arms. Goldzwig and Cheney organised their analysis of the bishops according to their judgements of the bishops' efforts to articulate general moral principles, allow for a range of responses, balance the concerns of the transitional Church and national Church groups, and weigh collegiality and pluralism with hierarchical authority (1994: 17).

A second characteristic of rhetoric important in the work of rhetoric scholars studying public relations has been the characteristic of dialogue or exchange of ideas between individuals. Bryant's definition of rhetoric and the definition of corporate rhetoric by Crable and Vibbert (1986) are dialogical in the sense of both sides entering the exchange. For Pearson (1989), dialogue is a precondition for the ethical conduct of organisations toward their publics.

In 1980, Heath described the paradigm of corporate advocacy, concerned with "the management of issues on behalf of corporate, educational, special-interest, governmental, and non-profit organisations" (1980: 370) as based on the assumption that "ideas, opinion, understanding, and judgement may be refined through open and vigorous debate" (*ibid.*). Heath envisioned this debate as a form of dialogue or argumentation with "carefully researched support for theses and arguments and well-designed strategies of refutation" (Heath 1980: 374).

The characteristic of dialogue has been central to Heath's works, including his three propositions in 1993 for rhetoric's place as the dominant paradigm for the study and practice of pubic relations. In each of the propositions below, Heath emphasised the creation of influence through a give-and-take process between individuals and organisations. Dialogue occurred through the persuasive language choices of public relations practitioners. Persuasion was an interactive, dialogical process through which thoughts and actions grew, merged, and divided in the metaphor of the courtship.

1   Because practitioners help establish meaning by which people define their private and communal actions as well as public policies, a rhetorical paradigm is vital to the study and practice of public relations.

2   A rhetorical perspective views public relations as a form of social influence, a view that treats persuasion as an interactive, dialogic process whereby points of view are contested in public. Because it avoids a linear influence model whereby senders are assumed to be dominant, a dialogic view of persuasion counterbalances the view that it is inherently manipulative.

3   A rhetorical perspective assumes that thought and actions are predicated on facts, values and policies that establish limits and opportunities for asserting self-interest; this assertion grows out of the dialectic of merger and division, which is a rationale for

courtship by which each voice in the environment of organisations appeals for persons to become identified with it.

(Heath 1993: 143–4)

Heath has been sensitive in his writings to the "sender-oriented" notions which suggested that rhetoric was one-way and manipulative of audiences. While not ducking the notions of self-interest in the sender's messages, Heath argued that self-interest was tempered by the responses of audiences to these messages. Heath (1992c: 317) argued that the self and self-interest were at the heart of rhetoric. However, these self-interests were not static. Self-interests in the form of "rewards, costs, privileges, and constraints" (Heath 1992c: 318) were negotiated in the open contest of ideas because in the context of our system of free enterprise and representative governments, all ideas ran the risk of being ignored, derogated and challenged, even if one side might appear to have more power and influence to bring to bear. For example, Heath felt that even the advantage that corporations might have with the ability to spend great amounts of money could not overcome the resistance of better rhetorical strategies:

> Even given the fear that corporations have disproportionate influence because of their ability to engage in "deep-pockets" spending, they do not dominate the opinion arena, and may even be at certain disadvantages because of their apparent size and questionable credibility.

(Heath 1992c: 318)

Third, rhetoric was symbolic. Rhetoric was composed of verbal or non-verbal and visual symbols. It occurred in all media: film, television, radio, painting, sculpture and architecture (Heath 1992a: 21). Rhetorical scholars believed that symbolic behavior created and influenced relationships between individuals, audiences, and more currently organisations. Heath argued that a rhetorical perspective on public relations addressed the impact of words and other symbols (1993: 141).

Recently, Heath has provided another argument for the symbolic nature of organisational rhetoric by discussing "zones of meaning"; that is, shared interests of social realities that limit and shape people's interpretation of reality (1993: 142). Some ways of observing zones of meaning are through the analysis of metaphors, narratives, and terms high in abstraction such as productivity and excellence, that were interpreted specifically by managers in one way and by subordinates in another (Heath 1994: 141). Heath argued that "organisations consist of zones of meanings" or social realities had to be developed if individuals in departments or interpersonal relationships were to be able to coordinate their activities (1994: 45).

Tompkins (1987) argued for symbolism over substance in our efforts to understand organisations. In his article on the centrality of symbolism in understanding organisations, he drew heavily on the work of Kenneth Burke, who defined rhetoric's function as that of inducing cooperation through symbolic means:

> rhetoric is rooted in an essential function of language itself, a function that is wholly realistic, and is continually born anew; the use of language as a symbolic means of inducing co-operation in beings that by nature respond to symbols.
>
> (Burke, in Tompkins 1987: 78)

Tompkins concluded that "organisational theory is an extension of the classical concerns of rhetorical theory and that recent considerations of culture and symbolism are consistent with the 'new rhetoric' of symbolic action" (1987: 86).

A fourth characteristic of rhetoric has been that rhetoric is critical. Rhetorical scholars believed in the influence of rhetoric on society and its value to society, so much so that they treated critically how the outcome was achieved and whether the means justified the ends. Heath described this process as "evaluative frameworks that give continuity to society" (1993: 149). According to Heath, these evaluative frameworks, a contribution of the rhetorical perspective, addressed the "ways opinions create continuity or discontinuity of events" which an information-centred approach to public relations failed to do.

Heath gave as an example the inability of information to help solve the problems of public misunderstanding of risk situations (Nathan *et al.* 1992). Based on a random telephone survey of Texas City residents that tested their support of a proposed construction of a $200 million copper smelter, Nathan *et al.* found that knowledge had little to do with risk tolerance (1992: 253). Instead, they concluded that other qualitative factors, such as whether policy makers had dealt openly and honestly about risk, predicted public response to risk and not necessarily the factual details or formal risk estimates (1992: 255). Although Nathan *et al.* did not suggest the application of rhetorical research directly, their conclusion regarding the credibility of the policy makers or rhetors does fall within the evaluative rhetorical domain.

Heath proposed five points of departure with which to criticise the rhetorical nature of public relations: the dimensions of the rhetorical problem or situation; standards of truth and knowledge; rhetoric for good reasons; discovering the perspective embedded in the claims made; and the quality of the narrative form (1992b: 39–60).

Sproule (1990) proposed that two critical questions pertaining to social influences were required of all organisational scholars who wanted to try out rhetorical approaches. These two questions concerned the relationship of organisational communication to an idealised society, and the relationship of private interests with the public sphere:

> (1) how do managerial communication patterns relate to the idealised rational-democratic society and (2) to what extent have private institutional interests and privately controlled communication campaigns become so dominant in society that the public sphere may be weakened?
>
> (Sproule 1990: 130)

Sproule urged organisational scholars studying management discourse as a species of public rhetoric to use five schools of thought for criticising the "rhetorical products of today's organisations" (1990: 129). These were the progressive, practitioner, polemical (politically oriented) and rationalist approaches that questioned the public's ability to deal with institutionally based symbolic action.

Pearson (1989) gave two standards for producing ethical inter-organisational communication. One was that organisations must promote dialogue in which participants were free and equal to challenge one another's positions, attitudes and beliefs. Second, organisations must never take for granted existing structures to promote dialogue, but continually monitor the impact of these organisational structures on dialogue.

Rhetorical theories applied to public relations

The corporate advocate

In studying the contributions of rhetorical perspectives to the field of public relations, the predominant thinking has concerned a corporate advocate or person. While traditional rhetorical theory focused on identifiable individuals as senders or speakers, rhetorical scholars studying public relations have argued that organisations use individuals to craft messages that will represent the corporation or organisation in the contest to win public opinion.

In 1980, Heath argued that speech communication curricula were advantageous to the corporate advocate because he/she "must be a skilled writer and reflecting critical judgement and standards of form, appreciate effective and excellent expression" (1980: 374). Likewise, "the corporate advocate needs to understand the adversary's strategies and may be employed to aid the advocacy efforts of single-issue groups as they work for or against corporations" (Heath 1980: 374).

While Heath's perspective on individuals employed to create messages on behalf of organisations continued in speech communication textbooks as reasons for studying speech communication, the corporate advocate as a rhetor who performed certain roles did not continue to be developed very much in subsequent rhetorical research on public relations. Cheney and Dionisopoulos did exhort corporate communication specialists to "be aware of the assumptions and the effects of their symbols in the 'marketplace' of corporate discourse" (1989: 139). However, they changed direction in their research. Rather than consider the roles of individual public relations practitioners, Cheney and Dionisopoulos studied organisations as "texts" and the use of corporate communications texts to evaluate the images and the identities of organisations.

In a discussion of the maturing of the corporate person, Cheney and Dionisopoulos referred to our society's developing support for and belief in corporate entities. They concluded that "the proportion of power by individuals has decreased related to that enacted by corporate persons (or organisations)" (1989: 140). According to Cheney and Dionisopoulos (1989), corporations in this new more powerful role have begun to promote issues, aggressively court public opinion, and attempt to shape the public and social debate.

For communication scholars, the replacement by institutions of persons as rhetors came about with the US Supreme Court's (1978) Bellotti decision that supported the right of corporations to publish views in attempts to influence the public debate. This led to a reshaping of our beliefs about who or what is attempting to communicate, and our subsequent acceptance of the role of corporations as speakers – with personalities, identities and images that we treat as we do those of individual speakers.

Ascribing to this view, Cheney and Vibbert (1987) proposed four terms to analyse corporate public discourse: value, issue, identity and image. The working definitions of these terms were the following. A value was something that was prized by a person or collectively, as revealed through the ongoing discourse of the individual or collective (*ibid.*: 175). Identity was what was commonly taken as "representative of a person or group" (176). Image meant something projected by an individual or group, something perceived or interpreted by others and more temporary or basic than an identity (176). An issue was created when one or more human agents attached significance to a situation or perceived problem (175).

Instead of studying the corporate advocate or public relations practitioners, rhetorical theorists refocused their analyses toward corporate advocacy or the products of individuals employed by organisations to speak or produce corporate views. Cheney (1992) referred to this shift as the "decentering of the individual in theory and in practice" (1992: 170). Instead, the corporate person represented itself – the corporate, rather than the individual speech. The products of this speech, such as the images of corporations, became the evidence for rhetoricians to examine critically so as to reveal certain rhetorical strategies at work.

Rhetorical scholars began to assess also the proactive role of organisations in shaping issues and values. Heath and Nelson (1986), Crable and Vibbert (1985), Vibbert (1986), Heath (1988), and Crable and Faulkner (1988) considered the processes through which organisations managed public policy issues. Crable and Vibbert assumed that issues were creations given life "when one or more human agents attached significance to them" (1985: 5). Corporations "made" issues through the shaping of mass-mediated messages, sometimes through advocacy advertisements and sometimes through producing statements or actions that were distributed through the mass media. Vibbert (1987) created an issues model that illustrated the managed process of creating and resolving issues (to the corporation's benefit) through a process of definition of issues, legitimisation, polarisation and resolution.

Rhetorical strategies

There have been several studies of the application of rhetorical studies to public relations actions or products of organisations. In one of the earliest rhetorical studies of public relations practices, Crable and Vibbert (1983) established the messages of organisations as a proper domain for the analysis of rhetorical strategies. Crable and Vibbert analysed Mobil Oil Corporation's "Observations" half-page Sunday magazine ads during the years 1976–80. Their essay focused on four ideas: "Observations" as a response to a rhetorical situation; the argumentative approach of "Observations"; the cultural foundations of those arguments; and a summary assessment of "Observations" (1983: 260).

The authors described the economic and social climate of the time as one of increasing public criticism and potentially tighter federal government regulations on exploration and production of oil. Mobil responded by purchasing space in a channel of communication trusted by the "average" American, the Sunday supplement. According to Crable and Vibbert, among the self-helps, travel features, cartoons and recipes, Mobil intended to create a set of appeals to the American value system.

Crable and Vibbert described Mobil's rhetorical strategy as epideictic, the purpose of which was to increasingly associate itself with the values held in common with the audience. The authors described several instalments specifically in order to conclude that each ad helped to build the premise of Mobil having the same values and beliefs as the Sunday reader. Mobil used non-controversial messages to reflect the warrant-establishing and warrant-using arguments of rhetorical art. The purpose of these instalments was to build toward a fuller blown advocacy campaign for more specialised audiences that were to come later.

Following this article, Bostdorff and Vibbert (1994) again summarised the advantages of epideictic or values advocacy, but also cautioned public relations practitioners to consider carefully the honesty of their organisation's values advocacy and its contribution to societal interests. Their four ethical implications of values advocacy were:

1   values advocacy may create a misleading portrait of the organisation;
2   values advocacy may divert public attention from serious questions about an organisation's practices;
3   values advocacy may lay the groundwork for public support of policies that do not have social merit; and
4   values advocacy should raise concern because it persuades without seeming to do so.

(Bostdorff and Vibbert 1994: 53–154)

Conrad (1983) posited that the public relations materials of the Moral Majority used the rhetorical strategy of the romantic form. The Moral Majority Inc., a political action group led by the Reverend Jerry Falwell, published in its widely distributed newsletters and reports arguments made up of romanticised spiritual and secular myths. These myths depicted a demonic world and an idyllic world based on a reconstruction of individually satisfying past experiences. Conrad illustrated how Moral Majority rhetors took advantage of these two myths in its messages regarding political decision making and the First Amendment, molding public institutions, and representing persons who could not represent themselves. In the later set of messages, for example, the Moral Majority asserted that it had a spiritual guardianship for many groups of Americans, "Blacks, native Americans, the poor ... children threatened by four groups of demonic agents – pornographers, illegal drug dealers, abortionists, and militant homosexuals" (Conrad 1983: 167).

Peterson referred also to the rhetorical strategy of arguments through the use of "myths" in her analysis of the interpretative program at Grand Teton National Park, "a major public relations effort, providing information for current and potential visitors through publications, museums, and audio-visual devices" (1988: 121). Peterson applied Burke's dramatistic framework of act, scene, agent, agency and purpose to analyse human motives as expressed through language. She concluded that the in-house materials and interpretative program materials indicated efforts to argue the myths of protection and preservation. For example, the park's specific natural resources are linked to terms that focus on the "state of being" of the nature resources: "perfect, natural, meaningful, interdependent, native and wild" (Peterson 1988: 125). Peterson criticised this strategy as attempts to manage the incongruity between the myth of an idyllic state and the reality of destructive acts that might better be helped with visitor participation and intervention.

Dionisopoulos and Crable (1988) identified the rhetorical strategy of "definitional hegemony" in their study of the rhetorical strategies involved in the Three Mile Island aftermath of 1989. The nuclear power industry published speeches and brochures and sought through mass-media messages to alleviate public fears that followed the near-disastrous accident caused by a malfunctioning cooling pump.

Dionisopoulos and Crable (1988) surveyed the rhetorical context in which the nuclear industry's pre-accident rhetoric focused on a believing public which held nuclear power in high regard. The immediate post-accident context revealed that industry advocates had so understated the risks of reactor accidents that public opinion became quickly convinced that safety was a major concern. Dionisopoulos and Crable identified as "definitional hegemony" an attempt to influence public discussion by dominating the way in which the attendant issues are defined, as the rhetorical strategy used. As viewed through the messages of the newspapers, magazines, advertisements and pamphlets, Dionisopoulos and Crable argued that the nuclear industry redefined the safety of nuclear power and the "need" for nuclear energy. For example, "the industry offered its own version of what really happened, suggesting the facts had been kept from the American public" (1988: 140). The authors concluded that while it was difficult to assess the effort in the campaign to dominate the issues, nuclear power essentially became a non-issue in the 1980 elections.

Ice (1991) extended the application of rhetorical theories to public relations by examining the Union Carbide public relations response to the tragic gas leak from its Bhopal, India plant in 1984. Ice defined Union Carbide's rhetorical situation as its need "to justify itself in order to repair its damaged reputation" (1991: 341). Of particular interest to Ice were the multiple publics involved in the situation and a variety of reactions that would have to be treated separately. Ice used Grunig and Hunt's four-type conceptual scheme to identify publics: enabling, functional, normative and diffused (1984: 139–43). Then Ice applied Ware and Linkugel's (1973) typology of rhetorical strategies used in apologia discourse.

> These four factors include denial (denying the alleged wrong or event), bolstering (reinforcing the existence of a fact or relationship), differentiation (separating facts, sentiments, and relationships from some later context), and transcendence (moving an audience away from particulars toward some abstract principle).
>
> (Ware and Linkugel 1973: 344)

After identifying how Union Carbide applied the Ware and Linkugel typology to the four types of organisational publics, Ice cautioned against using multiple rhetorical strategies without also seeking to manage the strategies used. In the case of Union Carbide, Ice found that the use of certain rhetorical strategies of apologia repaired some relationships while alienating other publics. Similarly, Cheney (1991) published an in-depth analysis of how the US Catholic bishops managed multiple identities, both individual and collective.

Included among the rhetorical strategies used in public relations products, then, have been epideictic or values advocacy, the myths of the romantic form and myths more generally, definitional hegemony, apologia discourse applied to multiple publics, and the need to choose distinct rhetorical strategies for multiple publics.

Organisational rhetoric applied to the practice of public relations

The application of organisational rhetoric to the practice of public relations relied on a metaphor distinct from the traditional rhetorical view of a contest or wrangle in the public sphere. Organisational communication scholars (Bantz 1989) believed in Weick's (1969; 1979) contention that organisations were not simply things or containers, but rather they were created and reviewed through the communication of their participants. Sproule (1989) referred to Weick's view of organisations as the "private sphere." The modern organisation was made up of individuals' private or self-interests that motivated them to use rhetorical strategies. Rather than the rational-democratic sphere of the traditional rhetorician, the organisation was an arena made up of individuals who created organisational realities and culture with others through symbols.

> Weick presents organising as a human impulse that allows individuals to create mini-publics within the space of the organisations. People's behaviours are interlocked and they negotiate viewpoints in ways that overcome managerial meddling. In this way, the organisation really is more an invention of people than a structure having a fixed nature. To Weick, the organisation is inside one's head.
>
> (Sproule 1989: 26)

Weick's theories led communication scholars to renew their interest in the speech act, particularly the everyday talk in the routine contexts of organisations. These contexts have been referred to as "zones of meaning" (Heath 1994), provinces of meaning, interpretative schemes or symbolic fields (Tompkins 1987). Tompkins referenced Berg's (1985) cultural approach to the organisation as a symbolic field that has three important characteristics:

1 it consists of coded and stored experiences;
2 it is the result of the transformation of experienced reality into symbolic reality; and
3 it is the collective symbolisation of reality.

(Tompkins 1987: 84)

An earlier piece by Cheney (1983b) illustrated how Burke's rhetorical strategy of "identification" was used to establish the individual–organisational relationship. Whereas traditional rhetoricians had considered the strategies of public speakers to link their interests with those of their audiences, Cheney broadened Burke's writings to consider identification as "the function of sociality" (1983b: 154). Identification helped an individual respond to the divisions of society by permitting that individual to "belong" to some special body or bodies that granted him/her personal meaning. Cheney used as his example Erving Goffman's statement: "The so-called 'I' is merely a unique combination of partially conflicting 'corporate we's'" (1983b: 145). Finally, individuals revealed their identities through labels, such as "I work for Exxon" which provided shorthand meanings of values and interests. Our corporate identities served to enhance or lend prestige to the self; that is, praise of the organisation by implication provided praise to us.

Cheney (1983b) introduced the concept of "consubstantiality" that, according to Burke, represented the area of overlap between an individual and a group. Cheney defined consubstantiality as "a product or state of identification that leads an individual to see things from the perspective of a target" (1983b: 146).

While Cheney described Burkean identification as primarily receiver-oriented, Cheney concluded that "organisations frequently help facilitate identification through their myriad means of communication" (1983b: 146). Organisations stimulated the inducement process of their employees through their communicating of values, goals and information. The process became complete when the individual did what was "best for the organisation."

Cheney (1983b) described three identification strategies and tactics derived from Burkean theory to be found in organisational messages. The first was "the common ground technique." The organisation linked itself to the individual employee in an overt manner, as for example when management told employees that the corporation shared their values for economic security. The second strategy was "identification through antithesis." Cheney gave as an example corporate documents which emphasised threats from outsiders, stressing the need to unite and accept organisational values (1983b). The third strategy from Burkean theory was the assumed or transcendent "we." The word "we," an almost unnoticed appeal to identification, connected and linked the corporation and employee against the corresponding "they" (1983b: 148–9).

Cheney (1983b) applied these strategies to an analysis of corporate house organisations or newsletters. His was a rhetorical analysis of ten newsletters from ten different corporations, although he did include quantitative as well as qualitative measures. What defined his analysis as rhetorical was the prominence of his personal judgements about the texts and the motivations and intentions of the corporations as found in the texts.

Cheney (1983b) posited for example that the most important of the rhetorical strategies to be found in the newsletters was that of "the common ground technique." He stated that in terms of frequency, variety of types of articles, and diversity of ways common ground was expressed, there were the following six uses of common ground. First, ⁺here were expressions of concern for the individual as an integral member of the organisation. Second, the newsletters contained recognitions of individual contributions that highlighted the shared values of the corporation. Third, there was an espousal of presumably shared values: for example, the Chairman of Bank America, John W. Fisher, wrote: "I firmly believe that an awareness of and involvement in public affairs is a responsibility that each of us owes to ourselves, our families, our country and our company" (Cheney 1983b: 151). Fourth, Cheney listed "advocacy of benefits and activities that assumed the similarity of employees' values with these of the corporation." Fifth, Cheney found praise by outsiders (a form of third-party endorsement) to illustrate encouraging employees to identify with their organisations. Cheney's sixth category was testimonials by employees expressing dedication and commitment to the organisation.

Cheney (1983b) followed his analysis of common ground techniques by showing how identification by antithesis was used to unite the individual and the organisation together against a common enemy or threat from outside the organisation. All ten newsletters contained this strategy. Cheney also found the assumed "we," and such unifying symbols as guidelines on how to use the corporate trademark and logo.

Cheney (1983b) completed his argument for the application of the Burkean theory of identification to communication between the corporation and its employees, by broadening the role of such strategies to the "larger processes at work in the organisational setting." He posited that organisations took the task of employee identification seriously. "Corporations invest significant amounts of time, money and creative energy in the production of internal publications" (1983b: 156). Corporations have the ability to portray their priorities "not as the products of real choices but as the way things are and the way individuals want them to be" (*ibid.*). Speaking in 1983, Cheney concluded that top-level managers count on identification on the part of employees with their organisations. Organisations that can socialise their employees to think of the organisation's values and goals first, certainly had the advantage in terms of motivating and retaining employees.

With this study of identification strategies found in newsletters, Cheney began to develop his position for the use of rhetorical theory in the study of organisations. However, a more central contribution to our understanding of the distinction between fundamental rhetorical analysis and organisational rhetoric was evident in Cheney's (1983a) field study to reveal the "process" rather than "product" nature of identification.

Cheney proposed to explore the use of identification and other related processes, such as "decision making, persuasion, control, alienation, and communication in large contemporary organisations" (1983a: 342). Cheney posed the research question: "To what extent does the process of organisational identification explain the process of decision making by organisational members?" (1983a: 347–8). Mailed questionnaires collected data from 149 employees of a large industrial and high-technology corporation ranked in the "Fortune 500." Then, Cheney conducted twenty-nine face-to-face interviews. The results linked organisational goals and values as relevant in the process of employees making decisions. He found that "the company's interests figured prominently in the decision making of the majority of employees interviewed" (1983a: 353).

When Cheney attempted to trace the source of the decisional premises and identification, employees reportedly pointed to themselves as sources – "for my own satisfaction," "the way that is best" (1983a: 354). Employees reported that most decisional premises were made on the basis of daily communication with others. Changes in decisional premises came over time, because of direct communication phenomena and because of the actions of the organisation. Cheney concluded that this study suggested further evidence of an organisational identification and decision-making process. By identifying and describing this process, management could intervene symbolically and reinforce employee images and values.

Although Cheney (1991) and others (Goldzwig and Cheney 1984; Cheney 1992; Dionisopoulos and Goldzwig 1992) developed other fundamental rhetorical studies of public relations, there seemed to be little new to report in the research to extend Cheney's (1983) examination of the rhetorical nature of inter-organisational communication.

Instead, studies of organisational communication turned critical of organisations throughout the 1980s and into the 1990s. Critical theorists such as Deetz (1992) and Mumby (1988) had begun to examine the motivations of those most powerful in organisations. They posited that those in control did not contribute to the interests of their employees or society, but to their own private self-interests. Critical theorists believed that the central concept to be studied in organisations was power. Those in power sought to create and maintain organisational structures of power and domination.

One example of a research study that used critical perspectives to help illuminate the day-to-day decisions and activities of the modern organisation was published by Barker and Cheney (1994). This study linked up with the Tompkins and Cheney (1985) rhetorical idea of 'unobtrusive control through the use of organisational symbols. While organisational symbols represented an outward strategy for creating organisational cooperation, Barker and Cheney (1994) looked at the use of discipline to create organisational cooperation through internal or self-control.

Barker and Cheney (1994) applied Michel Foucault's perspective on "discipline" to the modern organisation. Foucault defined discipline as a communication construct. Discipline was defined by Barker and Cheney (1994) as both a set of activities and an outcome based on communication meant to train, control and bring about orderly conduct. Three methods for creating discipline according to Foucault were power, knowledge and rules of right.

Barker conducted an ethnographic research project in an organisation called Tech USA, which had changed its managerial culture in late 1988 from that of a traditional hierarchy to that of self-managed teams. Barker conducted in-depth worker interviews to learn whether the communication and control practices in Tech's new structure differed from the communication and control practices of the prior hierarchical structure. The teams were fully and equally responsible for all of the tasks required to produce Tech's information circuit transmission boards. Barker provided an in-depth description of how the new team members developed their own attendance policies.

> Without the first-fine supervisor to ensure that all members came to work on time, the teams had to develop a means of accomplishing this element of control themselves. They did this by developing a collaborative, value-laden discourse to discipline their actions; a novel, but powerful system of power relationships, knowledge, and rules of right that ensured they would meet their own attendance standards.
>
> (Barker and Cheney 1994: 33)

These particular teams created their own attendance rules through subtle interpersonal exchanges. By analysing the meanings given to the exchanges by the team members, Barker illustrated the centrality of communication to create rules, knowledge and organisational power. Thus his study continued in the line of organisational rhetorical research because it focused on the power of symbols in an organisational setting.

The application of rhetorical theories to public relations problems

The rhetorical perspective to emerge from this analysis of fifteen years of research was that of corporate rhetors who consciously chose specific symbolic, dialogical strategies that would more effectively persuade audiences. The more traditional rhetorical scholars assumed that there would be debate to establish decisions and resolutions of issues, given the social institutions and government of a democratic society. The debate might have been less than eloquent, hence Burke's reference to the "barnyard." However, the debate would have established mutually agreed decisions for the interests of the publics that made up a democratic society – if certain standards were followed. By analysing the rhetorical strategies of individuals and organisations alike, rhetoricians sought to help elevate the debate so that indeed the publics' interests would be recognised and protected.

The organisational communication scholars who have applied the study of rhetoric to organisational settings focused on another part of the practice of public relations. These organisational rhetoricians have described and brought rhetorical theories to our understanding of how organisations create, through communication, cooperative behavior among employees and managers so as to achieve organisational goals. The emerging theories of organisational rhetoric provided public relations people with a clearer understanding of the importance of managerial symbolic behavior. Some of these theories dealt with externally powerful symbols, such as the use of identification to motivate and enlist employees. The emerging more critical rhetorical scholars studied the use of power and discipline as communication constructs to reveal how organisational practices emerge and subsequently change.

Both fundamental rhetorical studies of public relations and organisational rhetorical studies focused on the symbolic nature of the messages distributed or exchanged interpersonally. This represented a distinct contribution to an understanding of public relations. Rhetorical scholars assumed that the meanings and language choices of public relations products were important elements in the dialogue and decision-making processes of public relations. This elevation of the symbolic has been missing from other types of research. The symbolic intentions and results of public relations products should be appreciated for their value in understanding the strategies of public relations people, as well as the effects such meanings will have on audiences.

While there was a mix of quantitative and qualitative research found in these rhetorical studies, they were dominated by the assertions of humanist scholarship. The scholars presented their interpretations of often broader and more global concepts such as discipline, power, cooperation and persuasion. Theirs is a qualitative view of public relations and its role in society. Rhetorical scholars make valuable contributions to our understanding of the forms and elements of symbol-making, rather than resting on an assumption that communication is little more than an exchange of information.

The peculiarities of organisational rhetoric should be clearly understood as less tied to the typical public relations products of newsletters, mass-mediated messages and annual reports. Organisational communication scholars have provided a distinct and useful contribution with their critical turn toward management motivations and power. Public relations is managed communication. Therefore public relations people are either part of the management function of organisations, or desire to work with managers so as to function effectively. Understanding managerial motives as evidenced in their communication practices is a first step to ensuring that public relations will have a voice in organisational decisions.

This rhetorical research of nearly fifteen years assumed an all-powerful role for public relations in society. Such is the critic's role – to give us ethical and moral standards to which we can aspire. In this way, according to the rhetorical perspective, we might see public relations achieve a desired professional status. However, rhetorical studies of public relations may have reached their greatest concentration in the early 1990s. Little followed the book of articles by Toth and Heath published in 1992. It may be that the rhetorical perspective has been too critical of public relations without the directions provided in these studies to further rhetoric's critical aims.

References

Arnold, C. C. and Frandsen, K. D. (1984) 'Conceptions of rhetoric and communication', in C. C. Arnold and J. W. Bowers (eds) *Handbook of Rhetoric and Communication Theory*, Boston MA: Allyn and Bacon.

Bantz, C. R. (1989) 'Organizing and the social psychology of organizing', *Communication Studies*, 49 (4) 231–40.

Barker, J. R. and Cheney, G. (1994) 'The concept and the practices of discipline in contemporary organizations', *Communication monographs*, 61, 19–43.

Berg, P. (1985) 'Organization change as a symbolic transformation process', in P. J. Frost, L. F. Moore, M. R. Louis, C. C. Lundberg and J. Montese (eds) *Organizational Culture*, Newbury Park CA: Sage.

Bitzer, L. F. (1971) 'More reflections on the wingspread conference', in L. Bitzer and E. Black (eds) *The Prospect of Rhetoric*, Englewood Cliffs NJ: Prentice Hall.

Blair, C. (1992) 'Contested histories of rhetoric: the politics of preservation, progress and change', *Quarterly Journal of Speech*, 78 (4) 403–28.

Bostdorff, D. M. and Vibbert, S. L. (1994) 'Values advocacy: enhancing organizational images, deflecting public criticism, and grounding future arguments', *Public Relations Review*, 20 (2) 141–58.

Burke, K. (1969a) [1945] *A Grammar of Motives*, Berkeley CA: University of California Press.

——(1969b) [1950] *A Rhetoric of Motives*, Berkeley CA: University of California Press.

Cheney, G. (1983a) 'On the various and changing meanings of organizational membership: A field study of organizational identification', *Communication Monographs*, 50, 342–62.

——(1983b) 'The rhetoric of identification and the study of organizational communication', *Quarterly Journal of Speech*, 69, 143–58.

——(1991) 'Rhetoric, identity, and organization', in *Rhetoric in an Organizational Society: Managing Multiple Identifies*, Columbia SC: University of South Carolina Press.

——(1992) 'The corporate person (re)presents itself', in E. L. Toth and R. L. Heath (eds) *Rhetorical and Critical Approaches to Public Relations*, Hillsdale NJ: Lawrence Erlbaum.

Cheney, G. and Dionisopoulos, G. N. (1989) 'Public relations? No, relations with publics: a rhetorical-organizational approach to contemporary corporate communication', in C. H. Botan and V. Hazelton Jr (eds) *Public Relations Theory*, Hillsdale NJ: Lawrence Erlbaum.

Cheney, G. and Vibbert, S. L. (1987) 'Corporate discourse: public relations and issues management', in F. M. Jablin, L. L. Putnam, K. H. Roberts and L. W. Porter (eds) *Handbook of Organizational Communication: An Interdisciplinary Perspective*, Newbury Park CA: Sage.

Conrad, C. (1983) 'The rhetoric of the moral majority: an analysis of romantic form', *Quarterly Journal of Speech*, 69, 159–70.

——(1985) *Strategic Organizational Communication*, New York: Holt, Rinehart and Winston.

Crable, R. L. (1990) ' "Organizational rhetoric" as the fourth great system: theoretical critical, and pragmatic implications?', *Journal of Applied Communication Research*, 18 (2) 115–28.

Crable, R. L. and Faulkner, M. M. (1988) 'The issue development graph: a tool for research and analysis', *Central States Speech Journal*, 29, 110–20.

Crable, R. L. and Vibbert, S. L. (1983) 'Mobil's epideictic advocacy: "observations" of Prometheus-bound', *Communicaton Monographs*, 50, 380–94.

——(1985) 'Managing issues and influencing public policy', *Public Relations Review*, 11, 3–16.

——(1986) *Public Relations as Communication Management*, Edina MN: Bellweather Press.

Deetz, S. (1992) *Democracy in the Age of Corporate Colonization*, Albany NY: State University of New York Press.

Dionisopoulos, G. N. and Crable, R. E. (1988) 'Definitional hegemony as a public relations strategy: the rhetoric of the nuclear power industry after three mile island', *Central States Speech Journal*, 39 (2) 134–45.

Dionisopoulos, G. N. and Goldzwig, S. R. (1992) 'The atomic power industry and the NEW woman', in E. L. Toth and R. L. Heath (eds) *Rhetorical and Critical Approaches to Public Relations*, Hillsdale NJ: Lawrence Erlbaum.

Ehninger, D. (1968) 'On systems of rhetoric', *Philosophy and Rhetoric*, 1, 131–44.

Goldzwig, S. and Cheney, G. (1984) 'The US Catholic bishops on nuclear arms: corporate advocacy, role redefinition, and rhetorical adaptation', *Central States Speech Journal*, 35, 8–23.

Grunig, J. E. (1992) 'Symmetrical systems of internal communication', in J. E. Grunig (ed.) *Excellence in Public Relations and Communication Management*, Hillsdale NJ: Lawrence Erlbaum.

Grunig, J. E. and Hunt, T. (1984) *Managing Public Relations*, New York: Holt, Rinehart and Winston.

Grunig, J. E. and White, J. (1992) 'The effect of worldviews on public relations theory and practice', in J. E. Grunig (ed.) *Excellence in Public Relations and Communication Management*, Hillsdale NJ: Lawrence Erlbaum.

Heath, R. L. (1980) 'Corporate advocacy: an application of speech communication perspectives and skills – and more', *Communication Education*, 29, 370–7.

——(1988) 'The rhetoric of issue advertising: a rationale, a case study, a critical perspective – and more', *Central States Speech Journal*, 39 (2) 99–109.

——(1991) 'Public relations research and education: agendas for the 1990s', *Public Relations Review*, 17 (2) 185–94.

——(1992a) 'Critical perspectives on public relations', in E. L. Toth and R. L. Heath (eds) *Rhetorical and Critical Approaches to Public Relations*, Hillsdale NJ: Lawrence Erlbaum.

——(1992b) 'The wrangle in the marketplace: a rhetorical perspective of public relations', in E. L. Toth and R. L. Heath (eds) *Rhetorical and Critical Approaches to Public Relations*, Hillsdale NJ: Lawrence Erlbaum.

——(1992c) 'Visions of critical studies of public relations', in E. L Toth and R. L. Heath (eds) *Rhetorical and Critical Perspectives to Public Relations*, Hillsdale NJ: Lawrence Erlbaum.

——(1993) 'A rhetorical approach: zones of meaning and organizational prerogatives', *Public Relations Review*, 19 (2) 141–55.

——(1994) *Management of Corporate Communication: from Interpersonal Contacts to External Affairs*, Hillsdale NJ: Lawrence Erlbaum.

Heath, R. L. and Nelson, R. A. (1986) *Issues Management*, Beverly Hills CA: Sage.

Ice, R. (1991) 'Corporate publics and rhetorical strategies: the case of Union Carbide's Bhopal crisis', *Management Communication Quarterly*, 4 (3) 341–62.

144   *Contemporary perspectives*

Mumby, D. K. (1988) *Communication and Power in Organizations: Discourse, Ideology, and Domination*, Norwood NJ: Ablex.

Nathan, K., Heath, R. L. and Douglas, W. (1992) 'Tolerance for potential environmental health risks: the influence of knowledge, benefits, control, involvement, and uncertainty', *Journal of Public Relations Research*, 4 (4) 235–58.

Pearson, R. A. (1989) 'Business ethics as communication ethics: public relations practice and the idea of dialogue', in C. H. Botan and V. Hazelton Jr (eds) *Public Relations Theory*, Hillsdale NJ: Lawrence Erlbaum.

Peterson, T. R. (1988) 'The meek shall inherit the mountains: dramatistic criticism of Grand Teton National Park's interpretive program', *Central States Speech Journal*, 39 (2) 121–33.

Redding, W. C. and Tompkins, P. K. (1988) 'Organizational communication – past and present tenses', in G. M. Goldhaber and G. A. Barnett (eds) *Handbook of Organizational Communication*, Norwood NJ: Ablex.

Sproule, J. M. (1988) 'The new managerial rhetoric and the old criticism', *Quarterly Journal of Speech*, 74, 468–86.

——(1989) 'Organizational rhetoric and the public sphere', *Communication Studies*, 4, 258–65.

——(1990) 'Organizational rhetoric and the rational-democratic society', *Journal of Applied Communication*, 18 (2) 129–40.

Tompkins, P. K. (1987) 'Translating organizational theory: symbolism over substance', in F. M. Jablin, L. L. Putnam, K. H. Roberts and L. W. Porter (eds) *Handbook of Organisational Communication: An Interdisciplinary Perspective*, Newbury Park CA: Sage.

Tompkins, P. K. and Cheney, G. (1985) 'Communication and unobtrusive control in contemporary organizations', in R. D. McPhee and P. K. Tompkins (eds) *Organizational Communication: Traditional Themes and New Directions*, Newbury Park CA: Sage.

——(1993) 'On the limits and sub-stance of Kenneth Burke and his critics', *Quarterly Journal of Speech*, 79, 225–31.

Tompkins, P. K. and Redding, W. C. (1988) in G. M. Goldhaber and G. A. Barnett (eds) *Handbook of Organizational Communication*, Norwood NJ: Ablex.

Toth, E. L. (1994) 'The normative nature of public affairs: a rhetorical analysis', in W. Armbrecht and U. Zabel (eds) *Normative Aspeckte der Public Relations*, Opladen: Westdeutscher Verlag.

Vibbert, S. L. (1986) 'Corporate communication and the management of issues', paper presented to the International Communication Association, Montreal.

Ware, B. L. and Linkugel, W. A. (1973) 'They spoke in defense of themselves: on the general criticism of apologia', *Quarterly Journal of Speech*, 59, 273–83.

Weick, K. E. (1969) *The Social Psychology of Organizing*, Reading MA: Addison-Wesley.

——(1979) *The Social Psychology of Organizing*, 2nd edn, Reading MA: Addison-Wesley.

5 Psychology and public relations

Jon White

Exploring the links between psychology and the theory and practice of public relations

Psychology in its modern form is a relatively new discipline, having emerged in the 1880s from philosophy and physiology as a separate area of study. Its early preoccupations were with the study of sensory capabilities and perception, through psychophysics which concentrated on detailed examination of the limits of human sensory capabilities.

Modern psychology's early proponents were ambitious. They believed that the new science would quickly come to provide a complete account of human behaviour, and the thoughts, feelings, attitudes and intentions which gave rise to it. It would also allow for all other studies to be reduced to psychology, since – for example – economics depends on an understanding of how people behave as they enter into certain kinds of exchange relationships, and make rational decisions about the use and disposition of finite resources, and political science requires a knowledge of how people behave as they organise for political activity and government.

Now psychology is more modest in its aspirations, partly as a result of the practical difficulties that have been encountered in over a hundred years of trying to study, and establish general laws about, human behaviour. Philosophers have continued to cast doubt on the possibility of discovering such general laws (see, for example, the doubts expressed by Ayer [1964]) and psychologists have not had great success in establishing general explanations of behaviour. Now, psychologists tend to set out to investigate behaviour by asking very specific questions under a number of more limited headings. Psychology has become focused, on a practical level, on trying to find useful answers to questions about behaviour in educational, occupational or clinical settings (e.g. Kakabadse *et al.* 1988; Handy 1993).

Public relations has a modern history of similar length to that of psychology. It is generally regarded in current texts on the subject (Cutlip *et al.* [1994] providing a typical example) as having emerged as press agentry in the mid-1880s, in the United States, and later elsewhere as a process involving the provision of public information, for example, in the United Kingdom in supporting the work of the Empire Marketing Board in the 1920s.

It might have been expected that the developing practice of public relations would be informed by parallel developments in psychology. To some extent this did happen. Grunig and Hunt, reviewing the historical development of public relations in their 1984 text, *Managing Public Relations*, suggested the First World War Creel Committee on Public Information, a propaganda agency, 'achieved great success because it made use, without knowing it, of psychological principles of mass persuasion'. Grunig and Hunt go on to propose that experience on the Creel Committee 'suggested to a new generation of public relations practitioners that mass persuasion was possible and that it could have its base in social science'.

One of the members of the Creel Committee who went on to explore this possibility was Edward Bernays, who could trace a direct link to contemporary developments in psychology through his relationship to Freud. Ernest Jones, Freud's biographer, describes (1964) how Freud's 'brilliant nephew, Edward Bernays' offered to, and was allowed to translate his *Introductory Lectures* for American publication.

Bernays' 1923 book, *Crystallizing Public Opinion*, shows the extent to which he had absorbed some of the thinking then current in psychology. His book tried to set down the broad principles governing the new profession of public relations, principles which he believed were substantiated by the findings of psychologists and sociologists. He also argued for the practitioner to play a role similar to that of the psychologist: 'the public relations counsel is first of all a student ... his field of the study is the public mind' (1923: 52). He went on to argue that the public relations counsel must call on his knowledge of individual and group psychology in understanding the interactions between individuals and groups. His aspirations that the book would go some way towards establishing the scientific basis of public relations practice were dealt with critically some years later by Tedlow (1979), who described the book as 'a sociological, psychological pastiche of speculations, drawn from the author's career' (see also Ross [1959] for a further critique of Bernays' use of psychological theories).

Crystallizing Public Opinion also shows the influence of the recently published *Public Opinion* by Walter Lippmann (1997). Cutlip *et al.*

(1994) point to the importance of the work of social scientists at this time in the development of public relations practice, and to the techniques that would be of use to the practice in its tasks of social analysis, as they began to explore questions relating to the formation and influencing of public opinion.

At the time, Bernays felt that the formation of public opinion was a largely emotional process, based not on a rational consideration of facts, but on emotional reaction to a simplified presentation of the facts. In this judgement he was influenced by the thinking and writings of his uncle, Freud, whose contribution to psychological thinking was to point to the unconscious, emotional and non-rational basis of behaviour believed to be rational.

Since the 1920s, psychology and public relations seem to have diverged, while both going through expansive development. Psychology's development has been through schools of psychological investigation and thought, such as psychoanalysis and behaviourism, and through study of areas of special interest, such as the behaviour of people at work, or in response to developments in mass communication and techniques of persuasion. Psychology has developed a repertoire of research techniques which are capable of wide application in areas such as market research, the study of group dynamics, assessments of personality and intelligence, and the measurement of attitudes and opinions (see, for example, Fisher 1974; Hoinville and Jowell 1982; Oppenheim 1992). These techniques are used to some extent in public relations practice, but more generally by public relations academics who point to their value in practice (e.g. Broom and Dozier 1990; Pavlik 1987).

Public relations in the United States, according to reviews provided by Pimlott (1951), Raucher (1968) and Tedlow (1979), developed in response to the needs of business for support in political struggles, and later to provide support to the war effort. Practitioners in the United Kingdom point to the significance of the country's wartime experience in the Second World War in giving impetus to the development of the practice in the United Kingdom, which is still felt to draw on, but lag behind US practice.

By 1968, Carlson, writing in the *International Encyclopaedia of the Social Sciences*, described practitioners' 'disarming willingness to pick and choose (their) intellectual antecedents'. He said that, while practitioners claim special skill in assessing, interpreting and modifying public opinion, they still draw on a small reservoir of academic studies for their intellectual rationale. His strongest criticism referred to the failure of practitioners to realise that the intellectual content and theoretical basis of their field have been singularly lacking in 'exciting new ideas, research practices or even impressionistic essays on understanding human behaviour and the communication process' (1968: 213).

Carlson suggests (1968) the need for closer collaboration between public relations and the social sciences, a need still felt in the 1990s and expressed by practitioners responding to a Delphi study in the United Kingdom in 1994 (White and Blamphin 1994). In 1968, Carlson suggested that where dialogue between practitioners and social scientists had taken place it had been sporadic and barren of results.

In part this has been due to what Cutlip identified in 1957 as 'an ignorant anti-intellectualism' to be found at the beginnings of a profession. In part it is also due to what Carlson described in 1968 as the variegated work experience and educational background of practitioners, which has meant that practitioners as a group have not been inclined to draw on social science research and findings. It is also possible that the few social scientists who would recognise themselves in this description, working on the study of public relations practice, have not yet found suitable channels through which they can communicate the results of their work to practitioners.

Public relations as an applied social psychology

If psychology is the study of behaviour, and the study of the way people think, feel and behave, then arguments can be put forward to suggest that public relations is an applied psychology. In practice, it is concerned with the behaviour of members of groups in relation to each other, within the groups of which they are members, and between groups. Practitioners are concerned with trying to influence the way people think, feel and behave, and make use of managed communication to try to do this. Practitioners set intermediate goals for themselves, such as building the reputation of the organisations and clients served, and developing awareness, understanding and goodwill.

In public relations, and business practice generally, a practical concern is how to take account of and respond to the interests of groups of people implicated in organisation decisions and actions. There is a growing body of evidence, brought out in the Excellence Study (Grunig 1992; Dozier *et al.* 1995) and by studies such the Royal Society of the Arts study of *Tomorrow's Company* (RSA 1995) that the effective and successful company or organisation is 'inclusive', that is it takes account of the interests of all groups with which it has relationships. The RSA study in particular has advocated that in future a measure of performance will be the extent to which the interests of significant groups are taken into account and met.

Like psychology, public relations sets out hypotheses regarding human behaviour which could be, and sometimes are, investigated using a variety of scientific methods, such as direct observation, experimentation and field studies. Supported hypotheses form the basis for the development of theory, statements about the world, which allow for explanation, prediction and control.

There are some interesting implications involved in viewing public relations as an applied psychology, rather than as an interdisciplinary study that draws on management studies, communication and cultural studies. The first is that it can finally be acknowledged that public relations practice is mainly concerned with influencing behaviour, as some practitioners and students of the practice have been arguing in the United States in recent years. There is still confusion about the scope and basis of public relations practice.

In the United Kingdom, debate about the scope of public relations practice surfaced in a Delphi study conducted among practitioners and academics in the country. White and Blamphin (1994) carried out a study to try to identify research priorities in UK practice. The group questioned for the study felt that there needed to be an adequate statement of the scope of the practice for progress to be made on developing the practice. A number of comments made illustrate the feeling among the group:

'Only problem is, it seems to be like navel gazing (looking at definitions, roles of PR). Yet, if there is no general agreement on what PR is, how can we call ourselves a profession'. For this practitioner, and one academic, defining public relations was the priority. Without an adequate definition of the practice, how could other questions be asked? 'The problem is that until there is common agreement on what PR is for, it is difficult to assess outcomes'.

(White and Blamphin 1994)

Others had different opinions: 'Public relations is no longer applicable in describing the function and is past its sell-by date. Communication is what we do.'

Another practitioner felt that the whole Delphi study presupposed there is such a thing as public relations, which he saw as a general term given to a number of management competencies associated with the promotion of ideas and reputations: 'Client companies will continue to select those competencies which are perceived to help them achieve their goals.'

Yet another practitioner felt that 'in a client-focused business, the customer will describe. Anything else is internal posturing that does not move us ahead at all. That said, if we are to define what we do, we must also decide at the same time how we plan to capture and police it.'

In current discussion of public relations practice on both sides of the Atlantic, public relations is variously described as a marketing discipline (in the UK's trade publication, *PR Week*), as a communication practice, as an exercise in the development of mutual understanding, or in terms of one of the specialised practices which make up the practice, such as public affairs. Recent books on corporate communications (Gayeski 1993; van Riel 1995) describe public relations as 'the use of communications techniques to build a positive public image' (Gayeski 1993: 7) or under the general heading of organisational communication.

Practitioners, for example in response to the Delphi study mentioned above, do become impatient with any discussion of definitions, since, as respondents to the Delphi study made clear, they know what they do and are not prepared to set time aside to clarify terminology referring to their work.

Among academics involved in the teaching and study of public relations, there has been a long-running discussion about where public relations fits into academic institutions in the United States, a debate that is beginning to take place in other countries such as the United Kingdom, as numbers of programmes aimed at teaching and carrying out research in public relations develop. In the United Kingdom, public relations, after less than ten years of university teaching in the subject area, is being taught in departments of social science, communications, advertising and marketing, journalism, business and management.

Genuine diversity of viewpoints regarding the nature of public relations practice is desirable in the development of a new subject area and what is still a relatively new practice, but some current views of practice are based on evasions, on an unwillingness on the part of practitioners to come to terms with the nature of the practice. This is a hard statement to justify in a chapter such as this, but the writer has had the experience in discussions of the scope of the practice with practitioners, in in-company training activities, and in work with national professional associations, of finding them reluctant to accept that they are ultimately concerned to have an effect on behaviour. The Institute of Public Relations in the United Kingdom admitted but obscured this recently when it redefined public relations as 'about reputation: the result of what you do, what you say and what others say about you'. Following this definition, practice is 'the discipline which looks after reputation ... with the aim of earning understanding and support, and influencing opinion and behaviour'.

A second important implication of accepting that public relations is an applied psychology is that this opens up the entire field of psychological investigation as a source of research findings relevant to the practice. At present, students of public relations – academics and practitioners – draw piecemeal from psychology. While this is productive of insights, it means that exposure to all that psychology has to offer is limited and raises questions about the criteria used in any search through the psychological literature. For example, Gayeski (1993) suggests that the theories with which corporate communicators should be familiar include theories of communication, learning and management, and organisation development. While these are important areas, why are theories of social interaction, group dynamics, attitude and opinion formation not included?

A conclusion drawn from the Delphi study in the UK (White and Blamphin 1994) was that there was a need for a translation of findings from the social sciences into terms that would make them accessible to practitioners. This exercise would continue the work begun in the United States to attempt to develop the body of knowledge which should underpin practice.

An interesting further implication to be drawn from regarding public relations as an applied psychology is one already referred to by Carlson (1968) but left unexamined. It is that public relations practice involves a study of social behaviour which could enrich psychology itself. Carlson suggested that collaboration between social scientists and practitioners could be more fruitful:

> one of the ironies of public relations practice today is that it continues to draw from the same small reservoirs of studies for its intellectual rationale, while all the time having within its own files raw data that might make a significant contribution to communication theory.
>
> (Carlson 1968)

It is possible to go further than this and suggest that practitioners' observations of organisation behaviour, management decision making, group relations, communications, and social impact, could inform development of theory in a number of areas of psychology.

Psychology itself has developed over the past century into a number of main 'schools', or areas of interest, the concerns of which have entered popular imagination, particularly those from psychoanalysis and the work of Freud. These include:

- psychophysics
- social interactionism
- gestalt psychology
- physiological psychology
- psychoanalysis
- cognitive psychology
- behaviourism
- social psychology and sociology

In a number of areas, public relations could contribute what Carlson refers to as raw data from practice files.

Discussion following the Delphi study in the UK (White and Blamphin 1994) suggested that an ideal to be strived towards would be for practitioners to be as confident in their theoretical and research bases as management consultants now are in theirs. To move towards this ideal, practitioners would need to be able to draw on the research findings available in psychology and other social sciences, but the point which has just been made suggests that practitioners could contribute relevant findings to the social sciences from which they intend to draw.

The practice of public relations has not exploited the findings of psychology to the extent that it could, in the opinion of participants in the Delphi study. While efforts have been made to draw on psychology (the Excellence Study is a good recent example), psychological theories and research findings have been absorbed, if at all, ill digested into the practice (for an example of this, see the description of a public relations programme carried out by a chairman of the Public Relations Consultants Association in the United Kingdom through his company, in which he is clearly referring to an approach based on diffusion of innovations but which shows no knowledge of diffusion research [PRTV Training Video, 1991]). This may change in future as graduates from programmes of education in public relations, in which there has been some exposure to psychological theories and methods, become more widely dispersed through the practice. Their exposure will depend on the content of the programmes through which they have passed, and the qualifications of faculty to provide them with instruction in psychology.

Psychology itself is less confident of its potential contribution. George Gaskell, a psychologist at the London School of Economics, suggests (in a discussion, June 1995) that many psychological findings are applicable, rather than applied. His suggestion is that psychology fails to involve itself sufficiently in a dialogue with practitioners, which means that many findings are left uncommunicated. Psychology also tends, he believes, to focus on narrow questions or interest areas and now fails to make links between them. He cites as an example the study of group dynamics which fails to make adequate reference to the role of communication in groups, because psychologists interested in group dynamics may not also be interested in communication.

The speculative nature of early psychological theories has now been recognised, and a number of the founders of psychological thought have been subjected to fierce criticism, on the grounds that their work, at best, was unscientific and, at worse, fraudulent. Early psychological theory was, we saw earlier, influential in an indirect way: for example, it informed the work of wartime propagandists who, if not public relations practitioners already, transferred their skills to public relations practice in peacetime.

Future links between psychological theory and public relations practice

It sometimes seems that public relations will be defined by whoever is trying to define it according to their own special interests. A successful practitioner will claim that the practice is whatever he or she practices. Academics will define it on the basis of their professional experience, or on the basis of their disciplinary background (which is partly what I am trying to argue here), or perhaps to meet the requirements of the institutions in which they teach.

A way forward towards definition of the practice is suggested in current thinking about management, and the findings emerging from reports such as the *Tomorrow's Company* report in the United Kingdom. The report suggests that in future managers will have to attend to and manage important relationships. Public relations is that part of the overall management task concerned with the management of important relationships.

To carry out this task, public relations practitioners will need the ability and access to techniques that will enable them to understand and act upon relationships. This chapter has argued that understanding and techniques relevant to the practitioner's tasks are to be found in psychology. By recognising this, practitioners gain access to a body of knowledge which can enrich practice, and which can in turn be enriched by observations and findings derived from practice.

References

Ayer, A. J. (1964) 'Man as a subject for science', Auguste Comte Memorial Lecture, London School of Economics, 7 February.

Bernays, E. L. (1923) *Crystallizing Public Opinion*, New York: Boni and Liveright.

Broom, G. and Dozier, D. (1990) *Using Research in Public Relations: Applications to Programme Management*, Englewood Cliffs NJ: Prentice-Hall.

Brown, R. (1986) *Social Psychology*, New York: Collier Macmillan.

Carlson, R. O. (1968) 'Public relations', in D. L. Sills (ed.) *International Encyclopaedia of the Social Sciences*, London and New York: Macmillan.

Cialdini, R. (1988) *Influence: Science and Practice*, London: Scott, Foresman.

Cutlip, S. (1957) 'The university's role in public relations education', *Journalism Quarterly*, 34, 68–73.

Cutlip, S., Center, A. and Broom, G. (1994) *Effective Public Relations*, 7th edn, Englewood Cliffs NJ: Prentice-Hall.

Dozier, D. M., Grunig, L. A. and Grunig, J. E. (1995) *Manager's Guide to Excellence in Public Relations and Communications Management*, Mahwah NJ: Lawrence Erlbaum Associates.

Fisher, B. A. (1974) *Small Group Decision-Making: Communication and the Group Process*, New York: McGraw-Hill.

Gayeski, D. (1993) *Corporate Communications Management*, Boston MA and London: Focal Press.

Grunig, J. E. (ed.) (1992) *Excellence in Public Relations and Communication Management*, Hillsdale NJ: Lawrence Erlbaum.

Grunig, J. E. and Hunt, T. (1984) *Managing Public Relations*, New York: Holt, Rhinehart and Winston.

Handy, C. (1993) *Understanding Organisations*, London: Penguin.

Hoinville, G. and Jowell, R. (1982) *Survey Research Practice*, London: Heinemann.

Jones, E. (1964) *The Life and Work of Sigmund Freud*, London: Penguin.

Kakabadse, A., Ludlow, R. and Vinnicombe, S. (1988) *Working in Organisations*, London: Penguin.

Lippmann, W. (1997) *Public Opinion*, New York/London: Free Press Paperbacks.

Oppenheim, A. N. (1992) *Questionnaire Design, Interviewing and Attitude Measurement*, London: Pinter.

Pavlik, J. (1987) *Public Relations: What Research Tells Us*, Newbury Park CA: Sage.

Pimlott, J. A. R. (1951) *Public Relations and American Democracy*, Princeton NJ: Princeton University Press.

Raucher, A. R. (1968) *Public Relations and Business 1900–1929*, Baltimore: Johns Hopkins Press.

Rogers, E. M. (1983) *Diffusion of Innovations*, 3rd edn, New York: The Free Press.

Ross, I. (1959) *The Image Merchants*, Garden City NY: Doubleday.

Royal Society of the Arts (1995) *Tomorrow's Company: The Role of Business in a Changing World*, London: Royal Society of the Arts.

Tedlow, R. S. (1979) *Keeping the Corporate Image: Public Relations and Business 1900–50*, Greenwich CT: Jai Press.

van Riel, C. B. M. (1995) *Principles of Corporate Communication*, London: Prentice-Hall.

White, J. and Blamphin, J. (1994) 'Priorities for research into public relations practice in the United Kingdom: a report from a Delphi study carried out among UK practitioners and public relations academics in May, June and July 1994', unpublished paper, City University, London.

Part III

International perspectives of public relations

6 Public relations

The cultural dimension

Toby MacManus

Introduction

Culture is a fundamental concept in sociology, identified by Giddens (1987) as one of the four central influences on modernity, and is a much used term forming the basis for a wide range of scholarly reflection and research on the nature of human society. The contributions of Williams (1958), Geertz (1973), Hall (1986) and Bourdieu (1984) indicate its diverse and complex nature.

Just as fundamental a concept is communication which is said to have emerged as an area for research when J. Dewey, G. Mead, R. Park and others came together in the late 1880s (Carey 1989). Subsequent inquiry has also been wide ranging and substantial, as exemplified by the scholarship of Dewey (1927), McLuhan (1964) and Habermas (1984).

This chapter addresses these two areas of social inquiry, for the purpose of examining the interrelationship between culture and communication in the form of public relations. The topic's broad scope limits the extent of this article to a selective and very much an outline assessment of some theories or approaches with a cultural foundation or relevance which may be applied as methodologies in public relations research, or more simply, provide supporting insight into the nature of public relations.

Culture in this discussion is understood as referring to:

> those patterns of organisation, those characteristic forms of human energy which can be discovered as revealing themselves ... within or underlying all social practices.
>
> (Williams, cited in Hall 1986: 35–6)

It represents a 'collective programming of the mind' (Hofstede 1984: 23) that has the effect of enabling one group of people to be distinctive from another. The discussion is approached by working from broad sociological or social theory perspectives to disciplines that progressively become more closely related to public relations, concluding with a recent theory of public relations as a multicultural activity.

Broad evolutionary perspectives

The first perspective examined is socio-economic in that it seeks to relate the emergence of modern public relations in its current form to broad evolutionary explanations of social change and structure. Two theories offer complementary insights into how the increasing complexity of human society can account for the conditions which gave rise to modern public relations: Giddens' analysis of the development of modernity (1990) and Beniger's theory of the control revolution (1986).

Giddens explains the consequences of modernity by identifying the sources of dynamism underlying its processes. The central dynamic being the increasing separation of space and time in history, represented by a movement of human society away from the conditions of primitive cultures, closely bound in face-to-face interaction, to the present insular society with little conscious awareness of their past. Developing forms of communication (writing, print, electronic media) provided the means of extending communication across distances and traditions, and enabled a sense of 'co-presence' with others to be continued. As societies become more complex and separated, occupational cultures evolved whose purpose was to mediate communication. These were journalism, advertising and public relations.

In Beniger's analysis of modern social evolution, the rapid expansion of communication infrastructures at the end of the nineteenth century resulted from a crisis of control in the economy, and in society in general, after the industrial revolution (Van Dijk 1993). The industrialisation of the mid-nineteenth century led to bottlenecks of mass production, which had outpaced the ability of social systems to create awareness and demand for products (material or conceptual) and the means for their effective distribution. The crisis was resolved through three sets of innovations: bureaucratic organisation, transport and communication infrastructure, and mass communications and research.

These theories, in particular their interwoven elements of culture, communication and technology, offer an understanding of the origins of modern public relations that adds to the notion of the inequalities created by industrialisation. Such inequalities caused public hostility towards emergent corporations, that, in turn, led to the response of hiring journalists to justify their purpose and methods, and in doing so build a positive reputation for the corporation (Baskin and Arnoff 1992). Public relations is therefore an outcome of the processes of nodernisation: the spatial expansion of society; the market economies that created large organisations; and with them bottlenecks of mass production; and the necessity for organisations to identify their presence – to themselves (constituent sub-systems) and to significant external systems (publics) (Rühl 1992).

While these theories provide socio-economic explanations for the origins of modern public relations, a deeper appreciation of the relationship between culture, communication and technology, leading more directly to public relations, can be accessed through the perceptive and eloquent essays of James Carey (1989). Much of his analysis echoes the theories of Giddens and Beniger.

Carey identifies communication with culture through the observation that a primary goal of communication is to understand another person or culture: 'you look at practices people engage in, the conceptual world embedded in and presupposed by those practices, and the social relations and forms of life that they manifest' (Carey 1989: 85–6). For public relations this can be taken to mean that the cultural context in which a public is embedded needs to be grasped for communication with the public to have the possibility of maximising effectiveness, a theme addressed in one of the early discussions of public relations and culture by Mackey (1994).

In explaining the development of modern communication in the USA, Carey emphasises the influence of the expansion of the railway and telegraph transportation systems. These became the nerves and arteries of society through which the mass media could be channelled. They are elements in the solution to the control dilemma referred to by Beniger. The large size of the USA compared to industrialised countries in Europe, and the imperative for effective long-distance systems of communication give some indication of why public relations became so widely established there, and not to the same extent in Europe.

Baskin and Arnoff (1992) offer further reasons, claiming the USA as the perfect crucible in which to mould public relations because of its strong democracy and free-market economy. But other countries in the late nineteenth century were democratic, had powerful economies, and because of their colonial territories, had far-flung outposts to communicate with. So it seems that the emergence of public relations was also an American cultural outcome or response to its social, political and economic circumstances. However, the historical development of communication is a story of global, cross-cultural influence (Sreberny-Mohammadi 1995), and in the case of public relations this is revealed in the two-way pattern of influence between Europe and America.

The meanings attributed to communication in Beniger's framework are, however, only a part of the picture in Carey's understanding of the relationship between communication and culture. He separates communication into two forms: transmission and ritual. Transmission is the dissemination of messages in space to reduce the limitations of distance and to influence or control people. It became the dominant form of communication in the USA, and indeed, Carey criticises American culture for being obsessed with transmission forms of communication and neglecting communication in its ritual form. Public relations as a persuasive or manipulative form of mass communication can be placed within this model. The ritual form of communication, on the other hand, has the purpose of creating, or sustaining cohesion in society; drawing people together to share fellowship and commonality. The model of public relations seeking to effect mutual understanding or two-way symmetrical communication is very close to the concept of ritual communication. Transmission and ritual communication as expressions of contrasting cultural perspectives are therefore similar to Grunig's identification of a conservative dominant worldview of public relations (transmission), and in contrast an open, liberal worldview (1989).

However, a different set of explanations for the nature of contemporary public relations can be found in postmodernist theory.

Postmodernist thinking as social inquiry was a reaction to the optimism that characterised modernity: the belief in progress and the liberation of people from ignorance and superstition (Dickens and Fontana 1994). The world wars of the twentieth century are largely considered to have shattered this optimism and laid the foundations for postmodernism. While postmodernism is regarded as being firmly in place in advanced capitalist countries after World War II, there is a notable lack of consistency in both definition and analysis of its effects. But that need not prevent a brief critical examination of the relevance of two prominent theorists labelled as postmodernist: Jean Baudrillard and Fredric Jameson.

Baudrillard has a deeply pessimistic view of a postmodern culture that no longer represents reality; one that is not conditioned by outside influence, but instead constructs its own imaginary universe. In his analysis, cultural development has moved from 'signs which dissimulate something to signs which dissimulate that there is nothing'

(Baudrillard 1983: 12). Postmodernism is defined by the new technologies enabling objects and images to be subject to unlimited
reproduction. The result is a 'hyper-real' society where the distinction
between the real and the unreal is obscured in an endless flood of signs
and simulations. It is not necessary to share Baudrillard's gloomy
vision to see substance in his observations, and to recognise the role
public relations can play in constructing this 'weightless' culture. Both
the bizarre disinformation strategy of Hill and Knowlton during the
Gulf war, constructed around the falsified story of babies taken out of
incubators and left to die, and the activities of celebrity publicists
feeding the media with invented stories of the 'hyper-real' nature of
their clients' lives, gain a deeper meaning when interpreted through
the lens of Baudrillard's postmodernist theory. In this context communication is not a system of control, as in transmission, nor does it act to
bond through ritual; it is, through the media, a creator of myths.

> What counts now is how we label people and objects, not the
> things themselves ... we live by feeding off the images that the
> media constantly make for us.
>
> (Gottdiener 1994: 168)

Many public relations educators would, however, argue that the significance of Baudrillard applies to only a segment of the public relations
industry. Professional public relations seeks to legitimately identify an
organisation; to enable it to be seen, heard and understood in an over-
loaded information society. Creating real rather than 'hyper-real'
reputations is the aim. But how far notions of professional public relations have become established in practice is unclear and will vary from
country to country.

Fredric Jameson defines postmodernism as a periodising concept
'whose function is to correlate the emergence of new formal features in
culture with the emergence of a new type of social life and a new
economic order' (1983: 113). Its historical position is as the cultural
logic of multinational capitalism. His critique is based on Marxist principles: postmodern society is 'late capitalism' which has progressed into
the penetration and colonisation of *Nature and the Unconscious* (Dickens
and Fontana 1994). 'Nature' refers to the destruction of the agricultural
systems in their pre-capitalist farm in underdeveloped countries. The
'Unconscious' refers to the growth and influence of mass media
communication on the individual, the term colonisation suggesting a
gradual and insidious infiltration of ideas, principally manufactured by
commercial interests within the system of 'late capitalism'. Jameson's

portrayal of media influence owes much to Baudrillard's ideas, but his position is distinctive because of the emphasis given to the globalising nature of capitalism and the commodity form.

Criticisms of Jameson have focused on his analysis being in part founded on a 'base to superstructure' model of society, the traditional Marxist position that economic forces are the fundamental determinant of the cultural, political and legal characteristics of society. Quite apart from the argument that it may be culture that shapes economic structure, Jameson's critics have questioned such a reductionist view where no distinction is allowed between culture's dominant and oppositional modes.

What does Jameson's perspective on postmodern society signify for public relations and culture? Clearly, alongside advertising and journalism public relations becomes one of the tools used by the colonisers of 'late capitalism' to penetrate the territory of the unconscious. The essential notion of the successful persuasion and manipulation of mass audiences by mass communication is not original; research on the related issue of agenda-setting effects dates back to the 1960s (Windahl and Signitzer 1992). Agenda-setting addresses the relationship between the media agenda and the public agenda and proposes that the more prominence the media give to an issue or event, the more important it becomes in the minds of the public. Gandy (1992) attributed a substantial role to public relations in this process, suggesting that as much as 50 per cent of media coverage originates from public relations sources who use information in the form of a subsidy. However, while agenda setting may influence the subjects that people think about and discuss, cultural studies research has illustrated how audiences create their own meanings from media content.

A further problem for public relations cast in the role of agent for multinational corporations (Jameson's vanguard of 'late capitalism') is that its activities are not confined to business. The skill of the environmental organisation Greenpeace in setting media, political and public agendas is well known and exemplified by its apparent ability to focus national attention in Germany and other countries on the multinational company Shell's recent decision to sink a redundant oil platform in the North Sea as a means of disposing of it – a decision that the company subsequently reversed.

Greenpeace's activities represent the potency of counter-hegemonic cultural activity that Gramsci (1971) recognised as a possibility, and whose flourishing presence in the USA is discussed by Downing (1995).

The utility of Jameson's social world for analysing public relations is therefore limited by evidence for the existence of a plurality of possible 'colonisers' of the unconscious. But even the effectiveness of 'colonisation' is in some doubt, given the ability of audiences to be ¬elective in the way they use and interpret mass media messages. This ¬s exemplified in research traditions, such as effects research, uses and gratifications research and reception analysis, which from different positions have investigated the nexus between the mass media and its audience (Jensen and Rosengren 1990). All of this highlights the fundamental weakness of Jameson in giving so much emphasis to a universalising concept of culture.

If the importance attached by Jameson to a global culture is suspect, what is the case for cultural diversity, especially in economically advanced societies, and its impact on public relations? To examine this question, the next section narrows the focus to theories that address 'national' characteristics of culture.

Theories identifying characteristics of national culture

One of the common themes among postwar social theorists is the application of language in the explication of social life (Giddens 1987). The anthropologist Edward Hall (1976; 1990) used language to differentiate between cultures, examining the relationship between language and its context; 'the information that surrounds an event' (1990: 6). He noted that the degree to which a message contained explicit or implicit communication depended on whether the speaker operated in a high- or low-context culture, where different cultural rules would apply. In low-context cultures, the receiver is not expected to gain understanding of a message by using the external context to aid interpretation. In high-context cultures the receiver has a cognitive map of the context and needs much less background in the content of the message to understand its meaning. Low-context situations require explicit communications; in high-context situations communications are more implicit.

Differences in levels of context occur in everyday life, but Hall's proposition is that the degree of high/low context is also a facet of culture; countries vary in levels of assumed contextuality that surround conversation. At the low-context level is Switzerland, where verbal communication is characterised by precision in respect of time. The low-context culture of Switzerland may partly explain why it was among the first, if not the first, to introduce a statutory licensing system specifying exact requirements to be met for legal recognition as a professional public relations practitioner. By contrast, in Japan context is high: much is left to inference or the manner of speaking. This will change according to the age, sex and social status of the partner (Usunier 1993).

Context has obvious importance for public relations because of the high degree of interpersonal skills needed in forming relationships with clients, stakeholders and other strategic publics. The often delicate negotiation with publics, the persuasion inherent in lobbying, become high-risk activities in international public relations where the degree of context associated with communication may differ markedly between the countries involved. The same risks will apply where such differences arise between cultures within a country.

There is, of course, nothing new in the observation that care is required in intercultural activity; indeed it is possible to regard all communication as intercultural (Windahl and Signitzer 1992). Hall's work is valuable because it provides at least a framework for identifying relative levels of potential sensitivity in inter-cultural public relations. What it cannot do, however, is provide the public relations practitioner with the cultural skills needed for successful communication. It is a powerful argument for the use of local input and support when planning and implementing foreign campaigns (Banks 1995), or conversely, being aware of the pitfalls of ethnocentrism in international public relations and marketing.

While Hall's context framework is usually applied to illuminate major differences between cultures such as Japan and North America, there is some evidence that it can be successfully applied in comparative research on countries where context distinctions are less marked. Its sensitivity to differences in European business culture between countries with low- and low-middle context cultures is suggested by Djursaa's study of Britain, Denmark and Germany (1994). On the basis of data from in-depth interviews, she argues that communication processes involve trust building, and that networking can be understood as differences in 'contexting patterns'. Her conclusion that German and Danish business cultures are generally more low-context than the British counterpart confirms their positions on Hall's continuum of low- to high-context cultures. In a high-context business environment, the establishment of personal relationships is a prerequisite for conducting business; what is of central importance in low-context cultures is the contract and its small print. The value placed on developing personal relationships and building networks in Britain as opposed to Germany or Denmark emerged as one of the main findings of Djursaa's study, and supplied vivid illustrations of how frustration and offence resulted from failures by businessmen to recognise and accept the changes in cultural context and its implication for business communication and behaviour.

A number of criticisms can be levelled at the methodology and onclusions of the research: the small sample on which broad claims about culture were made, the doubtful conclusion – given Meech and Kilburn's observations (1992) – that differences between Scottish and English businessmen lacked significance, and the inferences made about German business culture derived only from the opinions of Danish businessmen. The inclusion of a German cohort would have given the research greater symmetry. But for all its weaknesses, it remains a thought-provoking study with direct implications for public relations strategy when applied on a pan-European basis.

Hall's theory of context has also been used in a comparison of media effects in economically underdeveloped and advanced countries by Gozzi (1992). He reasons that the influence of mass media in high-context countries will be generally to subtract context, and in low-context countries to add context. These effects are illustrated by television reducing street life and community interaction in high-context communities where each household owns a television (Gozzi 1992). However, in low-context cultures there is relatively less shared communication, and mass media 'often provide a background of shared stories, symbols and characters that people will have in common, thus increasing context' (Gozzi 1992: 62). The research concepts of agenda-setting and spiral of silence which have been applied to the media in low-context countries give support to the media's, and by extension, public relations' effect of adding context. In fact whether through mass media, or more singular forms of communication (exhibitions, events), public relations assists in cultural production as well as being influenced by it.

Hall's framework of high/low cultural context and his complementary concept of polychronic and monochronic perceptions of time (Hall 1983) do not appear to have received much attention in public relations research. But the work of Geert Hofstede (1984; 1991) on the consequence of culture for psychology, organisational behaviour and management science has attracted some interest and recognition (Sriramesh 1992; Coombs *et al.* 1994; MacManus 1994). In particular, Coombs *et al.* applied Hofstede's dimensions of national culture, with concepts of profession, to conduct a comparative analysis of Austria, Norway and the USA. The strength of Hofstede's work derives from the scope and thoroughness of his project, a study of the values of people working in local subsidiaries of IBM across sixty-six countries in two stages, 1967–9 and 1971–3. His influence on organisational and management thinking has been substantial (Søndergaard 1994), so it was perhaps only a matter of time, with the expansion of international public relations research, before his four main dimensions on which national cultures could exhibit differences became known and applied.

While there are notable limitations in the methodology of Hofstede's study summarised by Søndergaard (1994), it is nonetheless a valuable tool for the inter-cultural analysis of public relations. But a more powerful methodology might be obtained by applying both Hall's context and Hofstede's dimensions. Even so, in the case of Coombs *et al.* (1994), Hofstede's dimensions can be applied as a methodology to differentiate perceptions of public relations that appear culturally determined, as opposed to those relating to a professional attitude, transcending culture. Further research might also help define or confirm existing notions about which types of strategy work best in a particular culture. Sriramesh and White (1992), in their analysis of public relations and culture, have already proposed that 'excellent' public relations is more likely in cultures with 'low power distance', 'low individualism', 'low masculinity' and 'low uncertainty avoidance'. It is interesting to note in this respect that neither the USA nor the UK match the elements of 'individualism' (where with Australia they have the highest scores) or 'masculinity', where at 62 and 66 respectively they are both well above the mean of 49.

Of course the notion of what is 'excellent' and professional public relations may, as with views of what constitutes excellent management, be culturally derived, emerging in one culture but not applying in another. In addressing the problem of whether generic principles of public relations can be held to exist, Verčič *et al.* (1993) began developing a theory that occupies the middle ground between ethnocentrism and cultural relativism. Drawing on Brinkerhoff and Ingle's (1989) structured flexibility theory of management, they speculate on the possible extension of the characteristics of excellent public relations, identified in the large-scale study by J. Grunig and colleagues (1992). They concluded with an assessment that the developing professional culture of public relations may have as its basis a number of generic principles applicable across 'most cultures and political systems' (Verčič *et al.* 1993: 35).

Within the frame of the national studies, the proposals of Coombs *et al.* (1994), Sriramesh and White (1992) and Verčič *et al.* (1993) represent a sound agenda for further international research to explore differences and similarities between countries practising public relations.

Organisational culture

While culture has acquired many different meanings, a fundamental distinction is made between culture as the result of socialisation into a society's values, symbols and customs – Hofstede's mental programming – and the conception of organisations as cultural entities (Sorge 1994). The latter is another dimension to the discussion of culture and public relations. Organisational culture has become a significant area of study, building on research in the 1930s into corporate culture in the USA (Mayo 1933; Roethlisberger and Dickson 1939) to the more recent classic studies of the 1980s (Deal and Kennedy 1982; Peters and Waterman 1982; Schein 1992). Its connection to public relations has since been considered by Sriramesh *et al.* (1992); Heath (1994) and Banks (1995).

A central role for public relations is communicating corporate values and encouraging mutual understanding throughout an organisation. The intention is that employees come to know what is expected of them, what they may expect from others, and that they identify positively with the organisation – its structure and mission (Heath 1994). The subcultures of organisations, categorised by Martin and Siehl (1953) as enhancing, orthogonal and counter-cultural, give a conceptual focus for analysis in the formation of an internal communications strategy. Awareness and understanding of these subcultures ought to lead to more effective strategies, but their identification and who belongs to them is problematic since they may have no formal boundary, or be recognised as a group. The same need for understanding applies to relationships with other organisations and has special importance for public relations consultants, who are likely to find the task of analysing subcultures in the organisations they provide a service to more difficult than in-house practitioners.

One of Schein's conclusions about organisational culture is the observation that mid-life organisations, whether consciously or not, tend to develop by identifying the strengths and weaknesses of different subcultures and biasing the total culture in favour of one of the subcultures (1992). Public relations can contribute to this process, although whether through assisting in strategy formulation, or just as a means of implementation, depends on the level of acceptance of its strategic function by the dominant coalition within the organisation. It is also possible for a public relations department to get out of step with the organisation and operate itself as a counter-culture. Sriramesh *et al.* (1992) suggest this may happen when the public relations manager is not part of the dominant coalition and the department's professional approach to public relations conflicts with the organisational culture's understanding of the role of public relations.

From a theoretical standpoint (Grunig 1992; Heath 1994) an effective organisation maintains an open culture, where employee feedback is encouraged and senior management listens to questions, especially those that challenge the status quo. As all individuals are members of different groups at the same time and so 'carry several layers of mental programming within themselves of culture' (Hofstede 1991: 10), the more responsive an organisation is to its members, the more flexible it will be in recognising and responding to changes in the external environment. Such a normative view of public relations is easily stated, but can be difficult to communicate to management. A rigid organisational culture may be blind to external changes because the messages from outside are interpreted in a way consistent with the internal culture. Information does not come to a company packaged; 'it must be discovered and interpreted' (Heath 1994: 256). Not all organisations feel comfortable with openness and may, perversely, even be influenced into this way of thinking by the local culture within which they are embedded.

A limitation of the organisational culture perspective is that the interrelationship between internal cultures and the culture of the locality (regional or national) may become sidelined. The effect of national cultures on subsidiaries of IBM, demonstrated by Hofstede (1984; 1991), has already been mentioned. It is therefore expected that the culture of the locality of an organisation helps shape its outlook and behaviour. This contextual relationship is illustrated by Barsoux and Lawrence's analysis of the corporate culture of traditional French companies. Their finding that these companies were 'remarkably reticent by UK or USA standards' (1990: 186) concurred with earlier research by Ehrmann (1957) and Horovitz (1980), the former stating 'France was the country of counter-publicity'. Other comparisons include General Motors, described as very Mid-Western in management style and image, and Nestlé, in spite of having 96 per cent of its employees working outside of Switzerland, regarded as very Swiss in that it limits foreign shareholders with voting rights to only 3 per cent (Whittington 1993).

The importance of the link between locality and organisational culture is further highlighted in Whittington's (1993) examination of the corporate strategy-making process, with its clear implications for public relations.

Whittington presents four theoretical approaches to strategy: classical, evolutionary, processual and systemic. Classicists regard strategy as a process of long-term rational planning, while evolutionists challenge the practicality of making distant assumptions about the future, and advocate focus on maximising possibilities of survival in the present. Processualists agree with the evolutionary view of long-termism, but suggest strategy should be comprehended as an emergent process involving learning and adaptation. Finally, in the systemic approach, while long-term planning is recommended, relativity is emphasised; strategies are dependent on cultural contexts; they reflect the social systems through which they are enacted, hence approaches to strategy will vary, influenced potentially by aspects of layers of culture such as social class, profession, ethnicity and nationality (Whittington 1993).

A systemic approach means that managers have a heightened sociological sensitivity: 'every manager should analyse his or her immediate social system, in order to grasp the variety of social resources and rules of conduct available' (Whittington 1993: 38). Managers are also careful not to assume the strategic logic of competitors will be the same as their organisation's.

Although Whittington does not refer to Hall or Hofstede's work, he also makes a strong connection between culture and its effects on organisations through the people who work in and around them. Because the focus of Whittington's work is on strategy, the connection with public relations is much closer, although his discussion does not extend in this direction. As a systems theory perspective, the systemic approach validates the boundary-scanning role of public relations, monitoring external (and internal) environments to identify strategically important issues whose consequences may affect the autonomy of the organisation. But it implies as well that managers should develop their own personal sensitivity to public relations issues.

Whittington's discussion of strategy serves to highlight the value for public relations practitioners of being aware of how strategy is formulated in their organisation. Different approaches are likely to have separate implications for a communications strategy. An organisation adopting a predominantly processual approach may allow strategy to emerge at more than one level or, for example, through the activities of one or more project groups given considerable autonomy. In such a scenario, the task of the public relations function of monitoring and participating in these developments becomes more complex than a formal 'top-down' strategy-making structure.

In challenging the universality of any one model of strategy, the systemic view warns against ethnocentrism. To press home the point, Whittington cites Anglo-American studies on leadership which do not translate well into other cultures (1993). His observation provides further evidence for caution against being too accepting of any one model of public relations.

Banks' social-interpretative approach to public relations

So far there has been an examination, albeit in brief, that has largely focused on propositions of scholars whose ideas have been grounded in the disciplines of sociology (Giddens, Beniger), social theory (Baudrillard, Jameson), cultural anthropology (Hall), organisational behaviour (Hofstede), and corporate strategy (Whittington). This last section assesses a theoretical framework of public relations proposed by Banks (1995) that uses culture as one of its central elements.

Banks' understanding of the purpose of public relations develops from Kruckeberg and Stark's (1988) thesis that it should recreate or maintain the sense of community that became eroded by the effects of modern mass communication and transportation. He argues that this limits the legitimacy of public relations to non-profit and non-governmental organisations. On the basis that all organisations, for better or worse, help to constitute the fabric of communities, he concludes that all organisations have a social responsibility for 'nurturing the development of positive and supportive communities' (1995: 20–1). Public relations communication should therefore be directed to that end, as well as seeking to secure for the organisation a favourable reputation. It is a conception of public relations as ritual communication – helping to sustain and celebrate cultural identity. Culture is brought into the equation through being defined as 'systems of meanings group members acquire through experiential membership' (Banks 1995: 10). Defining culture solely in terms of systems of meaning enables a small group to become a culture, and so a public. Public relations is therefore a multicultural activity, since it operates in a social environment of multiple systems of meaning.

The stress on the construction of meaning derives from the 'social-interpretative' approach adopted by Banks. It is a subjectivist perspective that rejects the positivist philosophy of knowledge where social phenomena are considered to be subject to natural laws that operate independently of individual wishes. In the social-interpretative view, the predictive value of a theory is of less significance than the description and explanation of social phenomena.

Banks' discussion of the nature of public relations leads to identification of five core characteristics that he uses to explain his intercultural theory of public relations: institutional, representational, ideological, integrational and cultural.

In considering cultural characteristics, he makes the important distinction between the various senses in which culture can be applied to public relations: in communicating with publics, it is operating in an intercultural context; public relations acts to produce and shape culture (documents, logos, exhibitions and events are cultural artefacts, in whole or in part created by public relations); and in the process of communication, public relations proposes to the audience a way of contextualising a part of the social world. In the third sense it is cultural because of existing beliefs held about public communication, such as the right of an organisation to communicate publicly, and the value attached to gaining support through persuasion as opposed to coercion.

The social-interpretative approach is a useful theoretical framework, as it successfully integrates aspects of existing research into the social/cultural dimension of public relations (White 1987; Kruckeberg and Stark 1988; Mackey 1994; Botan 1992), and offers propositions for further research (Banks 1995). Moreover, it constructs a view of public relations that stands in contrast to its actual role as implied by Baudrillard (1983).

The concluding chapter of Banks' book attempts to chart a course between the apparent actuality of public relations and the ideal state. It is accepted that practice is varied (Hallahan 1993), diversity is poorly recognised by the profession (Banks 1994) and professional membership in the USA probably represents only 5–10 per cent of the public relations workforce (Seitel 1992). What follows are laudable observations on the need for improved training and education, and for a firmer professional body that accredits education and programmes; and an argument for ethical communication. These are presented for the benefit of practitioners, educators and students.

While educators may be sympathetic to Banks' prescriptions for a multicultural approach to public relations, and students open to persuasion, enthusiasm could well be muted amongst practitioners. Important, too, are the people who hire and manage public relations practitioners. How many members of the dominant coalition of commercial organisations recognise the primary goal of public relations to be 'building strong communities within a more humane global society' (Banks 1995: 116)? Public relations as a transmission form of communication may well have more direct appeal.

Although the criticism of idealism may be levelled at this understanding of public relations, it is also possible to see it as its main strength, which derives from the social-interpretative approach. Support for this approach is found in Carey's essay on 'Reconceiving mass and media' (1989) and more fundamentally in the critical response of Adorno and later Habermas to Popper's affirmation of 'pure' science (Holub 1991). In essence, they argued that reality cannot exist as a separate entity from ethics in sociology, because the study of society has to crystallise around values about a just society. So the realms of existence and ethics have to be thought together – a process that Banks has followed. By giving emphasis to a methodology that should enable a deeper understanding of the diversity of the everyday character of public relations, Banks encourages caution in perceiving public relations as a discipline capable of being defined through a set of unshakeable truths. Similar reasoning on the nature of sociology is presented by Cuff *et al.* (1990), who suggest there is no uniform set of terms, concepts or theories that encompass sociology; instead its meaning is best approached by assessing the different ways proposed for trying to understand the world. As a younger and narrower discipline, there are few public relations-specific theories or perspectives to draw on, but a wealth of material from surrounding disciplines, of which the study of culture is one.

Conclusion

This chapter has sought to illustrate how the discipline of public relations is embedded within a broader framework of social theory and culture. Cultural content and context have been identified as inherent in communication; a link with public relations has been made by explaining how the two basic representations of communication, transmission and ritual relate to theoretical frameworks of public relations. It has also been noted how the cultural dimension is relevant to decisions at international level about the extent to which a public relations programme should be customised or standardised, and through the influences on the organisation of its internal subcultures and external locality culture. In the final section, a theoretical approach to public relations grounded in the concept of its multicultural diversity has been examined. Its representation of public relations has been justified against the criticism of unrealistic idealism, by relating to the arguments of Adorno and Habermas against 'positivism'. In the way that Habermas, in his early work, used the idealised notion of the 'public sphere' as a foundation to critically evaluate western society, so Banks' notion of an idealised community-oriented public relations offers a basis for a critical evaluation of public relations.

References

Banks, S. P. (1995) *Multicultural Public Relations: A Social-Interpretative Approach*, Thousand Oaks CA: Sage.

Baskin, O. and Arnoff, C. E. (1992) *Public Relations: The Profession and the Practice*, 3rd edn, Dubuque IA: W. C. Brown.

Barsoux, J. L. and Lawrence, P. (1990) *Management in France*, London: Cassell.

Baudrillard, J. (1983) *Simulations*, New York: Semiotext(e).

Beniger, J. (1986) *The Control Revolution: Technological and Economic Origins of the Information Society*, Cambridge MA: Harvard University Press.

Botan, C. (1990) 'Public relations as a science: implications of cultural differences and international events', paper presented to the Quandt Foundation Communication Group, Salzburg.

——(1992) 'International public relations critique and reformulation', *Public Relations Review*, 18 (12) 149–59.

Bourdieu, P. (1984) *Distinction: A Social Critique of the Judgement of Taste*, London: Routledge.

Brinkerhof, D. W. and Ingle, M. D. (1989) 'Integrating blueprint and process: a structured flexibility approach to development management', *Public Administration and Development*, 9 (5) 487–503.

Carey, J. W. (1989) *Communication as Culture*, London: Unwin Hyman.

Coombs, W. T., Hollady, S., Signitzer, B. and Hausenauer, G. (1994) 'A comparative analysis of international public relations: identification, interpretation of similarities and differences between professionalisation in Austria, Norway and the USA', *Journal of Public Relations Research*, 6 (1) 23–9.

Cuff, E., Sharrock, W. and Francis, D. (1990) *Perspectives in Sociology*, 3rd edn, London: Routledge.

Deal, T. E. and Kennedy, A. E. (1982) *Corporate Culture: The Rites and Rituals of Corporate Life*, Reading MA: Addision-Wesley.

Dewey, J. (1927) *The Public and Its Problems*, Chicago IL: Swallow.

Dickens, D. R. and Fontana, A. (eds) (1994) *Post Modernism and Social Inquiry*, London: VCL Press.

Djursaa, M. (1994) 'North European business cultures: Britian vs Denmark and Germany', *European Management Journal*, 12 (2) 138–46.

Downing, J. (1995) 'Alternative media and the Boston Tea Party', in J. Downing, A. Mohammadi and A. Sreberny-Mohammadi (eds) *Questioning the Media*, 2nd edn, Thousand Oaks CA: Sage.

Ehrmann, H. W. (1957) *Organised Business in France*, Princeton NJ: Princeton University Press.

Gandy, O. H. (1992) 'Public relations and public policy: the structuration of dominance in the information age', in E. L. Toth and R. L. Heath (eds) *Rhetorical and Critical Approaches to Public Relations*, Hillsdale NJ: Lawrence Erlbaum.

Geertz, C. (1973) *The Interpretation of Cultures*, New York: Basic Books.

Giddens, A. (1987) *Social Theory and Modern Sociology*, Cambridge: Polity Press.

——(1990) *The Consequences of Modernity*, Stanford CA: Stanford University Press.

Gottdiener, M. (1994) 'Semiotics and postmodernism', in D. R. Dickens and A. Fontana (eds) *Postmodernism and Social Inquiry*, London: UCL Press.

Gozzi, R. (1992) 'Mass media effects in high – and low – context countries', in F. Korzenny, S. Ting-Toorney and E. Schiff (eds) *Mass Media Effects Across Cultures*, Newbury Park CA: Sage.

Gramsci, A. (1971) *Selections from the Prison Notebooks*, trans. Q. Hoare and G. Nowell-Smith, New York: International.

Grunig, J. E. (1989) 'Symmetrical presuppositions as a framework for public relations theory', in C. H. Botan and V. Hazlton Jr (eds) *Public Relations Theory*, Hillsdale NJ: Lawrence Erlbaum.

——(ed.) (1992) *Excellence in Public Relations and Communication Management*, Hillsdale NJ: Lawrence Erlbaum.

Habermas, J. (1984) *Theory of Communicative Action*, trans. T. McCarthy, Boston MA: Beacon Press.

Hall, E. T. (1976) *Beyond Culture*, New York: Doubleday.

——(1983) *The Dance of Life*, New York: Anchor Press.

Hall, E. T. and Hall, M. R (1990) *Understanding Cultural Difference*, USA: Intercultural Press.

Hall, S. (1986) 'Cultural studies: two paradigms', in R. Collins, J. Curran, N. Garnham, P. Scannell, P. Schlesinger and C. Sparks (eds) *Media, Culture and Society: A Critical Reader*, London: Sage.

Hallahan, K. (1993) 'The paradigm struggle and public relations practice', *Public Relations Review*, 19, 197–205.

Heath, R. L. (1994) *Management of Corporate Communication: From Interpersonal Contacts to External Affairs*, Hillsdale NJ: Lawrence Erlbaum.

Hofstede, G. (1984) *Culture's Consequences: International Difference in Work Related Values*, London: Sage.

——(1991) *Culture and Organisations: Software of the Mind*, London: Harper Collins.

Holub, R. C. (1991) *Jurgen Habermas: Critic in the Public Sphere*, London: Routledge.

Horovitz, J. (1980) *Top Management Control in Europe*, London: Macmillian.

Jameson, F. (1983) 'Postmodernism and the consumer society', in H. Foster (ed.) *The Anti-Aesthetic*, Port Townsend WPI: Bay Press.

——(1992) *The Geopolitical Aesthetic: Cinema and Space in the World System*, London: BFI Publishing.

Jensen, K. B. and Rosengren, K. E. (1990) 'Five traditions in search of an audience', *European Journal of Communication*, 5 (2–3) 207–38.

Kruckeberg, D. and Stark, K. (1988) *Public Relations and Community: A Reconstructed Theory*, New York: Praeger.

Mackey, S. (1994) 'A theory of public relations theory', paper presented to the Public Relations section of the ICA/ACA conference, Sydney NSW.

McLuhan, M. (1964) *Understanding Media: The Extensions of Man*, Cambridge MA: MIT Press.

MacManus, T. (1994) 'A comparative analysis of public relations in Austria and the United Kingdom', paper presented to the International Public Relations Research Symposium, Lake Bled, Slovenia.

Martin, J. and Siehl, C. (1983) 'Organisational culture and counter-culture: an uneasy symbiosis', *Organisational Dynamics*, 12, 52–64.

Mayo, E. (1933) *The Human Problem of an Industrial Civilization*, New York: Macmillan.

Meech, P. and Kilburn, R. (1992) 'Media and identity in a stateless nation: the case of Scotland', *Media, Culture and Society*, 14 (2) 245–59.

Peters, T. J. and Waterman, R. H. (1982) *In Search of Excellence: Lessons from America's Best Run Companies*, London: Harper and Row.

Roethlisberger, F. J. and Dickson, W. J. (1939) *Management and the Worker: An Account of a Research Program Conducted by a Western Electric Company, Hawthorne Works, Chicago*, Cambridge MA: Harvard University Press.

Rühl, M. (1992) 'Stepping stones towards a theory of public relations', paper presented to the Confederation of European Public Relations Associations, Education Section, Brussels.

Schein, E. (1992) *Organisational Culture and Leadership*, Englewood Cliffs NJ: Prentice-Hall.

Seitel, F. (1992) *The Practice of Public Relations*, 5th edn, Englewood Cliffs NJ: Prentice-Hall.

Søndergaard, M. (1994) 'Research note: Hofstede's consequences – a study of reviews, citations and replications', *Journal of Organisational Studies*, 15 (3) 447–56.

Sorge, A. (1994) 'Editorial', *Journal of Organisational Studies*, 15 (3) vii–x.

Sreberny-Mohammadi, A. (1995) 'Forms of media as ways of knowing', in J. Downing, A. Mohammadi and A. Sreberny-Mohammadi (eds) *Questioning the Media*, 2nd edn, Thousand Oaks CA: Sage.

Sriramesh, K. (1992) 'Societal culture and public relations: ethnographic evidence from India', *Public Relations Review*, 18 (12) 201–11.

Sriramesh, K. and White, J. (1992) 'Societal culture and public relations', in J. E. Grunig (ed.) *Excellence in Public Relations and Communication Management*, Hillsdale NJ: Lawrence Erlbaum.

Sriramesh, K., Grunig, J. E. and Buffinton, J. (1992) 'Corporate culture and public relations', in J. E. Gruning (ed.) *Excellence in Public Relations and Communication Management*, Hillsdale NJ: Lawrence Erlbaum.

Tayeb, M. H. (1988) *Organisations and National Culture: A Comparative Analysis*, London: Sage.

Usunier, J-C. (1993) *International Marketing: A Cultural Approach*, Hemel Hempstead: Prentice-Hall International.

Van Dijk, J. A. G. M. (1993) 'Communication networks and modernisation', *Communication Research*, 20 (30) 384–407.

Verčič, D., Grunig, L. A. and Grunig, J. E. (1993) 'Global and specific principles of public relations: evidence from Slovenia', paper presented to the

Association for the Advancement of Policy, Research and Development in the Third World, Cairo.

Whittington, R. (1993) *What is Strategy – and Does it Matter?*, London: Routledge.

Windahl, S. and Signitzer, B. H. (1992) *Using Communication Theory: An Introduction to Planned Communication*, London: Sage.

White, J. (1987) 'Public relations in the social construction of reality', paper presented to a conference of the Association for Education and Journalism in Mass Communication, San Antonio TX.

Williams, R. (1958) *Culture and Society, 1780–1950*, London: Chatto and Windus.

7 Preliminary Delphi research on international public relations programming

Initial data supports application of certain generic/specific concepts

Robert I. Wakefield

Introduction

Today, even though societies are moving into an increasingly interactive global environment, there is still considerable confusion over the concept of international public relations. A few years ago, an American public relations executive argued that "there simply is no such thing as 'international public relations'" (Angell 1990: 8). Another countered, "international public relations is one of the most rapidly growing areas of the [public relations] profession, and one of the least understood" (Pavlik 1987: 64).

What is practised in the name of international public relations can vary from simple hosting or promotions to diplomacy and relationship building. To some, public relations programs "only sound international if you're on the other side of the ocean" (Anderson 1989: 414). To others, international practice is merely a media relations role or a support for marketing, as opposed to public relations, objectives (L. Grunig 1992a). Only in rare cases does a multinational make international public relations a strategic part of executive management, or position it as stated by British executive Paul Winner, "to try to resolve, or at least minimize conflict ... to avoid the need for forceful intervention" (1990: 20).

Few people have tried to define international public relations. Wilcox *et al.* called it "the planned and organized effort of a company, institution, or government to establish mutually beneficial relations with publics of other nations" (1992: 409–10). Other scholars have emphasized the idea that international public relations involves practitioners taking a broad perspective that will allow them to work in different countries or cultures, or collaborate with others from different nations. Booth said that the only true international practitioners "understand how business is done across national borders" and perform in that context (1986: 23). For the purposes of this chapter, international public relations is defined as:

> a multinational program that has certain coordination between headquarters and various countries where offices and/or publics are located, and that has potential consequences or results in more than one country.

Whether or not the field is ready, rapid change and complex forces are shaping an uncertain international environment in which effective public relations is needed. The people of the world are increasingly interdependent (J. Grunig 1992a), while simultaneously asserting their cultural independence (Hill 1992). Communication technologies, intertwined market systems and realignments of economic power have helped to bring individuals and societies together more frequently. Governments and businesses compete and collaborate at the same time. Yet more interaction is also generating greater cultural divides and more hostility between and within national boundaries (Hennessy 1985; Kohara 1989).

Some byproducts of this environment are issues and conflicts. Some issues, like AIDS and the environment, help to bring people together across cultural and national boundaries in a fragile attempt to find common solutions (Haywood 1991; Epley 1992). Other issues pull people apart. Recent strife within Russia, Bosnia and Rwanda, the Persian Gulf conflict, and racial tensions in the United States exemplify the conflicts that result when cultures live together but fail to understand each other. Similar dissension can occur between distant cultures – as exemplified by the trade friction between the United States and Japan.

For organizations, it is almost impossible to escape the increasing array of issues in the international context. Multinationals are even more vulnerable to hostilities and crises than domestic organizations because of the increased numbers and complexities of those stakeholders who can oppose them, and the necessity for dealing with them in cross-cultural contexts (Dilenschneider 1992; Nigh and Cochran 1994). Traverse-Healy explained, "issues which ... demand a public relations response ... more often than not are global in development and expression" (1991:

34). L. Grunig added that the global environment is characterized by "dissensus rather than consensus, heterogeneity rather than homogeneity and rapid rate of change rather than stability" (1992a: 130).

Crises like the explosion at the Union Carbide plant in Bhopal, India, or the bombing of Pan Am Flight 103 over Lockerbie in Scotland in 1989, indicate how important it is for organizations to have communication programs that cross cultural boundaries. The Bhopal crisis fostered activist groups in countries as diverse as the United States, Japan, Malaysia, the Netherlands and the United Kingdom (Sen and Egelhoff 1991). Likewise, groups from Scotland, England, America, West Germany, Finland, Israel and the PLO were involved in the perpetration, operations or investigations of the Lockerbie disaster (Pinsdorf 1991).

Cross-border issues and publics have fostered the growth of international public relations. Considering the pitfalls, and with no consensus on the nature of cross-border public relations, organizations venturing into this environment do so with no real guidelines for success. Practitioners who lack expertise fail to gain the trust of senior managers who desperately need solid advice and performance in the maze of international relationship-building. Worse, they become vulnerable to making – or repeating – costly and embarrassing mistakes. It should be apparent, then, that for the field to gain maturity and credibility, research is needed to determine what makes international public relations effective.

Literature on international public relations

Writings and seminars on international public relations have increased significantly in recent years. At least three books and several dozen articles have discussed international practice.[1] *Public Relations Journal* highlighted the growing interest with several cover articles.[2] Professional conferences – including the 1991 and 1993 annual conferences of PRSA – have emphasized the increasingly transnational nature of the field. And the *Public Relations Review* of summer 1992 was a special edition about international issues and practice.

Despite this activity, efforts to build theory in international public relations are still limited and haphazard. This is partly because public relations has just begun to expand internationally and is uneven in its development (Botan 1992). But also, public relations scholarship is still in a youthful state (Kunczik 1990; J. Grunig 1992b). Articles addressing international concerns are often anecdotal, or what Kunczik called "scientifically 'non-serious' sources" (1990: 24). Many tell how to avoid cultural blunders or to apply certain tactics to achieve "success" in campaigns in a given country. Such superficial discussions offer little theoretical insight into how public relations should be practised across borders.

Most scholarly attempts at research have been country-specific, discussing public relations in a particular country and how it varies from other countries. If conducted well, these studies contribute to the growing body of knowledge about public relations from country to country. They also assist the understanding of transnational practice. After all, even when public relations programs are strategically positioned to cross borders, the execution of those programs must always occur within borders. However, the studies do not fully satisfy the knowledge base about all the complex issues and problems inherent in strategically coordinating campaigns across borders (Anderson 1989; Botan 1992).

Global vs local practice

One of the fundamental strategic questions in the multinational organization is whether to centralize or localize strategies and operations (see e.g. Ovaitt 1987; Dilenschneider 1992). This question is commonly discussed in such disciplines as comparative management, cultural anthropology, development management, etc. In comparative management literature, for example, the poles are referred to as "culture-specific" or "culture-free" (Adler *et al.* 1986). It is also debated in advertising (Ovaitt 1988) and marketing (Baalbaki and Malhotra 1993), fields similar to public relations.

In public relations, Anderson (1989) distinguished between the two poles as follows:

1   Global public relations emphasizes the concept that programs can and should be created at a central headquarters and, with only minor adaptations, be implemented in all local markets.
2   International public relations emphasizes the placement of resources and decision-making authority in the local markets, where local communicators best understand the needs of their audiences.

Practitioners and authors defend either side of the equation. Anderson argued that global imperatives "demand that programs in distinctive markets be interrelated" (1989: 413). Others argue that local politics and cultures are so strong that public relations must be localized.

Dilenschneider (1992) asserted that public relations should be performed by locals who better understand the customs, traditions and laws of each country. Multinationals often choose one of the two ,oles, and Americans, in particular, tend to view their global/local tructures as an either/or proposition, centralizing everything or allowing complete local autonomy (Hampden-Turner and Trompenaars 1993).

In practice, however, polarization can be harmful (Botan 1992). Centralization results in slow responses to issues and creates activities that are inappropriate for host country conditions. Complete autonomy indicates that the multinational perceives little risk of crisis. Coordination remains low and the "plans and programs are often not brought into question" (Botan 1992: 151). Handing over operations entirely to the locals fosters a "not invented here" mentality that undermines the mission of the organization (Hill 1992). Kinzer and Bohn agreed that "lack of global ... coordination within the corporation risks a public relations disaster" (1985: 5).

Bridges between global and local thinking

A good starting point for considering international public relations research in terms of the choice between a global or a local positioning was the "pole debate". However, it must be recognized that, in choosing one of the poles, a multinational organization would always have to settle for less than a comprehensive program.

It seemed that a few experts were right – that to be effective, international public relations programs must recognize and respond to both global and local needs (Ovaitt 1988). Traverse-Healy (1991) had said that international public relations should have a centralization of policies and messages, combined with local strategies and adaptations to language, customs and politics. It could be argued that the key to successful international public relations would be to discover exactly which combination of global and local variables are most effective. With this research, the field could move towards maturity, and its practitioners could understand how to perform so as to obtain credibility with management.

To determine the best combination of global and local structuring, cues can be taken from related disciplines. For several years, researchers in fields like sociology, comparative management, cultural studies and anthropology have been examining factors of effective international management (Ricks *et al.* 1990). Because these domains are far ahead of public relations in the international theory-building process, they could prove useful to public relations scholars trying to understand the complexities of cross-border practice.

Contingency theory is especially relevant to international organizations, which face particularly uncertain environments (Robertson 1990). L. Grunig characterized publics in the global environment as "increasingly more unfamiliar and more hostile, as well [as] more organized and more powerful" (1992a: 130). Negandhi (1983) claimed that contingency theory is the best approach for international management, because it accounts for the more complex and dynamic environment of a multinational organization.

One contingency model was Brinkerhoff and Ingle's (1989) theory of structured flexibility. This identified a combination of functions that were "generic to good performance" – that could be universally applied – or were "specific" to local markets. The generic variable in their theory included short- and long-term objectives, consensus on policies, establishment of responsibilities, overall strategic plans and budgets. The specific variable allowed for local flexibility to modify and implement programs as needed.

This chapter argues that a combination similar to the structural flexibility theory could prove useful to international public relations. If certain variables could predict effective generic and specific performance, it may also be possible to determine the appropriate combination of these variables for excellent international practice. It can also be argued that the foundation for the generic variable may already exist, from a multi-year study on excellence in public relations management.

Excellence in international public relations

In 1984, Grunig and others started to determine what comprises excellent practice in public relations (J. Grunig 1992a). Various aspects of the field had been studied previously, but no one had accumulated a comprehensive set of variables that would indicate successful practice. This examination was sponsored by the International Association of Business Communicators (IABC) Research Foundation. According to Carrington (1992), it was the most comprehensive study conducted in the industry. The authors identified variables that must be present among management, with practitioners, and in the organization for public relations to be effective. The study is contained in the book entitled *Excellence in Public Relations and Communication Management* (J. Grunig 1992c).

The Excellence Study predicted that successful programs will have certain characteristics. These are broadly described as follows:

1 a management predisposition to practise public relations strategically;
2 placement of the senior public relations practitioner among the organization's decision makers;
3 symmetrical communication with influential publics that can be threats to or supporters of an organization;
4 combining public relations functions into a single, integrated unit separate from marketing; and
5 development of organizational conditions that allow practitioners and other employees to function freely, including providing equal opportunities for women and minorities.

(J. Grunig 1992c)

The Excellence Study also identified positive effects of outstanding public relations programs. For organizations that practice excellent public relations, positive results will be:

1 achievement of communication objectives,
2 an ability to manage conflict and reduce the associated costs, and
3 greater job satisfaction for employees.

(J. Grunig 1992c)

With these effects, public relations can contribute to an organization's "bottom line" and thus overcome traditional questioning of public relations by senior executives (Baldwin 1991).

Recently, J. Grunig (1992a) related the Excellence Study to the structural flexibility theory mentioned above. He postulated that the Excellence findings could serve as the generic variables for effective international public relations. If this could be validated, then it would remain only to identify the specific variables. The resulting combination of generic and specific variables might then lead to a theory of excellent international public relations.

Possible specific variables

Beyond the universal foundation, effective public relations should also respond to specific variables that can affect local practice. Headquarters should generate clear policies, communication themes to support the overall mission, and guidelines for evaluation, controls and budgets.

Those policies then must be expressed in each location through strategic planning and specific interaction with local audiences. "The public is 'out there' ... and therefore 'out there' is where the action has to be," said Traverse-Healy (1991: 34). Local practitioners should be responsible for:

1   creating and maintaining local strategies and programs;
2   developing the machinery for implementing these programs, including the appointment of necessary staff or retaining an outside agency; and
3   establishing a training and evaluation system that corresponds with the central program.

(Epley 1992)

How can practitioners establish these local priorities, however, if they do not understand environmental factors that can affect their programs? Anecdotal sources currently show great confusion about what factors can affect local practices. Thus identifying these factors and learning what effects they create is vital to building a theory of effective international public relations.

So, what are the potential specific variables? Literature from various disciplines suggests six possibilities:

1   the level of development in a country;
2   the local political situation;
3   the cultural environment;
4   language differences;
5   the potential for activism;
6   the role of the mass media.

These variables are explained briefly below.

Level of development refers to what degree a nation has achieved economic and technological growth. Botan described development as "not only the level of economic development ... but development of the information infrastructure" (1992: 154). After examining public relations in Slovenia, Verčič *et al.* (1993) viewed level of development as a possible specific variable in international programming.

Development level often determines who controls public relations. In developed nations, public relations is a tool for market competition; in developing nations, it assists the government in rallying its citizens. Development levels also influence literacy rates and the media that are available for public relations activities. Developed countries have high literacy, competitive media, and access to those media (Botan 1992). But in nations like India, where half the population cannot read and many languages are spoken, it makes little sense to send messages through the media. Rather, practitioners usually employ more direct vehicles of communication.

After visiting several developing nations, Sharpe supplied examples of public relations there. In Brazil, "government ... approval is needed for almost every aspect of life" (1992: 104). Thus corporate public relations helps to obtain favors from the government. Turkish public relations is intended to show a positive face to audiences in Europe and the United States. Sharpe also claimed that public relations sometimes can benefit from lower levels of development because the field in these nations is not burdened by the roots of one-way journalism. Thus they can more quickly implement two-way communication and develop more rapidly than their western counterparts did.

Recent volatility in political systems has caused scholars to re-examine government and media relationships, the influence of global technologies, and public opinion within societies. Many claim that once authoritarian regimes start opening their societies, their citizens are exposed to images of freedom and prosperity through external sources. They also encounter external support for human rights. This encourages uprisings against the more suppressive regimes (Sharpe 1992). In many cases, techniques of western public relations were instrumental in some of the transitions away from authoritarianism (Hiebert 1992).

Verčič *et al.* argued that public relations is not possible in an authoritarian state. Authoritarian regimes foster propaganda, which, although often mistaken as public relations, is one-way information used to "make people aware of the system of constraints on their behavior" (1993: 23). Propaganda works because dictators use violence on their own citizens to enforce behaviors. By contrast, public relations requires "lateral" relationships, where the possibility of change in government is as great as among the people.

Sharpe (1992) argued that modern public relations can exist in authoritarian countries. He used China and Turkey as examples of nations where public relations is practised despite strong constraints. He admitted, though, that public relations has developed in these countries to gain necessary financing and because of the influence of global technologies. It can be argued that without outside influences, authoritarian states would still stifle public relations as practiced elsewhere. More research is needed to determine which view is right.

Culture is an ambiguous concept, and difficult to study. There are more than 160 definitions of culture (Negandhi 1983). Adler *et al.* (1986) viewed culture as:

1   something shared by all or almost all members of some social group;
2   something that older members of the group pass on to younger members; and
3   something (morals, laws or customs) that shapes the group's behaviors or views of the world.

Even with the confusion, the influence of culture on communication is widely accepted (Ellingsworth 1977). Hall linked the two concepts when he said "culture is communication and communication is culture" (1959: 191). This is important to public relations, because communication and public relations have also been seen as synonymous (J. Grunig and Hunt 1984; Sriramesh and White 1992).

One path of cultural study comes from Hofstede's (1980) dimension theories. He developed four classifications for cultural groups: the fostering of individualism or collectivism, the social distances between the powerful and the unpowerful (power distance), the extent to which uncertainty is avoided or welcomed (uncertainty avoidance), and the extent to which typically masculine or feminine characteristics are prevalent. Many scholars since Hofstede have studied dimension theory (Tayeb 1988; Adler 1991).

Hampden-Turner and Trompenaars (1993) identified dimensions like Hofstede's (1980), but their interpretations differed. They reasoned, for instance, that because Americans value individuality, universal standards are needed to codify behaviors and protect the mainstream from aberrances. This codification, in turn, leads to a focus on short-term results and an emphasis on bottom lines over the human relationships and cooperation.

The Hampden-Turner and Trompenaars (1993) dimensions could shed light on the specific variables in international public relations. For example, codified standards have fostered activist groups who seek to change the status quo (Schmid and de Graaf 1982). Thus public relations practitioners in codified societies need to deal more frequently with activist groups than do practitioners in other lands. They also face greater pressures to "justify" their practices through measurable research (Lesly 1986). By contrast, two-way symmetrical public relations may be more readily accepted in societies that already value the underlying principles of communication, cooperation and compromise (L. Grunig 1991).

Language is an obvious factor in the international arena. Many nations have multiple official languages, not to mention differing dialects and accents (Wilcox *et al.* 1992). Language translation prob-lems are a renowned nightmare in international practice (Howard and Mathews 1986). In the past few decades, English has become "the universal language of the world" (Naisbitt 1994: 26). The diffusion of English has led to direct interaction and communication that would not have been possible years ago.

Even with a "world language," intercultural misunderstandings can arise. Reed stated that "the first cross-cultural barrier has to do with words ... no matter how precise the translation" (1989: 13). Language differences can be tragic, or even fatal. Misinterpretation of one word between Colombian pilots and American flight controllers was largely responsible for a 1990 Avianca Airlines crash on Long Island that killed seventy-two people (Pinsdorf 1991). This reality of miscommunication in cross-cultural interactions is one of the main reasons that public rela-tions activities should be localized. Articulation of ideas and precision in communication is essential to effective public relations (Lesly 1986).

The potential for activism is another possible variable. L. Grunig defined activist publics as "two or more individuals who organize ... to influence another public or publics through action that may include education, compromise, persuasion, pressure tactics or force" (1992b: 504). These actions can be very damaging to an organization. However, the potential for activism can also create opportunities for public relations.

Activism can be particularly acute in the international realm. Nigh and Cochran stated that "since 1980 ... a multitude of interest groups and transnational organizations have increasingly figured in the deci-sion making of multinational enterprises" (1987: 5). These groups are organized, powerful and sophisticated in their tactics, and insist that organizations satisfy their desires (Dowling 1990). Where they once used to pressure governments for change, they now attack organiza-tions directly; thus organizations must identify and communicate with activists before significant damage occurs (Rose 1991).

Nigh and Cochran (1987) explained why responding to activists and issues is more difficult internationally. First, multinational organ-izations face more actual or potential stakeholders than domestic organizations, and it is more difficult to identify international issues and publics. Also, multinationals face transnational interest groups that quickly transcend boundaries but are of no concern to domestic organizations. Finally, issues resolution for the multinational organiza-tion must involve communication across cultures.

There is evidence that the type and extent of activism will differ from country to country. Activism can be affected by the imposition of standards that some groups resent (Duffy 1984), or by the degree to which a government allows public debate (Schmid and de Graaf 1982). Another influence is power distance (Hofstede 1980). Sriramesh (1992) reported that outside of conflicts between organizations and their labor groups, India has little activism. This is mostly because the managerial elite dominates their non-elite publics, who are not acculturated to press for changes.

The manner in which an organization responds to activism also can be influenced by local factors. In one country, a public relations staff might spend a great deal of its time monitoring the environment for sudden changes among its activist publics. In another country, practitioners may be able to devote most of their time to networking and relationship building, without constant worry about upcoming pressure.

Some may question the role of the media in society, but few would argue that the media have some influence on world affairs. Pavlik explained that media coverage "leads to action, not because of its effect on the ostensible audience, but because others believe it will influence its audience" (1987: 107). Hennessy concurred that "If enough people whose collective influence is great think that the *New York Times* editorials are important ... then these media presentations do become influential" (1985: 249).

Global technologies have carried the mass media, and the political and cultural ideologies they espouse, across the world at increasing speeds and lower costs. "Never before in history has so much been communicated so rapidly to so many people," said Martin and Hiebert (1990: 5). "Instant communications has made the planet's populace more knowledgeable and opinionated than ever before," added Epley (1992: 110).

This increased information and knowledge generates at least two results that could affect international public relations. The first is an apparent increase in activism and issues that are more global, as mentioned above. The second revolves around the nature of media messages in a global context. Added to these potential effects is the fact that media are different from country to country.

Interest groups have learned how to manipulate the media to achieve their goals (Pires 1989). They stage events such as protests, boycotts, marches and sometimes even violent demonstrations (L. Grunig 1986). The media do not purposely favor activist groups, but advance their causes by covering these events (Pires 1989). This coverage ensures an audience for activist ideologies and, as a result, special interest groups are now influencing opinions of decision makers throughout the world (Hiebert 1992).

The influence of the mass media is especially great when no other source of information is available (Kunczik 1990). People can check the "reality" of local coverage through other sources who know what happened. But globally, where incidents happen far away and cannot be personally verified, people depend solely on the media for information. A stark example was the media coverage that bombarded the world during the Persian Gulf conflict (Hiebert 1991). Yet media reporting can be quite different from "reality" (Kunczik 1990). Thus the media monopoly in foreign information can create unrealistic images about other countries, or about individuals and organizations from those countries.

In the end, effective public relations comes down to local communication. Epley stated that international practitioners must "jump beyond infatuation with modern gadgetry and learn how to use these new sophisticated communication vehicles to narrow our scope and better define very specific messages to targeted audiences" (1992: 115). Haywood added that "communication is extremely local and very personal" (1991: 22).

The Delphi study on international effectiveness

A comprehensive study on international public relations that examines the proper combination of generic and specific variables is sorely needed. With such a study, a normative theory of excellence in international public relations could be created. Normative theory explains how public relations should be practised, as distinguished from positive theory which describes how public relations is practised. However, the best normative theories realistically guide practice (J. Grunig and L. Grunig 1991). Thus an examination that creates good normative theory on international public relations should be useful for practitioners as well as scholars.

For exploration into a field that is poorly defined, qualitative methods are appropriate (Marshall and Rossman 1989). Qualitative research is essentially an ongoing dialogue; when one study is completed, other researchers are invited – indeed encouraged – to scrutinize, critique and add to the discussion. This is how knowledge expands in a dynamic field (Pauly 1991). Qualitative research was therefore used to answer the proposed questions and achieve an accurate picture of effective international practice.

Qualitative research is well suited for studying public relations in an international context. Lesly (1986) contended that public relations should use qualitative research because it deals with complex human processes that are always changing. In the international realm, the complexities of culture, politics and economics are compounded. Adler and Doktor (1986) argued that human interactions become more complex and communication is increasingly difficult as cultural and national boundaries are crossed. As public relations extends throughout the world, the "why's" become increasingly important as programs are tailored to meet the needs of specific publics (Sharpe 1992).

There are a number of practical reasons why qualitative research may be most appropriate for international public relations. When respondents speak different languages than that of the researcher, qualitative methods are adaptable to the changing and unknown circumstances (Rieger and Wong-Rieger 1988). Pauly (1991) and Agar (1980) suggested that any research is fraught with inherent problems of cultural biases of the researcher. Rather than apologizing for these biases, qualitative methods allow the researcher to distance personal perceptions and let the data emerge from the subject's own cultural perspectives. This improves the validity of the data (Babbie 1989).

The study reported in this chapter used the Delphi technique, a relatively new qualitative method. The Delphi is a structured group process "where individual judgments must be tapped and combined to arrive at ... decisions which cannot be made by one person," stated VanSlyke Turk (1986: 17). The method draws upon the knowledge of experts without having to gather these experts in one place. Responses can be obtained through technology. Therefore the process is particularly suited to a panel of experts who are geographically dispersed. Of course, such is the case in a global study of experts in international public relations.

A Delphi study typically involves four main steps: development of the initial Delphi question; determination of sample size and selection and contacting of respondents; development, distribution and analysis of three increasingly precise questionnaires to the respondents; and preparation of a final report. The process is fairly standard, but it can be modified according to the needs of a given research project. For example, many projects stop after the second questionnaire. Others use cassette tapes as a response method rather than self-administered questionnaires (Delbecq *et al.* 1975).

The Delphi technique is appropriate in a problem-identification situation in which there is a "lack of agreement or incomplete state of knowledge concerning either the nature of the problem or the components which must be included in a successful solution" (Delbecq *et al.* 1975: 5). VanSlyke Turk explained that "increasingly, situations faced by today's organization ... demand this kind of pooled judgment, for this is an age of 'maximum feasible participation'" (1986: '7).

For the study instrument fourteen propositions were created – eight dealing with the generic variable and six with the specific variable. Experts were asked to respond to the propositions based on their understanding of public relations in their own countries. The purpose was to begin a discussion on the appropriateness of the propositions in each country, with the aim of generating significant dialogue from the respondents – preferably including specific examples as to why the propositions would or would not be feasible in their country.

The propositions were as follows:

1   Excellent international public relations (IPR) is based on two-way symmetrical communication that pervades the organization worldwide. Top management at headquarters and senior managers in each market foster mutual trust, respect for others, and the need for establishing mutual benefits between the organization and all publics – internal and external – on whom its success or failure depends.

2   The two-way symmetrical philosophy will be reflected in the organizational culture and in internal communication worldwide. Management would foster participation and two-way symmetrical communication among its employees throughout the world.

3   Excellent public relations is a strategic management function working as part of and directly with senior management and the dominant coalition, worldwide. In an IPR program, the senior practitioner at headquarters will perform the managerial roles of boundary-spanning, counseling with the dominant coalition, and setting communication strategies that support organizational goals. Senior practitioners in each country must also perform strategic roles that identify local audiences, build relationships with them, and adapt quickly to changing local conditions.

4   Excellent IPR is integrated, meaning that worldwide, practitioners report to the public relations department at headquarters and work under a single umbrella.

5   An excellent public relations program is not subordinated to marketing, legal, or other organizational departments.

6   Senior practitioners all over the world will be qualified for their positions. They will be trained in public relations. They will understand the importance of advising senior managers and the dominant coalition, will be qualified to perform the managerial

roles of boundary-spanning and counseling, and will value and foster the use of two-way symmetrical communication. However, there will be variations in necessary qualifications directly related to the given culture.

7   In an excellent multinational, hiring and promotional practices would foster diversity by offering equal opportunities to women and "minorities" (those who typically are not accepted in the cultural mainstream) in every country.

8   Because the multinational organization faces a turbulent, dynamic environment, public relations is structured to be flexible and adaptable to that environment, worldwide.

9   A nation's level of development will affect the practice of public relations. A local component of an excellent IPR program will adjust to the particular nation's level of development and develop programs of communication to respond to that environment.

10   The political system of a given society will influence public relations. A local component of an excellent IPR program will respond to and build relationships with whatever political entity it faces.

11   An excellent IPR program will respond to varying indicators of cultural differences within and between each country. The way an organization deals with cultural indicators is important to the success or failure of the organization in each country.

12   Because language nuances vary from place to place, an excellent IPR program will place people in each country who understand those nuances and can deal with them most effectively (as opposed to transplanting expatriates, for example).

13   The potential for activism makes the international environment particularly turbulent, but the extent and type of activism may vary from society to society. Thus excellent IPR will contain a component in each country that can scan the environment, identify potential activist groups, and build programs to deal with them. The means for accomplishing this may vary from country to country and even within countries.

14   The mass media differ from country to country, with differing degrees of government control and of specialization and localization. Also, because of distance between host countries and organizational headquarters, media coverage can influence the way people think about multinationals. An effective local component of an excellent IPR program will build relationships with local media and with publics who may have received unrealistic pictures about the multinational organization.

(*Note*: Some of the propositions are condensed here to save space, and so they are not exact duplicates of those received by the respondents. The meaning is the same, however.)

A list of more than eighty names was produced, representing more han thirty countries. This list was divided into "A" and "B" candidates. Fifty were selected as "A" candidates, or those who could offer the most insight into public relations in their country. The remainder were placed in reserve in case an insufficient number of responses came from the first group. The instrument was sent with a cover letter to each of the fifty "A" candidates. Over the next six months, twenty-two responses were received from experts in eighteen countries – close to a 50 per cent response rate. Ten of the respondents were practitioners and thirteen were scholars in the field (some arguably fall into both categories). All but one sent written documents; the other sent a tape recording. Countries represented in the responses spanned five continents. They included the United States, Canada and Mexico in North America; Japan, Taiwan, Hong Kong and the People's Republic of China in Asia; the United Kingdom, the Netherlands, Germany, Spain, Slovenia and Yugoslavia in mainland Europe; Denmark and Norway in Scandinavia; Australia and New Zealand; and Saudi Arabia.

Initial results support generic/specific concept – with reservations and disclaimers!

A Delphi study is not a random, representative sampling that can be generalized to a larger population. Instead, it is a purposeful selection of respondents who are considered to be experts in a given field. Its main goal, as stated before, is not to discover all the answers, but to start a discussion on where a field is now and where it should be going. In this study a geographical balance of respondents and a balance of practitioners and scholars was sought. In this way it could be argued more confidently that the data were reflecting "pooled judgments" in an international context, as implied by VanSlyke Turk (1986). The downside, of course, is that in most cases the experts were the sole "voice" for a particular country.

Skeptics certainly could ask whether one practitioner or scholar represents the typical views in a given country. They could also ask whether scholars represent practitioners in any country, and vice-versa. They might argue that with the diversity of respondents, many of whose primary language is not English, there is a possibility for misinterpreting language and concepts in the instrument.

Also, the study is ongoing, and after analysis of the first round, a second instrument will be sent to all of the respondents. That instrument will contain declarative statements and a Likert scale with which the respondents can express the extent of their agreement or disagreement with the concept under discussion. From these responses can be obtained more comprehensive analyses of the respondents' feelings and suggestions about the state of international public relations.

As would be expected in a study of this type, the propositions were not greeted with consensus. Some of the propositions brought out polar extremes of thought in the responses. Some respondents gave examples that contradicted the examples supplied by others. In some instances the proposition itself did not seem to be well understood – or the respondents suggested that it was poorly worded.

Nevertheless, the information obtained so far is instructive. An examination of the preliminary data indicates certain patterns in the cumulative thinking of the experts. Thus, even at this stage, a summary of the data may be useful to the increasing numbers of public relations practitioners who are entering the international arena. The main trends are as follows.

Many respondents seemed to believe that the propositions were more valuable as normative statements than as current realities

One respondent summarized, "I think the propositions are all ideal in an ideal world – we do not have an ideal world." Another stated, "It is difficult to generalize about this. As a description of an ideal state I agree, but I would think that in most multinational companies, there is still a long way to go." And another: "To speak of mutual benefits is a speech easy to do but in normal activity is not applied." One respondent seemed to seek longingly for that perfected state, saying, "I think that it would be desirable, because only that kind of PR (and international PR) can be able to solve the future problems of the world. [But] this kind of international public relations will be possible only in the future."

Many of the comments about current management and public relations practices help to explain why the ideal is still far away. Several respondents said that for the propositions to be realistic, public relations people themselves must be qualified in all parts of the world. Apparently, this is not the case – even in the United States, where many of the modern practices were originated. Others said that it is virtually impossible – in some cases even undesirable – for management to foster a two-way symmetrical philosophy with all employees (one respondent said that some employees will never be loyal to the company, so why should the company foster equality with them?).

Two-way symmetrical communication was generally supported as a
foundation for excellent public relations, even though some seemed
uncomfortable with the term itself

The great majority of respondents seemed to value the concept of two-
way symmetrical communication – both as an organizational
worldview and as a way of practising public relations with important
publics. One stated that the ideal organization should not have only
one "dominant coalition," but several smaller, decentralized units with
"heterarchial, team/project-based" groups, "where power is dispersed"
(the respondent cited Tom Peters for this suggestion). Another
responded that to truly practice the two-way symmetrical model,
organizations have to go beyond mere "lip service by management.
Mission and vision statements are often an empty promise," she said.

According to some, one of the reasons symmetrical communication
is important is that excellent public relations cannot be achieved
without it. This is particularly the case in a transnational environment.
As one respondent stated,

> excellent international public relations can be achieved only
> through a top-down bottom-up collaboration. Each employee
> must be as committed as the top management at the local level or
> even the chairman of the board. Every single employee of the
> organization contributes to the success/failure of the company.

Some of the respondents pointed out that sometimes it is possible (but
not desirable) for organizations to foster the symmetrical culture in
their home country but not elsewhere. One discussed the situation
with some US companies who are known for a participative environment "at home," but in distant "developing nations" have been
charged with exploitation of the workers. Another said that he has seen
many multinationals who value and protect their expatriates at the
expense of local employees. This "ethnoarrogant" stance builds up
tremendous hostility in host countries and undermines everything the
organization is attempting to accomplish in its home territory.

Presumably the greatest reason for this discrepancy in most places is
that the organization moves abroad in the effort to expand sales while
reducing costs. One of the respondents explained that this philosophy
can backfire. He used a US multinational in his country as an example:

> In the US it is known for its participative culture, innovativeness
> and excellent employee policies ... but local behavior is

completely different: they have no commitment here and their only task is to increase sales. ... I also believe that at the end this is also hurting their sales here.

A few of the respondents, however, indicated that they would not even desire an organizational culture that practiced two-way symmetrical communication. One asked, "Is [proposition one] possible? No, I don't think so. Is it desirable? Well ... theoretically, yes, but in practice? No, I don't think so." Another argued that "international public relations is based on anything *other* than this philosophy [italics added]," because he viewed the practice as mostly "marketing, publicity, lobbying activity."

Some of the respondents noted that there are some problems with the term "two-way symmetrical communication." For example, one scholar in Europe said, "I'm not sure that you can describe two-way symmetrical communication in itself as a philosophy. It is underpinned by certain philosophical values which have their roots in Western philosophy, and this should be acknowledged." Actually, J. Grunig (1992c), the originator of the term insofar as public relations is concerned, has often acknowledged in his writings that the symmetrical theory was drawn from a variety of western philosophies and value systems. Indeed, it is not the term itself which is important, it is those very philosophies and value systems on which the term is based – as the respondent indicated:

More than one-third of respondents stated that "excellent public relations" and "excellent international public relations" are the same thing

Many of the respondents argued that "excellent public relations is the same as excellent international public relations." One explanation was that:

excellent PR in companies should be based on a philosophy of two-way symmetrical communication. ... Despite the fact that we still don't have large experience in international PR projects it is obvious that the same philosophy should be applied also in excellent international PR practice.

Another reason is "in the sense that these plans should be conceived and executed to achieve the same set of organizational goals."

Some of the respondents asserted that international public relations has essentially the same philosophy as domestic public relations, but differs in the way it is implemented. One stated that the main difference is in "relation to the location of the target groups as well as the range of effects of PR actions." Another added that "[international public relations] is exposed to a variety of environments so that there will be some spread in the specific way PR philosophy is carried out."

These statements are consistent with the arguments of J. Grunig, who explained that even within many countries, the circumstances and publics to which organizations must respond differ greatly. Therefore, boundary-spanning and symmetrical relationship building are foundations of excellent practice. The only elements added to international practice, he stated, are artificial borders that, as shown in recent years, can change quite quickly.

Some respondents, however, distinguished between domestic and international public relations more fundamentally, with the two-way symmetrical philosophy itself as the example. One debated whether "the two-way symmetrical model is really a suitable model to give insight in the nature of public relations," but acknowledged that for international public relations, "the idea of mutual influence and mutual trust is suitable." She said that excellent international public relations must include much more compromise, in this case between headquarters and host country, than is necessary domestically. Another concurred that "management's attitude to communication and hence the organization's structure and focus on communication probably has more importance in international than national public relations. ... Strong commitment to symmetrical two-way communication is required."

A major obstacle to effective public relations in almost every country is that organizations tend to position the function under marketing, instead of equal to it

This proposition generated strong feelings among respondents almost universally. The trend to position public relations under marketing creates problems for organizations, because they then focus on consumer audiences only and lose their ability to scan their multi-public environment for major threats to their operations. As one respondent said, in this reduced position public relations "is often an afterthought" and thus becomes "a waste of time." Another said that this "at the end hurts sales" – the very opposite effect to what organizations hope to achieve by placing public relations under marketing. The tendency is even worse for public relations scholars and practitioners, though, because it represents a strong threat to the very survival of the field.

Despite the strength of feeling, however, a "yes, but" attitude surfaced – yes, the functions should be separate, but realistically this may not happen for a long time. One respondent seemed to represent the views of many when he stated, "PR should be a separate function. I do no agree that this is possible because PR culture, even in large … multinational organizations, has not yet reached a standard of total excellence."

Another proposed that throughout the world, the emphasis on markets and customers is much greater than interest in public needs or expectations. Thus, as many respondents explained, public relations activities are often conducted within marketing perspectives and through marketing budgets. However, one respondent claimed that some multinationals are already separating the functions, either to contribute to national goals that are separate from headquarters goals or because they recognize the threats from outside the consumer publics.

There was only one counter-argument among the group. He said that public relations practitioners are not prepared to perform separate functions in an organization. He raised the question, "is it feasible to give a bunch of PR practitioners being specialists in everything from customer relations to staff and governmental relations? You cannot expect PR loners to give good advice … without having some sort of marketing background."

Recognition of the need for greater qualifications was almost unanimous, but there were disagreements on exactly what qualifications were needed

Several of the respondents said that public relations practitioners were not yet fully qualified to sit in management circles, develop organizational strategies, and carry out the delicate tasks of symmetry as proposed herein. One expressed the view that there are very few in any country who are qualified to perform the overall guidance and communication functions needed at headquarters. Most stated that public relations practitioners are still under-educated and under-qualified in most countries – including the United States, where public relations education supposedly abounds. Many of the countries are still hampered by the "ex-journalist" syndrome, where the emphasis is placed on writing and techniques other than strategic management and decision making.

As for what type of education is valuable for practitioners in the multinational – both at international and local level – there was wide debate. One person said, "Though an expert in public relations, the practitioner still needs to have good business sense so that all the work can ultimately be accounted for to the success of the organization." Another said, "I believe a practitioner must be a broad-gauged social scientist with highly developed communication and planning skills." Some respondents suggested that public relations ought to be taught at graduate level, after a broader undergraduate foundation had been established. One, however, argued that an MBA program with one course in public relations is insufficient academic training for the international public relations career.

The specific propositions elicited almost unanimous agreement, at least in terms of the variables mentioned being factors that influence local practice

To almost everyone, culture and language were obvious variables. One example of a memorable language failure was when an American-based multinational corporation attempted to run an advertisement in Denmark that asked, "Why does one man look at a waffle iron and think about breakfast, and another see a waffle iron and think about running shoes?" The advertisement made no sense to the Danes, who do eat waffles – but not for breakfast. Another discussed an advertisement that was supposedly adapted for New Zealand, but was actually a mere replay of an Australian advertisement. This offended the New Zealanders, whose culture is significantly different from Australia's but who are often considered by the rest of the world as a mere extension of Australia.

The proposition about activism was also mostly supported; nevertheless, it generated some interesting comments. Almost one-third of the respondents expressly stated that activism is a positive movement, and that it can also be positive for organizations that build relationships with activist groups. As one respondent summarized, "Without [activism] we may not need PR, and the level of activism can be a good predictor of the level of PR efforts needed." (Another expert, however, strongly objected to the phrase "deal with them" that had been used in the proposition. To her, that meant resorting to violent actions.)

The only controversy in the range of specific variables resulted from the proposition on level of development. An American summarized the apparent feelings of many by asking, "development in whose eyes?" A respondent from Europe pointed out that development can be defined differently by different people, and that it "will tend to vary with the environment." The gross national product used by economists to measure development is misleading and inappropriate, she said. As an example, she argued that in the northern United States, harsh winters raise the costs of keeping warm; "thus a thousand dollars is less of a value in northern Minnesota than in sunny Arizona." Generally, however, respondents agreed that level of development determines literacy rates, communication resources, education levels, etc. Therefore, they concurred, it is a factor in local public relations.

Closely allied to the level of development is the political system. Everyone agreed that political systems are a factor. Several argued that under a totalitarian government, public relations is not possible. Others offered views that organizations should not support or build relationships with oppressive dictators because it would be a violation of "higher ethical and moral standards" that should be universal.

The propositions concerning an integrated, worldwide public relations structure and the hiring of women and minority groups received the least agreement

Although the majority of respondents agreed, at least in part, to each of these concepts, these were the only two propositions that elicited more than half a dozen dissenting opinions. This seemed to be, at least in part, tied to the natural concern people have around the world to protect their own cultural mores and values. The integrated structure proposition seemed a threat to many of the respondents when they thought in terms of their own local autonomy. The proposition on employment of women and minorities seemed, to some, an imposition of western cultural values on their own long-held beliefs.

The structural proposition was interesting. The majority of respondents acknowledged that, in theory, integration of public relations is valuable. But when it came to practical implementation, there was widespread disagreement. Some argued that the local general manager is ultimately responsible for all operations in his or her country – that headquarters cannot and should not assume such responsibility. Others seemed worried that public relations driven from headquarters would somehow infringe upon the rights and strategies of the local unit. As one stated, "I cannot see how top-driven, 'consistent' programs can work. Again, this seems like the big boys' [US] view of the world."

In the case of employment practices, dissension arose mostly from strong cultural constraints within certain countries. The most adamant response to this proposition came from a country strongly influenced by Islam. This respondent said:

> multinational organizations should not hire women unless they are supposed to deal with the "women" public directly. In fact, they are not allowed to hire women for jobs where interpersonal communication with men is required and where men can do the job.

In Japan, where the constraints are not religious, the respondent said that women are "unfortunately still 'minorities' in the business world." Well-educated women there are hired by prestigious multinational organizations, "which are not as chauvinistic as Japanese counterparts."

One American respondent viewed this proposition as an attempt to impose American cultural values upon other countries with differing cultural values. But he extended the American influences beyond the mere hiring of minorities. "American values are resented and viewed as undesirable in many cases, with considerable justification," he said, and went on:

> Countries look at US unemployment rates, divorce rates, drug use, exposure of corruption in the media and politics, lack of cultural support for public health care, numbers of people in US prisons, etc. The result is that the values we honor are not seen as values but as reasons for decay.

Despite the arguments just presented, however, the majority of respondents agreed with the gist of each of these propositions. On structure, the caveat in the responses was echoed by one – that the proposition can work if "top PR management were well acquainted with the culture of each country," and sensitive to intercultural issues. With the hiring issue, many stated that an organization should value diversity, but ultimately should employ those who are the most qualified – regardless of race, religion or gender.

Discussion and summary

Only one round of this Delphi study has been completed. After the second round is completed and a more comprehensive analysis of the entire range of data is possible, the results and conclusions of this study may change. However, the data so far indicate general support for the generic and specific propositions. If support for the propositions carries through the next round, it should begin to lead to a theory of excellence in international public relations.

Somewhat surprisingly, agreement on most of the propositions seemed fairly universal. Of course there were exceptions, like the cultural reticence indicated by respondents around the idea of "equal employment practices." However, before the study began, it was anticipated that there would be much more diversity of thought that could be correlated to geographical differences. It was also anticipated that there might be resentment in some circles toward a study originating in the United States that proposes "universal" concepts. Some resentment did surface, but interestingly enough the strongest concerns came from North Americans!

Generally, however, it seems that the respondents support the notion that two-way symmetrical communication provides a foundation for excellence. This apparently holds true not only for domestic public relations activities, but for international practice as well. Certainly the concept needs more refining to be fully understood in an international context, but practitioners and scholars can be encouraged that a starting point is available.

As mentioned earlier, even when completed, a qualitative study is simply a starting point for further discussion. In the field of public relations, particularly, the international components of the practice are so new and complex that there is tremendous room for future research. Considering what respondents have indicated about the current expertise and qualifications of public relations practitioners, it seems that more research is desperately needed.

Notes

1 Some of the books written to date include: Kunczik 1990; Nally 1991; Wouters 1991. Recent articles include: Farinelli 1990; Wilkinson 1990; Fry 1992; Stanton 1992.
2 These include: Reisman 1990; Vogl 1990; Josephs and Josephs 1992; Hauss 1993.

References

Adler, N. J. (1991) *International Dimensions of Organizational Behavior*, 2nd edn, Boston MA: PWS-Kent.

Adler, N., Doktor, R. and Redding, S. G. (1986) 'From the Atlantic to the Pacific century: cross-cultural management reviewed', *Journal of Management*, 12 (2) 295–318.

Agar, M. H. (1980) *The Professional Stranger: An Informal Introduction to Ethnography*, San Diego CA: Academic Press.

Anderson, G. (1989) 'A global look at public relations', in B. Cantor (ed.) *Experts in Action*, 2nd edn, White Plains NY: Longman.

Angell, R. J. (1990) '"International PR": a misnomer', *Public Relations Journal*, 46 (10) 8.

Baalbaki, I. B. and Malhotra, N. K. (1993) 'Marketing management bases for international market segmentation; an alternate look at the standardization/customization debate', *International Marketing Review*, 10 (1) 19–44.

Babbie, E. (1989) *The Practice of Social Research*, 5th edn, Belmont CA: Wadsworth.

Baldwin, P. (1991) 'Corporate communications boost bottom line, study finds', *Dallas Morning News*, 12 February, 7-D.

Booth, A. (1986) 'Going global', *Public Relations Journal*, 42, 22–6.

Botan, C. (1992) 'International public relations: critique and reformulation', *Public Relations Review*, 18 (2) 149–59.

Brinkerhoff, D. W. and Ingle, M. D. (1989) 'Between blueprint and process: a structured flexibility approach to development management', *Public Administration and Development*, 9 (5) 487–503.

Carrington, J. (1992) 'Establishing a more strategic role in PR practice: why, how and when?', *Public Relations Quarterly*, 37 (1) 45–7.

Delbecq, A. L., Van de Ven, A. H. and Gustafson, D. H. (1975) *Group Techniques for Program Planning: A Guide to Nominal Group and Delphi Processes*, Glenview IL: Scott, Foresman.

Dilenschneider, R. L. (1992) *A Briefing for Leaders: Communication as the Ultimate Exercise of Power*, New York: HarperCollins.

Dowling, J. H. (1990) 'Public relations in the year 2000', *Public Relations Journal*, 46 (1) 6, 36.

Duffy, M. (1984) *Men and Beasts: An Animal Rights Handbook*, London: Granada.

Ellingsworth, H. W. (1977) 'Conceptualizing intercultural communication', in *Communication Yearbook I*, New Brunswick NJ: Transaction Books.

Epley, J. S. (1992) 'Public relations in the global village: an American perspective', *Public Relations Review*, 18 (2) 109–16.

Farinelli, J. L. (1990) 'Needed: a new US perspective on global public relations', *Public Relations Journal*, 46 (11) 18–19, 42.

Featherstone, M. (ed.) (1990) *Global Culture: Nationalism, Globalization and Modernity*, London: Sage.

Fry, S. L. (1992) ' '92 IPRA president tracks global issues', *Public Relations Journal*, 48 (3) 25–6.

Grunig, J. E. (1992a) 'Generic and specific concepts of multi-cultural public relations', paper presented at the Association for the Advancement of Policy, Research and Development in the Third World, Orlando FL.

——(1992b) 'A decade of accomplishment in public relations research: implications for other domains of communication', paper submitted to the *Journal of Communication*.

——(1992c) *Excellence in Public Relations and Communication Management*, Hillsdale NJ: Lawrence Erlbaum.

Grunig, J. E. and Grunig, L. A. (1991) 'Conceptual differences in public relations and marketing: the case of health-care organizations', *Public Relations Review*, 17 (3) 257–78.

Grunig, J. E. and Hunt, T. (1984) *Managing Public Relations*, New York: Holt, Rinehart and Winston.

Grunig, L. A. (1986) 'Activism and organizational response: contemporary cases of collective behavior', paper presented at the meeting of the Association for Education in Journalism and Mass Communication, Norman OK.

——(1991) 'Court-ordered relief from sex discrimination in the foreign service: implications for women working in development communication', in L. A. Grunig and J. E. Grunig (eds) *Public Relations Research Annual*, vol. 3, Hillsdale NJ: Lawrence Erlbaum, 85–115.

——(1992a) 'Strategic public relations constituencies on a global scale', *Public Relations Review*, 18 (2) 127–36.

——(1992b) 'Activism: how it limits the effectiveness of organizations and how excellent public relations departments respond', in J. E. Grunig (ed.) *Excellence in Public Relations and Communication Management*, Hillsdale NJ: Lawrence Erlbaum.

Hall, E. T. (1959) *The Silent Language*, Garden City NY: Doubleday.

Hampden-Turner, C. and Trompenaars, A. (1993) *The Seven Cultures of Capitalism*, New York: Doubleday.

Hauss, D. (1993) 'Global communications comes of age: five case histories prove power of integrated messages', *Public Relations Journal*, 49 (8) 22–6.

Haywood, R. (1991) 'Are the issues converging?', in M. Nally (ed.) *International Public Relations in Practice*, London: Kogan Page.

Hennessy, B. (1985) *Public Opinion*, 5th edn, Monterey CA: Brooks/Cole.

Hiebert, R. E. (1991) 'Public relations as a weapon of modern warfare', *Public Relations Review*, 17 (2) 107–16.

——(1992) 'Global public relations in a post-communist world: a new model', *Public Relations Review*, 18 (2) 117–26.

Hill, R. (1992) *We Europeans*, Brussels: Europublications.

——(1994) *Euromanagers and Martians*, Brussels: Europublications.

Hofstede, G. (1980) *Culture's Consequences*, Beverly Hills CA: Sage.

Howard, C. M. and Mathews, W. (1986) 'Global marketing: stop, look and listen', *Public Relations Quarterly*, 31 (2) 10–11.

Josephs, R. and Josephs, J. W. (1992) 'Spain gains world attention as public relations comes of age', *Public Relations Journal*, 48 (5) 18–22.

Kinzer, H. J. and Bohn, E. (1985) 'Public relations challenges of multinational corporations', paper presented to the International Communication Association Conference, Honolulu HI.

Kohara, T. (1989) 'International public relations: an overview', in B. Cantor (ed.) *Experts in Action*, 2nd edn, White Plains NY: Longman.

Kunczik, M. (1990) *Images of Nations and International Public Relations*, Bonn: Friedrich Ebert Stiftung.

Lesly, P. (1986) 'Multiple measurements of public relations', *Public Relations Review*, 12 (2) 3–8.

Marshall, C. and Rossman, G. B. (1989) *Designing Qualitative Research*, Newbury Park CA: Sage.

Martin, L. J. and Hiebert, R. E. (1990) *Current Issues in International Communication*, New York: Longman.

Naisbitt, J. (1994) *Global Paradox*, New York: William Morrow.

Nally, M. (ed.) (1991) *International Public Relations in Practice*, London: Kogan Page.

Negandhi, A. (1983) 'Cross-cultural management research: trend and future directions', *Journal of International Business Studies*, fall, 17–28.

Nigh, D. and Cochran, P. L. (1994) 'Issues management and the multinational enterprise', *Management International Review*, 27 (1) 4–12.

Ovaitt, F. Jr (1988) 'PR without boundaries: is globalization an option?', *Public Relations Quarterly*, 33 (1) 5–9.

Pauly, J. (1991) 'A beginner's guide to doing qualitative research in mass communication', *Journalism Monographs*, 125, February.

Pavlik, J. V. (1987) *Public Relations: What Research Tells Us*, Newbury Park CA: Sage Communication Text Series, vol. 16.

Pinsdorf, M. K. (1991) 'Flying different skies: how cultures respond to airline disasters', *Public Relations Review*, 17 (1) 37–56.

Pires, M. A. (1989) 'Working with activist groups', *Public Relations Journal*, 45 (4) 30–2.

Reed, J. M. (1989) 'International media relations: avoid self-binding', *Public Relations Quarterly*, 34 (2) 12–15.

Reisman, J. (1990) 'Taking on the world: global affiliates challenge the big guys', *Public Relations Journal*, 46 (3) 18–24.

Ricks, D., Toyne, B. and Martinez, Z. (1990) 'Recent developments in international management research', *Journal of Management*, 16 (2) 219–53.

Rieger, F. and Wong-Rieger, D. (1988) 'Model building in organizational/cross-cultural research: the need for multiple methods, indices and cultures', *International Studies of Management and Organizations*, 19 (3) 19–30.

Robertson, R. (1990) 'Mapping the global condition: globalization as the central concept', in M. Featherstone (ed.) *Global Culture: Nationalism, Globalization and Modernity*, London: Sage.

Rose, M. (1991) 'Activism in the 90s: changing roles for public relations', *Public Relations Quarterly*, 36 (3) 28–32.

Schmid, A. P. and de Graaf, J. (1982) *Violence as Communication: Insurgent Terrorism and the Western News Media*, London: Sage.

Sen, F. and Egelhoff, W. G. (1991) 'Six years and counting: learning from crisis management at Bhopal', *Public Relations Review*, 17 (1) 69–83.

Sharpe, M. L. (1992) 'The impact of social and cultural conditioning on global public relations', *Public Relations Review*, 18 (2) 103–7.

Sriramesh, K. (1992) 'Societal culture and public relations: ethnographic evidence from India', *Public Relations Review*, 18 (2) 201–11.

Sriramesh, K. and White, J. (1992) 'Societal culture and public relations', in J. E. Grunig (ed.) *Excellence in Public Relations and Communication Management*, Hillsdale NJ: Lawrence Erlbaum.

Stanton, E. M. (1992) 'PR's future is here: worldwide, integrated communications', *Public Relations Quarterly*, 37 (1) 46–7.

Tayeb, M. H. (1988) *Organizations and National Culture: A Comparative Analysis*, London: Sage.

Toth, E. L. (1986) 'Broadening research in public affairs', *Public Relations Review*, 12 (2) 27–36.

Traverse-Healy, T. (1991) 'The corporate aspect', in M. Nally (ed.) *International Public Relations in Practice*, London: Kogan Page.

VanSlyke Turk, J. (1986) 'Forecasting tomorrow's public relations', *Public Relations Review*, 12 (3) 12–21.

Verčič, D., Grunig, L. A. and Grunig, J. E. (1993) 'Global and specific principles of public relations: evidence from Slovenia', paper presented to the International Conference on The State of Education and Development, Association for the Advancement of Policy, Research and Development in the Third World, Cairo.

Vogl, F. (1990) 'Closing the gap: new approaches to international media relations', *Public Relations Journal*, 46 (7) 18–20.

Wilcox, D., Ault, P. H. and Agee, W. K. (1992) *Public Relations: Strategies and Tactics*, 3rd edn, New York: HarperCollins.

Wilkinson, A. (1990) 'Globalization: are we up to the challenges?', *Public Relations Journal*, 46 (1) 12–13.

Winner, P. (1990) *Effective PR Management: A Guide to Corporate Survival*, London: Kogan Page.

Wouters, J. (1991) *International Public Relations*, New York: Amacom.

Part IV

Historical-German perspectives of public relations

8 The origins and development of public relations in Germany and Austria

Karl Nessmann

The problems of writing a history of PR

It is necessary to start by pointing out that it is rather difficult to trace the historical development of "Öffentlichkeitsarbeit"/public relations (henceforth abbreviated to PR), and just as difficult to determine the origins of PR. This is because research in this field is still at an embryonic stage. A glance at the literature reveals that, although there are numerous publications on PR theory and practice, they contain very little information on the history of PR in German-speaking countries. Having said this, there are a few isolated references to the subject in various textbooks and reference books (cf. for example, Oeckl 1993a; 1993b; Brauer 1993) but they are generally not very comprehensive and rely too much on the history of American PR, which is treated in much greater detail than the German and Austrian history. Of course, evidence for and examples of the history of PR in German-speaking countries are cited but they are not followed up systematically (cf. also Barthenheier 1982; Binder 1993; Kunczik 1994).

The problems involved in tracing the historical origins and developments of PR are a consequence of the somewhat vague definition of PR and its ensuing identity crisis. Even today, it is still not clear what tasks, functions and activities can be assigned to the field of PR work, and uncertainty surrounds the antecedents of PR. If press offices are considered to be the forerunners of PR, then a historical overview must start in the nineteenth century. If, however, PR is interpreted generally as "relations with the public," then this is surely eternally relevant and PR is as old as human thought. In this case, PR would date back to Adam and Eve, to the point when people had to win over the confidence of others. With this non-scientific interpretation, historical figures and heroes are often quoted as the precursors of PR. Thus, for the American PR pioneer Edward L. Bernays, for example,

Julius Caesar was the original PR man. Albert Oeckl, one of the sages of German PR, cites religious examples (Moses, Buddha, Mohammed, etc.). Indeed, PR anecdotes range from classical antiquity through the middle ages right up to the nineteenth century. For other authors, the origins of PR coincide with the emergence of the term or the profession, such as the work of Edward L. Bernays and Ivy Lee in the United States at the beginning of the twentieth century, or Carl Hundhausen in Germany with his first PR publication in 1937 and again after the war in 1947. Such key moments are often identified as "the birth of PR." Admittedly, the appearance of a term or the inception of organizational forms does not say much about actual developments. Still, most researchers, including the author of this chapter, would agree that the form of communication or phenomenon known as PR evolved alongside, and in reaction to, the nascent European enlightenment in the seventeenth and eighteenth centuries, and the emerging industrialization and the development of mass media in the nineteenth century (cf. for example, Scharf 1971; Binder 1983; Saxer 1991; Hategan 1991; Stadler 1992; Ronneberger and Rühl 1992; Rühl 1994; Kunczik 1994; Liebert 1995a). Thus a historical survey of PR would start in the eighteenth century and, in view of the primary objective to concentrate on its origins, end in the mid-twentieth century with the establishment of PR as a profession. The proposed subdivision into three phases (eighteenth/nineteenth centuries to the start of the twentieth; 1914–45; 1945 onwards) should not be taken to suggest periodization along the lines of Oeckl (1993b), but merely serves as a pragmatic, and chronological, structural approach. Quite simply, the necessary research has not yet been done to present a fairly precise classification based on the substance of the history of PR. Furthermore, a well-founded history of PR would have to differentiate between various fields of activity, for example, PR in politics, business or administration, or the history of PR as a profession (cf. for example, Hategan 1991) and analyze the relevant social (economic, technical, political, cultural, etc.) conditions in society. In other words, it is not so much a question of determining a date for the emergence of PR as of uncovering a complex causal network. This is beyond the scope of this chapter, as research on the history of PR is still too preoccupied with gleaning historical data and facts. Thus this chapter is limited to a survey of the important key moments by which the origins and developments of PR in Germany and Austria can be traced in chronological order.

Phase 1: The eighteenth/nineteenth centuries to the early twentieth century

As stated above, the origins of the form of communication known as PR, in the modern sense of the word, must be considered in the light of political, cultural, economic and technical developments in the eighteenth and nineteenth centuries, in other words in terms of industrialization, new forms of technology and rationalization; increasing democracy, literacy and urbanization; and last but not least the emergence of mass media, journalism and publicity.

The origins of practical PR

Documentary evidence of the still very fragmentary history of PR dates back as far as the eighteenth century. Hategan, for example, writing on the beginnings of state-run PR (1991), refers to the systematic news policy of Frederick the Great (1712–86) who bolstered his foreign policy by circulating favorable items and suppressing bad news. Napoleon is also mentioned, as he always had a mobile printing press with him on his military campaigns and attempted to create a favorable atmosphere with the help of a news office. He did not only pursue a policy of actively providing information, but also ensured that foreign newspapers were scanned every day in what can be seen as an antecedent of modern press cuttings practice. Indeed, all these communicative activities can be regarded as forerunners of PR. Kunczik (1995) reported that sources exist which prove that Prussia initiated an image campaign of sorts as early as 1807. Furthermore, a certain Friedrich List is said to have suggested to a group of German factory owners in 1834 that they should pay more attention to the general public and set up newspapers for employees in their factories, amongst other things. Liebert (1995a) mentions the so-called "Amtsblätter," or official gazettes in the eighteenth and nineteenth centuries as early examples of municipal public relations work. These cases illustrate that communicative activities which can certainly be classified as PR took place at a very early date, even before the first press offices were set up in politics, business and administration and the term PR was actually coined.

According to Oeckl (1993a, 1993b), the first state-run information office in Germany (known as the "Ministerialzeitungsbüro" or Ministerial Newspaper Bureau) was set up in 1848; in 1851 it was renamed the "Zentralstelle für Preßangelegenheiten" or the Central Office for Matters of the Press. 1851 also saw the start of industrial

public relations, and Oeckl cites the participation of the German industrialist Krupp at the Great Exhibition that year in London as a
particularly original example of PR. Alfred Krupp took great trouble to
transport a two-ton block of steel to London. Krupp's stand was a real
sensation at the Great Exhibition and the company became a household
name throughout the world. It had crafted an image for itself, as we
would say today. In the mid-nineteenth century, other industrial
concerns, such as Henkel, Bahlsen, AEG, Siemens, etc. also devoted
their energies to communicative activities. In 1857, for example, the
industrialist Gustav von Mevissen demanded the "greatest possible
publicity" and a "comprehensive business report" for his company
(Haacke 1969: 6, quoted in Barthenheier 1982: 5). And the selfsame
Alfred Krupp, in an internal communication to his employees of 27
November 1866, wrote words to the effect that it was time to arrange
for the circulation of regular and truthful reports on the factory in the
newspapers (according to Hategan 1991). A few years later, on 7 March
1870, Krupp provided more important evidence of the company's
communication policies when he called for someone to be responsible
for evaluating international press reports on the Krupp concern, and for
dispatching brochures translated into various languages throughout the
world. The object of this work was to persuade important people and
authorities to appreciate Krupp's products. Hategan is justified in
stating that Krupp's words closely resemble the definition of international public relations work given in modern PR literature. As several
diploma and doctoral theses being written (in German) at present
include detailed analyses of the historical development of PR in various
German industrial concerns, we can look forward to a series of interesting contributions to the history of PR.

According to Klimek (1979; cf. also Haas 1987), the prehistory of
Austrian PR commenced in 1867 with communicative activities initi-
ated by the trade unions, in particular the union paper issued that year.
The informational activities of the state during the Austro-Hungarian
monarchy (1867–1914) are also cited as further evidence of embryonic
PR activities in Austria.

Back in Germany, a "Preßdezernat" or Press Department was set up
in the Foreign Ministry in 1871. The first press office in a German
company was established by Krupp in 1893. Other industrial concerns
followed suit and set up their own departments to carry out practical
PR tasks in the modern sense of the word, although, as Oeckl rightly
points out (1993b), it was not called public relations at the time
because the term had not yet been invented. Brauer (1993) states that
in those days three terms were used to classify these tasks, namely

press office or press department; economic department, and technical-literary department. In 1894, the German Reich Navy commissioned so-called "Press officers" to provide information and receive visitors on all the larger ships. The aim of their work was to "cultivate good rela-:ions with the general public" (Oeckl 1993b: 18). In 1906, the first municipal press office was opened in Magdeburg (cf. Liebert 1995b). In the early years of the twentieth century, associations also began to practice public relations work, the first being the Hanseatic League, set up in 1909 to promote trade and industry (Hansabund zur Förderung der gewerblichen Wirtschaft). Other associations and pressure groups followed (cf. Oeckl 1993b; Brauer 1993).

The origins of theoretical PR

Academics also began to show interest in the phenomenon of PR from the mid-nineteenth century. The subject of many a scientific analysis was the relationship between the media on the one hand and press offices on the other, in particular the influence of large commercial enterprises on coverage in the newspapers. The German communication scientist Michael Kunczik (1994) lists Heinrich Wuttke (1866), Tony Kellen (1908) and Max Weber (1911) as evidence that scientific interest in PR began at quite an early stage. In an article entitled "Die deutschen Zeitschrifen und die Entstehung der öffentlichen Meinung" ("German newspapers and the development of public opinion") Wuttke, for example, criticized the undue influence of press offices, and described the larger German newspapers as being "larded" with essays which can be traced back to a common source (Wuttke 1866, according to Kunczik 1994). In his article "Das Zeitungswesen" ("The newspapers") Kellen not only referred to state-run press bureaux or press departments as influencing public opinion, but also to the activities of political parties and commercial associations. In his speech to the First German Sociologists' Conference in 1910, Weber analyzed the interrelation between business and mass media, posing the question as to the actual source of news items in the final analysis. There was also discussion at the Seventh German Sociologists' Conference, held in Berlin in 1930, where the topic was press and public opinion. Analysis of the conference proceedings reveals that the delegates engaged in a very critical debate on the increasingly visible phenomenon of PR. In the lectures and discussions it was said, for example, that press offices had the habit of producing, doctoring and fashioning news and that the press was exploited by political and commercial interests. It was even claimed that the press could no longer do justice to its original task as a critic of public affairs, given such massive influence from outside. At the same time, the conference thoroughly analyzed the foundations of PR activities. Eckhardt, for example, stated that large businesses and associations required a certain degree of public confidence and recognition, and that without authority and popularity, no association or company could hold its own and generally maintain its economic policies (cf. Eckhardt 1931, according to Kunczik 1994). These arguments must appear very familiar today, as they are such an integral part of PR terminology.

The examples given above show that in German-speaking countries and in Germany in particular, a decidedly critical analysis of the phenomenon of PR was well under way, even before Carl Hundhausen introduced the term to the German language in 1937.

Comparison with the US

Thus this (first) developmental stage was not at all influenced by what was going on in PR in the United States. There PR had emerged in the mid-nineteenth century and reached its first pinnacle at the start of the twentieth century with Ivy Lee's "Declaration of Principles" in 1906. This phase of American development has been called the "public be damned" and the "public be informed" period (cf. Barthenheier 1982). One fundamental difference between the development of PR in Germany/Austria and the United States is that early PR activities in America were much more defensive in nature (e.g. PR in defense of and as a legitimation for "big business" versus criticism in the investigative journalism of muckrakers). In contrast, the early days of PR in Germany were characterized by active information work.

Thus the evidence presented here proves that it is possible to speak of an independent tradition of PR in Europe. In other words, the form of communication known as PR is not an American "invention," as many would have us believe, which was then exported wholesale to Europe many years later (after the Second World War, apparently), but could, at a pinch, be described as a "re-import" (cf. Liebert 1995a: 4).

Phase 2: 1914–45

According to Oeckl (1993b), the second developmental stage of PR in German-speaking countries started concurrently with the First World War in 1914. The evolution of press work from 1914 to 1918 was totally marked by the war. Thus a "Kriegspresseamt" or War Press Office was set up in Germany in 1915, followed by an information department under army command in 1916, a "Zentralstelle des reich-samtlichen Pressedienstes" or Central Office of the Reich Press Service, in 1917 and, shortly before the end of the war, the "Reichsamt für Presse- und Propagandatätigkeit beim Reichskanzler" or the Reich Bureau for Press and Propaganda Activities for the Chancellor of the German Reich, in 1918. These political (state-run) press or propaganda activities were, however, highly amateurish, without any clear objectives or knowledge of the laws of public relations work (cf. Oeckl 1993b).

Such detailed research on similar war information offices has not yet been carried out in the case of Austria. Fragmentary records of PR activities in Austria only reappear in connection with the First Republic (1918–38), when the Austrian government began to issue press reports in periodical publications. The government published parliamentary reports in its own information bulletins, and held press conferences (cf. Klimek 1979)

Between the wars (1918–38), the number of press offices in Germany shot up, in both the state and the commercial sector, with similar, smaller-scale developments in Austria (cf. Binder 1983; Oeckl 1993a; 1993b). First and foremost, it was the business sector which tried to foster understanding and build up confidence with the help of a wide variety of communicative activities, still unaware of the term PR but familiar with the concept of "media relations."

The Austrian Chamber of Commerce, for example, employed a journalist as a press spokesperson in 1927 who was not only responsible for press work but also edited an internal paper for the Chamber of Commerce (cf. Klimek 1979). In this period, new communicative methods were also tried out. The Austrian businessman Julius Meindl, for example, was very progressive in the way he dealt with journalists. He was always inviting the economic editors of the major daily newspapers to economic and political discussions in his office, thus guaranteeing journalistic sympathies (cf. Klimek 1979).

The National Socialist period and the Third Reich, which began when Hitler assumed power in 1933, saw to it that PR did not develop any further. Indeed, if anything, it took a step backwards towards propaganda. And even the first publication in German on the topic of PR, in 1937, could do nothing to change that. It was Carl Hundhausen who first introduced the American term to the German-speaking world when he came back from a trip to America and wrote his first article with the title "Public Relations: ein Reklamekongreß für Werbefachleute der Banken in der USA" ("Public relations: a publicity congress for advertisers in banking in the USA"), followed by a second paper a year later on "Public relations" (Hundhausen 1938). Neither article met with a visible response, because the English term was highly undesirable at the time, as Hundhausen later pointed out (cf. Oeckl 1993a). Developments in PR were also impossible for the reason mentioned above, namely that National Socialist propaganda methods prevailed and Goebbels forced the press and broadcasting corporation to toe the line by dictatorial means. The Third Reich was characterized by censorship, the outlawing of "critical" newspapers, professional bans for opposition journalists, linguistic regulations and silence decrees, or "Schweigegebote."

Comparison with the US – mutual influences

This (second) developmental stage in German-speaking countries also progressed fairly independently of events on the other side of the Atlantic. Indeed, the Americans had been working on methods of PR since the First World War and had initiated a very successful recruiting campaign. The "Committee on Public Information" founded by President Wilson did not only muster public opinion in favor of the necessary measures for the unpopular campaign in distant Europe, but also brought the "freedom loan" into being very successfully (cf. Oeckl 1993b). Between the wars, the PR branch experienced a veritable boom, with PR offices proliferating. Ivy Lee and Edward Bernays were the founders and at the same time the stars of the new profession. Bernays commenced academic work on PR and, as early as 1923, held his first lecture at New York University. Later he would divide developments in the United States at that time into four very different phases, namely "World War I," the "Rise of a new profession," "The public relations profession," and the "Period of World War II."

As far as the question of mutual influence is concerned, the Europeans did take note of American developments, especially the successful recruitment campaign (cf. Oeckl 1993b) and various communicative activities in municipal public relations work (cf. Liebert 1995a), but this had no effect on the professionalization of PR practice. In contrast, the development of American PR at the time was very strongly influenced by a German-speaker (from a theoretical point of view at least), namely the Austrian Sigmund Freud. Edward L. Bernays, a native Austrian born in Vienna, was the first, and for a long time undoubtedly the most influential American theorist in those early days of PR, and he also happened to be Sigmund Freud's nephew. Bernays, who helped Freud publish English versions of his work in the early 1920s, took over his uncle's theories of mass psychology in both his theoretical and practical PR work, sometimes to a very great degree. As Bernays later admitted in his biography, Freud had influenced him greatly (cf. Bernays 1967).

Phase 3: from 1945 onwards

According to Oeckl (1993a), the third stage of PR in German-speaking countries begins after the Second World War, in 1945. In Germany the history of PR must now be divided into east and west, just like the country itself, although no details will be given here of developments in the German Democratic Republic.

Again, it was Hundhausen who used the concept in German for the first time in 1947, in an essay entitled "Public relations" (Hundhausen 1947). Some authors take this date as the birth of PR in Germany, although references are always made to the influence of the western occupation forces and subsidiaries of American PR agencies. In his work on the history of PR, Oeckl claims that public relations work in Germany really began on the basis of practical suggestions from the occupying powers, the Americans in particular, after the currency reform in 1948 (cf. Oeckl 1993a). Of course, Oeckl here means the modern forms of PR, since communicative activities which are classifiable as PR have been around for much longer, as described above.

In Austria the developments began some years later and on a much slower scale, at least in connection with the business world (cf. Haas 1987). In the state and public sector, PR developed more briskly, in particular within pressure groups, the Chamber of Commerce, political parties and public offices. This specifically Austrian evolution of public relations work can be largely explained by socio-political circumstances. Austria has a virtually closed system of associations and political parties and a system of "Wirtschaft- und Sozialpartnershaft" or Economic and Social Partnership, which is unique in western industrialized countries. Even in Austrian businesses, institutions and organizations, PR is different from its German equivalent in terms of its tasks and functions. Whereas services for employees (cultural events, sports and continuation courses, etc.) constitute the major part of public relations work in the Federal Republic, other departments created especially for this purpose carry out these tasks in Austria (cf. Klimek 1979).

Back in Germany, the appearance of PR was accompanied by numerous attempts to Germanize the American term. At that time, foreign words, and Americanisms in particular, were generally unpopular, coupled with strong tendencies towards "linguistic puritanism." In this light, the weekly magazine *Die Zeit* announced a competition in February 1951 with the aim of finding a suitable translation for the term PR. Although 1,522 entries were submitted, the first prize was not awarded, as not one of the proposals was really satisfactory. On 24 April 1951, *Die Zeit* published the results. The jury considered the suggestion "cultivation of contacts" ("Kontaktpflege") to be the best of a bad bunch, followed by "cultivation of confidence" ("Vertrauenspflege") and "courting confidence" ("Vertrauenswerbung") (cf. Kunczik 1993: 6). In the same year, Albert Oeckl (head of the Press Office of the German Council of Trade and Industry, the DIHT, at the time) used the term "Öffentlichkeitsarbeit" in the DIHT's business report. Oeckl himself claimed that he had first invented the term the year before, i.e. in 1950, because the DIHT management at the time had rejected the American term "public relations" (cf. Oeckl 1993a). The idea behind Oeckl's term was that public relations work above all involves working in public, with the public and for the public (cf. Oeckl 1976). Even though many PR theorists and practitioners are still not very happy with the German translation "Öffentlichkeitsarbeit" (cf. Ronneberger and Rühl 1992), it is the only term which has managed to assert itself in German. In the meantime, the term "public relations" has become an acceptable word in colloquial speech and is used as a synonym for "Öffentlichkeitsarbeit." It is no longer regarded as a threat to German culture (cf. Kunczik 1993).

Developments from 1950 onwards

It is beyond the scope of this chapter to trace the rapid development of PR in theory and practice from this point onwards, given the aim of concentrating on the forerunners and origins of PR in Germany and Austria. However, a brief comment is warranted. After the war, press offices in politics, industry and administration were set up once again. The early 1950s saw publication of the first papers on PR (for detailed references cf. Oeckl 1993a; 1993b; Brauer 1993). Professional associations for PR were founded: in 1958 in Germany and as late as 1975 in Austria. The theoretical and practical development of PR took its course.

Taking the four models of PR defined by Grunig and Hunt (1984) as a starting point, the development of PR in German-speaking countries over the last fifty years (from 1945 to the present day) can be summarized as follows. PR has passed through all four phases of PR, namely publicity, information, asymmetrical communication and symmetrical communication, and is in the process of developing from a simple publicity/information activity into a complex, socially oriented symmetrical form of communication for management, echoing a similar evolution in the United States over a much shorter period of time.

Comparison with the US – mutual influences

As far as a comparison with the history of American PR is concerned, it is clear that the first two development stages in Germany and Austria (eighteenth/nineteenth centuries to 1945) proceeded largely independently of events in America. By contrast, the third stage (1945 onwards) is characterized by ideas travelling in both directions, with the Americans influencing Germans and Austrians much more than vice-versa in the past and present. In other words, PR theory and practice were devised by Americans, taken up by Europeans, especially German authors, and further developed in their own right in a European context. Here some examples from the early days of PR are cited.

Edward L. Bernays, above all others, strongly influenced German and Austrian authors and the pioneer Carl Hundhausen in particular, who not only used Bernays' theoretical approach in his work, but also in his terminology. Thus, in his book on the theory and systematics of PR (1969), Hundhausen used the terms "adjustment," "engineering of consent" and "feedback." In doing so he wanted to demonstrate above all that PR is a social process of mutual communication (quoted in Kunczik 1993). Oeckl, as the second great pioneer of German PR and the author quoted most frequently (cf. Signitzer 1992a), also followed Bernays' theories, particularly with reference to mass society.

Those working on PR in Austria after the war tended to be influenced by American developments in PR in a rather indirect manner, as they first looked to German colleagues for theoretical and practical inspiration. Of course, Edward L. Bernays also directly influenced the Austrian PR scene in the postwar period, as he happened to have been born in Vienna and cultivated his contacts with Austrian friends and relations on a regular basis.

In spite of the strong American orientation of German-speaking PR experts, it would be wrong to assume that American PR concepts were taken over wholesale and uncritically. It is truer to say that they were adapted and developed independently against the background of German and Austrian circumstances. Even the earliest publications in German made it clear that the will was there to develop PR in Germany and Austria in its own right. Herbert Gross, for example, wrote in his book on modern public relations work (1951) that it was not a case of transposing foreign methods, but of developing attitudes justified by the German situation and the German character (according to Oeckl 1993b). Even Hundhausen (1951) and other German pioneers (cf. Flieger and Ronneberger 1993) knew right from the start that the American situation could not be transposed to Germany or Austria, and that the prevailing conditions, prerequisites and forms of the media and communication society in Germany and Austria had to be taken into account. This comes out very clearly in the latest theoretical developments, although that topic must be left to another paper (cf. Signitzer 1992b; Ronneberger and Rühl 1992; Bentele 1994). Finally, the most recent intercultural comparative analyses (cf. Coombs *et al.* 1994; MacManus 1994; Nessmann 1995) reveal the great extent to which cultural aspects influence the development of PR in different countries.

The origins of PR in Germany and Austria – key developments

Phase 1: the eighteenth/nineteenth centuries to the early twentieth century

Practical PR

1712–86	Systematic news policy of Frederick the Great and Napoleon
1807	Image campaign in Prussia
1834	First PR consultation (Friedrich List)
1848	Ministerial Newspaper Office (March Revolution)
	Central Office for Matters of the Press
1851	Start of industrial PR in Germany
	(Krupp's block of steel at the Great Exhibition, London)
	(Gustav von Mevissen, 1857)
	(Krupp's principles of PR, 1866 and 1870)
1867	Start of trade union PR in Austria (first union paper and other PR activities)
1871	Press Department (Foreign Ministry)
1893	First press office in a German company (Krupp)
1894	First press officers (German Reich Navy)
1906	First municipal press office, Magdeburg (Germany)
1909	Start of PR in associations and pressure groups (Hanseatic League for the promotion of trade and industry)

Theoretical PR

1866	Heinrich Wuttke: the German newspapers and the development of public opinion
.908	Tony Kellen: "The newspapers"
1910	Max Weber: speech at First German Sociologists' Conference
1930	Seventh German Sociologists' Conference in Berlin on the topic of "The press and public opinion"

Phase 2: 1914–45

1914–18	First World War: information department and press service within army command
1918–38	Growing number of press offices in politics and industry
1937	First article in German on the topic of public relations, Carl Hundhausen
1939–45	Second World War: national socialist propaganda, censorship, outlawing "critical" newspapers, professional bans for opposition journalists, linguistic regulations and "Schweigegebote"

Phase 3: 1945 onwards

1947	Essay by Carl Hundhausen on public relations
1951	*Die Zeit* competition to find a suitable translation of the American designation
	Introduction of the term "Öffentlichkeitsarbeit" by Albert Oeckl (working in public, with the public and for the public)
	First books published on PR (e.g. Herbert Gross: *Moderne Meinungspflege*)
	Press offices in politics, industry and administration set up once again
1958–75	Professional associations for PR founded (1958 in Germany, 1975 in Austria) – courses developed at universities and private schools
	Professionalization and development of PR from a simple publicity/information activity into a complex, socially oriented symmetrical form of communication for management

References

Barthenheier, G. (1982) 'Allgemeine Grundlagen der Öffentlichkeitsarbeit', in G. Haedrich *et al.* (eds) *Öffentlichkeitsarbeit: Dialog Zwischen Institutionen und Gesellschaft, ein Handbuch*, Berlin/New York: de Gruyter.

Bentele, G. (1994) 'Public Relations und Wirklichkeit. Beitrag zu einer Theorie der Öffentlichkeitsarbeit', in G. Bentele and K. Hesse (eds) *Publizistik in der Gesellschaft: Festschrift für Manfred Rühl*, Konstanz: Universitätsverlag.

Bernays, E. L. (1967) *Biographie einer Idee: Die Hohe Schule der PR. Lebenserinnerungen von Edward L. Bernays*, Düsseldorf/Vienna: Econ Verlag (*Biography of an Idea: Memoirs of Public Relations Counsel Edward L. Bernays*, New York: 1965).

Binder, E. (1983) *Die Entstehung Unternehmerischer Public Relations in der Bundesrepublik Deutschland*, Münster: Lit Verlag Hopf.

Brauer, G. (1993) *ECON-Handbuch der Öffentlichkeitsarbeit*, Düsseldorf/Vienna/New York/Moscow: Econ Verlag.

Coombs, W. T., Holladay, S., Hasenauer, G. and Signitzer, B. (1994) 'A comparative analysis of international public relations: identification and interpretation of similarities and differences between professionalization in Austria, Norway, and the United States', *Journal of Public Relations Research*, 6 (1) 23–39.

Flieger, H. and Ronneberger, F. (eds) (1993) *Deutschland. Festschrift zum 100. Geburtstag von Carl Hundhausen*, Wiesbaden: Verlag für Deutsche Wirtschaftsbiographien.

Grunig, J. E. and Hunt, T. (1984) *Managing Public Relations*, New York: Holt, Rinehart and Winston.

Haacke, W. (1969) 'Public Relations – oder das Vertrauen der Öffentlichkeit', in *Politik und Zeitgeschichte, Beilage zur Wochenzeitung das Parlament*, B 48/69, 3–16.

Haas, M. (1987) *Public Relations Berufsrealität in Österreich*, Vienna: Orac Verlag.

Hategan, Ch. (1991) *Berufsfeld Öffentlichkeitsarbeit: Eingrenzung für die Aus- und Weiterbildung*, Hamburg: Tangens Systemverlag.

Hundhausen, C. (1937) 'Public Relations: ein Reklamekongreß für Werbefachleute der Banken in USA', *Die Deutsche Werbung*, Heft 19, 1054.

——(1938) 'Public Relations', *Zeitschrift für Betriebswirtschaft*, 2, 48–61.

——(1947) 'Public Relations', *Westdeutsche Wirtschaftskorrespondenz*, 2, 122, 2.

——(1951) *Werbung um Öffentliches Vertrauen: Public Relations*, Essen: Girardet Verlag.

——(1969) *Public Relations: Theorie und Systematik*, Berlin: de Gruyter.

Klimek, E. (1979) 'Öffentlichkeit und Öffentlichkeitsarbeit', dissertation, University of Vienna.

Kunczik, M. (1993) *Public Relations: Konzepte und Theorien*, Cologne: Böhlau.

——(1994) 'Public Relations: angewandte Kommunikationswissenschaft oder Ideologie? Ein Beitrag zur Ethik der Öffentlichkeitsarbeit', in W.

Armbrecht and U. Zabel (eds) *Normative Aspekte der Public Relations*, Opladen: Westdeutscher Verlag.

——(1995) 'Deutsche PR-Geschichte', lecture at the annual meeting of the German Society for Journalism and Communication Science (DGPuK), Stuttgart-Hohenheim, 16 June.

Liebert, T. (1995a) 'Über einige Inhaltliche und Methodische Probleme einer PR-Geschichts-schreibung (u.a. am Beispiel kommunaler Öffentlichkeitsarbeit)', paper presented at the annual meeting of the German Society for Journalism and Communication Science (DGPuK), Stuttgart-Hohenheim, 16 June.

——(1995b) 'History of municipal public relations in Germany', paper presented at the Second International Public Relations Research Symposium, Lake Bled, Slovenia.

MacManus, T. (1994) 'A comparative analysis of public relations in Austria and the United Kingdom', paper presented at the First International Public Relations Research Symposium, Lake Bled, Slovenia.

Nessmann, K. (1995) 'Public relations in Europe: a comparison with the United States', *Public Relations Review*, 21 (2) 151–60.

Oeckl, A. (1976) *PR-Praxis: Der Schlüssel zur Öffentlichkeitsarbeit*, Düsseldorf/Vienna: Econ Verlag.

——(1993a) 'Geschichte der Public Relations', in D. Pflaum and W. Pieper (eds) *Lexikon der Public Relations*, 2nd edn, Landsberg/Lech: Verlag Moderne Industrie.

——(1993b) 'Anfänge und Entwicklung der Öffentlichkeitsarbeit', in H. Fischer and U. Wahl (eds) *Public Relations-Öffentlichkeitsarbeit: Geschichte, Grundlagen, Grenzziehungen*, Frankfurt/Berlin/Berne/New York/Paris/Vienna: Peter Lang Verlag.

Ronneberger, F. and Rühl, M. (1992) *Theorie der Public Relations: Ein Entwurf*, Opladen: Westdeutscher Verlag.

Rühl, M. (1994) 'Europäische Public Relations: Rationalität, Normativität und Faktizität', in W. Armbrecht and U. Zabel (eds) *Normative Aspekte der Public Relations*, Opladen: Westdeutscher Verlag.

Saxer, U. (1991) 'Public Relations als Innovation', *Media Perspektiven*, 5, 273–90.

Scharf, W. (1971) 'Public relations in der Bundesrepublik Deutschland: ein kritischer Überblick über die gegenwärtig maßgebenden Ansichten', *Publizistik*, 16 (2) 163–80.

Signitzer, B. (1992a) 'Aspekte der Produktion von Public Relations-Wissen: PR-Forschung in studentischen Abschlußarbeiten', in H. Avenarius and W. Armbrecht (eds) *Ist Public Relations eine Wissenschaft?*, Opladen: Westdeutscher Verlag.

——(1992b) 'Theorie der Public Relations', in R. Burkart and W. Hömberg (eds) *Kommunikationstheorien*, Vienna: Braumüller.

Stadler, G. (1992) 'Kritik an Public Relations: Bestandsaufnahme und Systematisierung unterschiedlicher Positionen zur Öffentlichkeitsarbeit, eine Literaturanalyse', dissertation, University of Salzburg.

9 Public relations and the development of the principle of separation of advertising and journalistic media programmes in Germany

Barbara Baerns

Introduction

30 December 1994 was the last time that the aims and achievements of the German government were the subject of a four-page editorial-style advertisement which the press and information office placed in the tabloid *Bild* as well as, according to government spokesperson Dieter Vogel, in fifteen other daily newspapers in the eastern part of Germany. The opposition parties were outraged by the cost of DM2.5 million, and yet nobody said anything about the readers or the distinction between the editorial section of the paper and its advertisements.

On 8 October 1994 at 7.25 p.m., the TV channel Zweites Deutsches Fernsehen (ZDF) showed the first part of the soap opera *Wie Pech und Schwefel* ('*Thick as thieves*') featuring the actors Rainer Hunold, Saskia Vester, Burkard Heyl and others. It was either a coincidence, or the manifestation of a deliberate business strategy based upon synergistic effects, that Rainer Hunold appeared in the first spot of the advertising within the programme, endorsing the success of a special meal for slimmers. One might ask why so many television presenters in so many talk shows distance themselves explicitly from such 'plugging' of products, only to publicise the latest book and its publisher, or any other product produced by the guests they have invited to their shows.

Equally one might question whether the following example of the recommendations broadcast by radio editors amounts to advice or advertisement:

Sometimes, in the middle of the summer, you discover ugly blank spots in your garden because some of your plants have not grown properly while others have not survived the holidays due to pests, diseases or bad weather. However, these blank spots can be quickly filled. By so-called container plants. These are plants which – as the magazine *Flora* explained to us – have already grown in pots in the market-garden and may, therefore, be planted out any time, even when flowering. This is because the roots are not disturbed. The plant simply continues to grow. Nevertheless, *Flora* experts recommend making sure of a good start. This means putting the plant and the container into a bowl of water and in the meantime loosening the soil in the hole where the plant is to be put.

And so on. And what should we make of the following text? Is it a sound report, or is it a satire on those 'declarations of war against traditional ways of advertising' circulating in advertising departments?

Bild am Sonntag (BamS), the weekly tabloid from the Springer publishers, wants to try out a new advertisement format as from next year or possibly even before the pre-Christmas period: Product advertising disguised as a serialised novel. The author has already been chosen: Heinz Günther Konsalik, a popular writer who has written some 136 books mainly set in the worlds of doctors and soldiers. At the same time, the novelist wants to try out a new form of literature – an amusingly written soap opera consisting of separate episodes continued week after week. Title: 'The Wagner family – who else?' In each episode, ten products or service offers are to be included with their names and possibly also their advertising slogans. Small drawings of the products or firms in four colour print and clearly marked as an advertisement are supposed to make the text less monotonous. According to the head of the advertisement department of *BamS*, Peter Reckow, the publishers intend to explore by the end of September whether there are enough prospective customers among advertising agencies and producers of propriety articles. So far, the reactions have been rather 'restrained', says Reckow. The prospective customers will have to pay 17,000 Marks for having their products mentioned once. Accordingly, the publishers earn an average 170,000 Marks per double page. However, if space-buyers for at least 26 episodes cannot be found, then, according to Reckow, 'the project will be abandoned'.

(Martens 1989: 36)

Observations like these have led me to focus on public relations practitioners' and researchers' interest in the question of who should supervise and control the separation of advertising and programming. Here, it is recognised that the advertising sections of mass media may have their own information value. This chapter does not aim to condemn advertising *per se*, but calls for greater transparency regarding its source. In our society, the right to freedom of information for readers, listeners, and viewers is seen as secured solely by the fact that they are able to distinguish between editorial contributions and advertisements, or editorial programming and advertising respectively. This requires that audiences should be able to recognise the origin of what is presented to them.

Although it is not possible within the limitations of this chapter to explore this subject fully, I shall attempt to review some of main issues relating to the use of advertising and editorial in the media. The chapter comprises three sections. First, it will examine the results of research that highlights the difficulty, even for proficient media users, of differentiating between editorial output on the one hand and editorial-style advertisements on the other. Because of the limitations of the available research, I shall focus only on newspaper readers. Second, the chapter will examine the emergence of the problem, as well as examining the development of possible solutions historically. And third, in the form of scenario construction, I shall try to outline what approaches and possible solutions might be expected from the communicators of advertising, publishers, broadcasting stations, those in public relations and journalists who presently operate in the media industry.

Case study

> If the publisher or any person otherwise responsible ... for periodic printed material has received, demanded or was promised money for a published item, this item must be marked with the word 'advertisement', if it is not possible, in general, to recognise it as such by its arrangement and layout.

This law on the marking of published items which have been paid for, which is quoted here from the Berlin Press Law of 15 June 1965, §9, is found either verbatim or in analogous wording in all state press laws ('Landespressegesetze') of the Federal Republic of Germany. Besides the 1909 law against unfair competition, which prohibits misleading statements and actions that offend common decency, this law is part of the traditional body of regulations which establishes the clear separation of editorial and advertisement sections, and which furthermore includes regulations against articles that advertise, and regarding editorial additions to advertisements – not only in print media (Figure 9.1). However, ⁻he systematic proof of actual offences and their effects is still problematic.

Despite the unsatisfactory state of general research into the separation regulations, it is still surprising that the relatively easily answerable question of whether readers recognise editorial-style advertisements as 'advertisements' or as 'editorial contributions' has only once been researched empirically in Germany, and subsequently, has only been dealt with in case law within the courts. In such cases, the judges have deduced from the arrangement, layout, explicit special marking or non-marking how the so-called 'average superficial reader' (a legal construct which has also recently been called 'average unbiased reader') could possibly have perceived a controversial editorial-style advertisement. On the one hand, this form of argument revolves around perception, since it should be possible to establish at first sight and without doubt whether a contribution is an advertisement or not.

Laws

- Article 5 of the German Constitution
- Law against unfair competition
- State press laws
- State media and broadcasting laws
- Broadcasting treaty by the states

(Professional) codes of conduct

- Journalistic principles (press codes of conduct) and guidelines for journalistic work according to recommendations of the German Press Council
- Guidelines on editorial-style advertisements by the German Central Panel for the Advertising Industry
- Guidelines for editorial advice in newspapers and magazines
- Guidelines for broadcasting stations under public law, ARD and ZDF
- Joint guidelines of the state media supervisory boards

Figure 9.1 Legal foundations for the separation of editorial texts and advertisements (programmes and advertising)

On the other hand, it rests upon an estimation of the average experience and knowledge that a broad, heterogeneous and indistinct mass-media audience is supposed to have acquired. How many people really will recognise an advertisement as such and how many may be misled remains rather vague in jurisdiction, as long as such decisions rest on such concepts as 'not insignificant proportion' or a 'not absolutely irrelevant proportion' – and as long as sociological studies are not considered in trials concerning this subject. In the scientific literature on unfair competition legislation, some authors conclude that there is a deception when at least 12 per cent of the respondents are misled. Others are of the opinion that between 10 and 15 per cent is a 'not insignificant proportion'.

The study on which this chapter is based was carried out in the city of Essen in North Rhine Westphalia, where the Westdeutsche Allgemeine Zeitung publishing house is located. This company publishes the *Westdeutsche Allgemeine Zeitung* or *WAZ*, which is the largest subscription paper in Germany. Also in Essen, the *Neue Ruhr Zeitung* (NRZ) is published by the same company with the same advertising section.

To investigate the problem, editorial-style advertisements were shown to respondents who were subsequently interviewed face-to-face. All adults with a domicile in Essen were taken as the basis of the survey. This was because all residents could have some contact with the newspapers, be they regular readers, subscribers, or otherwise. A random sample of 515 targeted individuals was constructed, that is around two and a half times as many as would be necessary to reach the envisaged reliability and accuracy of the results for the given population size. This sample size was felt necessary, since a high non-response rate was expected due to the fact that the survey was to be carried out on a single weekend. The value of this sampling appproach was demonstrated later.

Given that the central aim of the study was to examine perceptions of the separation of editorial and advertising, respondents were asked to go through a sample issue of a newspaper and indicate for each page whether they could identify any editorial contributions.

This approach had two advantages. First, the respondents could only observe each page superficially, which would not necessarily be the case if individual contributions or individual advertisements were explicitly pointed out. Second, it enabled the researchers to discover whether respondents were able to distinguish editorial and advertising sections in general or not. However, the disadvantage with this approach was that entire pages had to be shown which consisted only of editorial-style advertisements.

Judging by previous experience, such pages mainly appeared in the weekend issues. On these pages, a number of editorial-style advertisements are compiled under headings such as 'Offers by local traders', 'Information on trades, crafts and manufacturing', 'People who ought to know', etc. The individual advertisements were not signified as such. Only the whole page was signified as advertisement, usually on its upper margin.

It should be noted that for the buyer of advertising space, the editorial style of the advertisements and their favourable placement in the context of the editorial section are used as an argument for their advertising effectiveness. Contents and journalistic make-up are coordinated with the advertisements according to the wishes of the customers. These kinds of advertisements are typically more expensive than others.

Two of these types of advertising pages, which we knew would appear on 25 January 1986, were chosen as subjects for closer scrutiny. The first test page was published on 25 January 1986 in the local Essen issues of *WAZ* and *NRZ*. The second appeared on the same day in the evening edition of the *Frankfurter Abendpost* (which has since ceased publication). By taking into account the Frankfurt paper, which was distributed only in very small numbers in Essen, it was possible to check whether editorial-style advertisements were recognised through their appearance in a well known or an unknown medium respectively.

When these pages were shown to respondents in the study, only about half thought that the pages taken from the local papers included editorial contributions. In other words, 110 of the 212 respondents did not recognise that these pages consisted of nothing but advertisements. Then, 136 of the 212 respondents, that is two in three, indicated that the second test page, which appeared in the non-local paper, included editorial contributions and did not realise that this page consisted solely of advertisements. There were 96 respondents, or 44 per cent, who came to wrong conclusions for both test pages. Only 61 respondents, 29 per cent, rightly considered both test pages as advertising pages (Table 9.1).

Table 9.1 Recognisability of two test pages as advertisement pages

	Test page 1: WAZ/NRZ		
	Recognised	*Not recognised*	*No. of respondents*
Test page 2: Abendpost			
Recognised	61	15	76
Not recognised	41	95	136
No. of respondents	102	110	212
p<0.001			

Table 9.2 Recognisability of test page 1 as an advertisement page

	Test page 1: WAZ/NRZ		
	Recognised	*Not recognised*	*No. of respondents*
Regular readers	76	57	76
Others	26	53	79
No. of respondents	102	110	212
$p < 0.001$			

In contrast, all other pages under consideration were usually correctly attributed. Only eight respondents thought the TV pages were advertising pages. And as far as the *Frankfurter Abendpost* night edition was concerned, ten respondents wrongly considered one page, two respondents two pages and two respondents three pages as advertising pages, though they were in fact editorial pages. One respondent made mistakes in judgement about both papers. Thus it might be concluded that the respondents had the elementary knowledge which is necessary to distinguish editorial and advertising sections; and consequently, that the large number of errors concerning editorial-style advertisements was, in fact, due to the make-up and layout of the pages.

Drawing further on marketing theory, we sought to discover whether regular readers were misled less easily. Just under one-third of the respondents described themselves as subscribers to one of the two Essen papers. Of these, 83 per cent referred to themselves as regular or irregular readers. Including non-subscribers, 133 indicated that they read this paper daily. Of the regular readers, 57 per cent (76 out of 133) recognised that the test page was an advertising page. Thus correct recognition and regular reading seem to be closely correlated. In spite of this, 43 per cent (57 of 133) of these regular readers were misled (Table 9.2). According to the guidelines presented earlier, this figure was unacceptably high.

No equivalent study has been repeated to date. But the results suggest that further research in this field is needed.

Historical developments

The different treatment of editorial and advertising material was probably consolidated in a historical development by which the editorial function crystallised as an independent organisational unit. The journalism researcher Otto Groth established that, during the last decade of the eighteenth century, a distinction came to be made between the content of a paper which is 'useful in general' and therefore free of charge, and that part which 'relates to the advantage of the contributor', for which a charge is made when printed. While the editorial section was reserved more and more for the 'unbiased judgement of an objective examiner', at the same time it became increasingly attractive is a context for advertisements, so that publishers demanded and received more money for advertisements on these pages. Incidentally, Hohmeister documented the increasing differentiation of the advertisement section of newspapers in the period 1830–50, and then around 1950 and 1975. In a first systematic historical case study on the *Giessener Anzeiger*, he established not only that a fundamental change in the layout of the paper occurred around the turn of the century, but also that 'the first professional journalists were employed' at this time (cf. Hohmeister 1981: *passim*).

Under French influence, the so-called 'Reklame' also came into use in the German press after 1821. Here, Heinrich Wuttke (1866; 1875) and also Karl Bücher (1926b), as well as Otto Groth (1928–30) saw the 'Reklame', in contrast to the 'Annonce' (advertisement), as a 'selfrecommendation' written in news style, opinion style, or other styles, which was sent together with a paid advertisement to the editorial section. The publishing of this 'self-recommendation' in the editorial section was made a condition for the insertion of the advertising. The book publishing business, which was the first to make use of this instrument to ask for editorial support for advertisements, was followed by other publishers. And Rudolf Mosse, a publisher from Berlin, who opened his business as a buyer of advertising space on 1 January 1867, announced that these so-called 'Reklamen' would accompany advertisements in all suitable journals free of charge.

First attempts at regulation

A new type of newspaper, the 'Generalanzeiger', emerged in Germany in the late nineteenth century and was advertising-oriented as well as financed through advertisements. This development, together with changes in business methods of the buyers of advertising space, gave impetus for the old-established publishers to unite in a syndicate in response to what they saw as a threat to their existence. According to its programme of 1901, the Verein Deutscher Zeitungs-Verleger (VDZV), or Association of German Newspaper Publishers, which was constituted in Leipzig in 1894, sought to reach unified regulations governing the use of free 'Reklamen' and the mixing of editorial and advertising sections, in order to counter this pressure. The association's goals were mirrored in the pronouncements of the organisation's

'Zeitungs-Verlag', which sought to contribute to the debate, particularly in terms of pieces like 'From practice for practice', 'Waste-paper offers, etc.', and 'Mail box'. Documentary records of these developments are still available today.

By the end of 1904, the board of the VDZV recommended to the 654 publishing houses which were by then members, not to publish 'local and editorial "Reklamen"', 'shop window reports for Christmas-advertisers', or 'advertisements within texts, or blurred advertisements'. The board rejected such devices as 'business methods that were partly inadmissible and partly not beneficial for the overall interest of the press'. Four years later one could read in the VDZV's newsletter that, thanks to their recommendations, 'Reklame' contributions have become rare. Furthermore, because of paper being in short supply and financial problems within the advertising business, there were agreements among newspapers that competed at local level to keep the editorial section as free from 'Reklamen' as possible.

It is remarkable that such characteristic publishers' initiatives occurred in a period when more and more German dailies were temporarily financed mainly by the profits from their advertisements, rather than from their distribution income. At the same time, general criticism was voiced regarding the mutual dependence and interlinking of the editorial and the advertisement sections in newspapers in the private sector. But by the mid-1920s, an attempt at free negotiations took place between newspaper and magazine publishers and the buyers of advertising space, negotiations which were directed towards the re-ordering of advertising. However, these negotiations failed. These attempts at negotiation also related to some degree to regulations about the placement of advertising in the editorial section. The German journalists' professional association, the Reichsverband der Deutschen Presse, took the decisions of the VDZV as a starting point, and suggested in 1927 that separation regulations should be established by law. It even called for 'legal sanctions against all kinds of press corruption'.

The following collection of case examples, involving controversial advertising techniques in the 1920s, reveals approaches that might still be used today by public relations firms seeking product publicity or event marketing:

- A standing order for a full-page ad by the sparkling-wine producers Söhnlein was accompanied by the following letter:

  > Without trying to influence the line of your paper we wish to bring to your attention that we are permitted to cancel our order

without notice should your paper publish anything against alcohol in general or against sparkling wine in particular.

(cf. Groth 1928–30: vol. 3, 308ff.)

» The national association of the German car industry asked the 'press and propaganda departments' of car and motorcycle manufacturers in 1928 to inform them which papers and magazines 'were: 1. supported through advertisements and included news about individual companies in their editorial section; 2. rejected news and articles which were propagandistically biased and therefore not based on advertisements' (cf. Groth 1928–30: vol. 3, 308ff.).

• On 30 January 1929, the Berlin paper *8-Uhr-Abendblatt* published on its first page news of the theft of a four-cylinder Chevrolet owned by a Berlin car dealer. The paper printed a picture of the car and reported over six issues on the hunt for the culprits. After the car had been found and the 'thief' caught, it turned out that the series was an advertising ploy contrived by the Berlin representative of General Motors and the *8-Uhr-Abendblatt* (cf. Heide 1940: 156).

After the attempt at free negotiations regarding the use of advertising and editorial material had failed in the 1920s, the matter was given a legal basis for the first time when the National Socialists came to power in Germany. This took the form of the so-called Editors' Law of 1933. Under the general conditions of the Editors' Law, it became the duty of editors to, among other things, keep their newspapers free from anything 'that mixes selfish purposes with those of the common benefit in a way that misleads the public' (Editors' Law of 4 October 1933, §14). In 1935, for the first time, the general conditions comprised 'guidelines on editorial advice in daily newspapers, magazines and correspondence'. These principles offered helpful advice about dealing with individual cases in sixteen fields (Figure 9.2). They were issued by the professional associations, which were subsequently 'streamlined' ('Gleichschaltung') in the Reich Press Chamber by an association between the Reich Press Chamber itself and the Advertising Council of German Trade and Industry which supervised the entire advertising business. In November 1938 the guidelines were issued in slightly amended form by the Reich Ministry of Propaganda and Instruction of the People, the Reich Press Chamber, and the Advertising Council. A supporting institution, the Office for Instructions on Editing Advice, belonging to the Advertising Council, was already in existence.

A OFFICIAL INFORMATION AND OFFICIAL RELEASES

B EVENTS, SPORTS, FASHION, THEATRE, FILM, ETC.

1 Entertainment, charity and popular instruction events
2 Programme surveys and the like
3 Health resorts, pleasure tours, etc.
4 Sports events
5 Theatre
6 Film
7 Fashion
8 Lottery
9 Auctions
10 Book and record reviews
11 Company events
12 Associations' events

C BUSINESS, TECHNOLOGY, ETC.

1 Information from the Reich estates, etc.
2 Instructive articles
3 Market reports
4 Fairs and exhibitions
5 Proprietary articles
6 Reports on new developments
7 Cars
8 Anniversaries
9 Cooperation with business leaders
10 Speeches held in companies, open door events, etc.
11 Explanations of photos by experts
12 Notes
13 Notes on business advertising
14 New buildings
15 Jewellery, handicrafts, etc.
16 Advice in supplements
17 Export magazines

Figure 9.2 Regulations for individual cases on the basis of the guidelines for editorial advice in newspapers, magazines, and by the correspondents (1935)
Source: Prüfer 1937.

Just a year after the introduction of broadcasting in Germany, the Broadcasting Advertising Service was established. The German postal service, to which sovereign rights over all wireless transmissions had been transferred as early as the end of the nineteenth century, had ounded the so-called German Reich Mail Advertising Ltd as early as 1920. This organisation was a form of postal service-owned advertising agency which had a branch in every main post office. This agency not only had the right to use all postal institutions for advertising purposes, it also negotiated radio advertising with the individual state-licensed broadcasting corporations. The broadcasting researcher Winfried B. Lerg found that within the different radio programmes, three advertising formats were possible:

1   Individual announcements, so-called 'Reklame-Rundsprüche' (literally 'broadcast speeches') were allowed to be only one minute, or ten typewritten lines, long. The basic price for such an announcement was 200 Marks. Discounts were given according to the extent and duration of the order. Repetitions of advertising slogans were possible only twice a week and at intervals of at least one day.
2   Advertising talks in a literary or popular scientific manner with a maximum length of fifteen minutes were supposed to offer useful information and to inject the advertising into the texts casually and unobtrusively. The company responsible also provided the speaker. The basic price of a fifteen-minute talk transmitted on weekday evenings or Sunday afternoons was 500 Marks, including a preview in the printed programme.
3   For advertising concerts there were special arrangements. The prices varied according to whether the advertiser provided an orchestra or used a recording (about 600 Marks) or employed the orchestra of the broadcasting corporation (about 700–800 Marks). Furthermore, there were extra charges for Sunday concerts (Lerg 1963: 129).

The first general agreement between the parent organisation of the broadcasting corporations, the Reich Broadcasting Corporation (founded in 1925) and the Reich Mail Advertising Ltd was reached in 1926, and included the following regulations to be observed in the transmission of radio advertisements:

1   The cultural significance of broadcasting must not be impaired by the practice of advertising.

2   For the broadcasting of advertisements, a continuous period with a
     fixed duration has to be agreed on.
3   The advertising announcements have to be clearly signified as such
     in the programme and be distinguished from the main programme.
4   The wording of the advertisements must not give the impression
     that the broadcasting corporation is the recommending agent.
     Rather it should be clear that it is the advertiser who is promoting
     his products (Lerg 1980: 139).

In the subsequent period, radio advertising was at first subject to
temporal limitations, that is, transmitted before midday and banned
on Sundays and holidays; and around the beginning of 1936 it was
banned generally. However, further research is needed to examine how
far the principle of the separation of advertising and editorial programming formulated in these guidelines was in fact implemented. A
degree of scepticism would seem appropriate, since if we look only at
the advertising of the Reich Mail Advertising Ltd, radio advertising
talks and advertising broadcasts in the music programme were being
offered well into the 1930s.

A new beginning and points of departure

After the collapse of the Third Reich, the allied occupying powers took
over responsibility for the setting up of a democratic German press.
The extinction of Nazi influences within the media was furthered by
press legislation. Regulations on how to deal with and signify advertisements were formulated by the American occupying authorities,
who also laid down guidelines regarding form and content of the periodicals licensed by them. After restrictions had been gradually
reduced, and the laws laid down by the occupying forces were replaced
by German laws in the American occupation zone, Bavaria and Hessen
were the first states to establish press laws which included the obliga-
tion to signify contributions for which a charge had been made.
Between 1964–6 the other West German states ('Länder') and also the
new Bundesländer in the DDR followed these earlier guidelines. As
early as 1952, the relevant professional associations produced their new
'Editorial guidelines for newspapers and magazines' (Figure 9.3). In
1964, the first version of the 'Guidelines on editorial-style advertisements' appeared. It placed a more explicit ban on the inclusion of
editorial support to advertisements.

In the second half of the 1970s, both the German Press Council and
the Federal Association of German Publishers expressed their inten-

1 Official information and official releases
2 Events, sports, fashion, theatre, film, etc.
3 Programme surveys and the like
4 Health resorts, pleasure tours, etc.
5 Sports events
6 Theatre, film and other events
7 Textile and fashion crafts
8 Lotteries
9 Auctions
10 Book and record reviews
11 Company and association events
12 General development of business, technology, etc.
13 Market reports
14 Fairs and exhibitions
15 Reports on new developments
16 Information sections
17 Cars, etc.
18 Anniversaries, birthdays, etc.
19 Cooperation with business experts
20 Company events, lectures, open door events, etc.
21 Explanations of photos by experts
22 Notes on business advertising
23 New buildings
24 Advice in supplements

Figure 9.3   Regulations for individual cases on the basis of the guidelines for editorial advice in newspapers and magazines (1952)

tions to reshape the guidelines more liberally, particularly those on editorial advice in newspapers and magazines, and particularly with regard to programme surveys, travel, theatre, films and other events, textiles, fashion, manufacturing, trade fairs and exhibitions. Conceptual challenges by independent weekly advertisers regarding the competitive nature of the medium, and arguments with the postal newspaper service about its criteria for differentiating between advertising and editorial, provided the impetus for keeping to the fixed professional norms. The criteria used by the postal newspaper service were tacitly amended later on.

As far as radio and television were concerned, a discussion about the principle of separation of advertising and editorial programming only came about after the introduction of private broadcasting, which was mainly financed through advertising. Since 1985, this principle has made its way into state media and broadcasting laws which regulate the admission of private broadcasting companies. By stretching the new advertising regulations that took these principles to their limits, many private stations tried to establish themselves in the advertising market with the help of 'unconventional' advertising formats which clearly flouted the separation principle. Looking at the range of offers by a selected private radio station, PRO Radio 4, Baum (1986) showed that the boundaries between editorial programming and advertising had become more and more blurred. Apart from the normal form of advertisement – i.e. a pre-produced commercial (costing between DM150–1,000) – the offers included the following formats and prices:

- Advertising presentation: commercials of 10–12 seconds within the programme read by the show's presenter (price DM50–100);
- Telephone advertising: an on-air phone-in and talk with the presenter about the advertised product (DM200–400);
- Feature advertising: a short radio play, interview or report of up to three minutes, 'a new advertising format with surprising effects and high attention value' (brochure) (DM500–2,000);
- Reminder advertising: 10–20 seconds; a short but effective reminder of earlier advertising messages (DM50–100);
- Live transmission from an outside broadcast vehicle: on air with live transmissions or with a recording on location, including presentation and, on request, artistes as well (price negotiable);
- Sponsored broadcast: short special features on a specific branch or topic, e.g. fashion, travel, leisure, recuperation, cars, house and garden ... or longer parts of programmes and shows which can be set up in cooperation with PRO Radio 4 (price negotiable).

At the same time, the presentation of products, equipment or services in a programme (product placement) and the financing of a show through a third party (sponsorship) were also the subject of a fundamental discussion about broadcasting and law. Earlier, public broadcasting only dealt with these topics, if at all, under the term 'plugs', in connection with problems of advertising placards at sports venues which had to be accepted in TV sports coverage. Excerpts from an interview that the communication periodical *Textintern* undertook with the director of ZDF, Dieter Stolte (Stolte 1986), indicate the new problems of delimitation and leeway of interpretation:

STOLTE: There will be no product placement. This does not mean that there will be no cooperation. Why should the ZDF not organise an event ... for example with the Westphalia Arena in Dortmund ... for which the owners cooperate to a certain degree? This has nothing to do with product placement. Product placement means that, for example in a series, a product is used not just because it is needed at this point but because it has been selected especially and it is brought into the picture so that an advantageous advertising effect comes about. And to this effect, a certain amount is paid. This will definitely be banned.

TEXTINTERN: Sums of money do not necessarily need to be taken. It would be possible to switch to services of other kinds.

STOLTE: It would be absurd to think that in the future we will drive American cars in a crime series such as *Derrick*, *Der Alte* or *Ein Fall für Zwei*; it would be absurd to think that a car could be popularised in such a way and nobody recognise the brand. But it makes a difference if the cars are driven such that the logo is brought into the picture permanently and insistently. Whether there is an advertising aspect or not, the ZDF will take no money from these car companies.

TEXTINTERN: But you would not reject cars that are offered by these companies?

STOLTE: As for cars, this question can be ignored, since the scale which we are talking about here is ridiculous compared with the entire production costs. There may be borderline cases in projects such as *Traumschiff*, a series about travellers on a cruise. We were not able to buy or even rent a whole ship. We need other forms of cooperation here. For *Traumschiff* we did not approach any particular company, but invited tenders from three shipping lines that were worth considering. Under such circumstances it is possible to set up a contract from which a financial advantage is gained. That has to be seen realistically; but if such a case occurs, it will in the future need my explicit authorisation. However, this is only relevant for larger projects and for subjects for which there is no alternative; otherwise it can only be realised with considerable financial effort. We will have to negotiate in individual cases. But: There will be no services in return within our programme.

Laws that were to safeguard the separation principle in public *and* private broadcasting were first laid down by the German states in their treaty for the reorganisation of broadcasting (the Broadcasting Treaty) in 1987 and – with fundamental changes in line with

European negotiations – in the Broadcasting Treaty of united Germany in 1991. Taking the latest amendment into account, which came into force in 1994, the core of the Broadcasting Treaty contains the following regulations which are binding on broadcasters in both public and private sectors:

- Advertising has to be clearly separated from the rest of the programme. Advertising has to be clearly signified by visual or acoustic means. It must not influence the rest of the programming as regards content or editing. Persons that regularly present news programmes and programmes on current political affairs must not take part in television advertising.
- It is regarded as a 'plug' to mention and present products, services, names, brands or activities of a manufacturer of goods or of a service company which are not necessary on journalistic or artistic grounds (product placement). And plugs are inadmissible.
- Sponsored programmes, that is radio and television programmes which are (part-) financed directly or indirectly by a third party, are an original creation alongside advertising and programmes and are admissible. At the beginning and end of the programme, the sponsor must be named. On television, not only company emblems but also trademarks may be inserted, and not just stills but also moving images may be used. The sponsor may advertise its products in the form of commercials within the sponsored show. News and current affairs programmes must not be sponsored.

Furthermore, the Broadcasting Treaty committed stations to produce guidelines on implementing the laws regarding the separation principle.

On 7 October 1994, the ZDF amended its previous guidelines on advertising and sponsoring of programmes that had been formulated in May 1993. (These in turn superseded ZDF's earlier guidelines on advertising programmes, as well as its guidelines on cooperation with third-party programmes of March 1989, which were based on the provisional guidelines concerning cooperation between ZDF programmes and third parties drawn up in March 1987.)

In November 1994, the directors of the committees of the broadcasting stations under public law in the Federal Republic of Germany (ARD) modified their guidelines on advertising, and the separation of advertising and programming and sponsorship, which had been passed on 24 June 1992. (These modifications superseded the ARD guidelines on the separation of advertising and programming of 23 March

1988. Earlier the ARD directors had agreed on principles for the separation of advertising and programming at their meeting on 22–3 October 1986. These principles supplemented the guidelines on cooperation in the combined ARD document 'German television' that had existed since 1971.)

The directors of the regional media supervisory boards, which were set up in 1984 along with the introduction of private broadcasting in Germany, and which are responsible for the admission and supervision of private broadcasting, met for the last time in January 1993, and agreed a set of common guidelines on advertising and the implementation of the separation of advertising, programming and sponsorship which were intended to apply first to television and second to radio. This agreement evolved because of the reformulation of the Broadcasting Treaty. At an earlier meeting in November 1988, the boards had published an outline of joint guidelines on the implementation of advertising regulations in the Broadcasting Treaty. This outline superseded the preliminary interpretation and implementation of guidelines issued (on 22 May 1987) by the directors of the regional media supervisory boards, on the separation of advertising and the rest of the programming and on sponsored programmes.

Expected sanctions and control mechanisms

It is generally understood that the control and realisation of the separation principle is primarily guaranteed by competition between business rivals. That is, publishers have to show regard for other publishers, stations for other stations, department stores for other department stores, pharmacological producers for other pharmacological producers; and they have to make sure that the rules of competition are obeyed since, otherwise, some competitors may gain an 'unfair' advantage. However, trials involving these competitors show that the separation principle has not always been followed. Indeed, legal decisions have been handed down regarding the use of editorial-style advertisements, reports that advertised, and the use of editorial support for commercials, not only in print media. Since 1965 there has been a guaranteed right to take legal action by, among others, consumers' associations ('associations with a legal capacity which, according to their statute, safeguard consumers' interests through instruction and advice'). Apart from the internal control functions exercised by the relevant organs of broadcasters under public law, and the external control functions of the regional media supervisory boards over the private broadcasting stations (which have had limited influence too), much of the implementation of controls has continued to rely on a set of voluntary norms adopted by the advertising business and the press.

Finally, in 1984, the Central Association of the Advertising Industry, which was founded in 1949 as an umbrella organisation of advertising agencies and all those who pursue, produce, carry out and procure advertising, and which had until 1991 been known as the Central Panel of the Advertising Industry (ZAW), published a handbook in cooperation with the publishers' associations. The handbook, entitled *Plugs*, contained regulations as well as specific cases, verdicts, expert comment and articles on the subject. The German Advertising Council, which was founded in 1972 by the ZAW, is a 'self-regulating institution' which passes on instances of offences against the separation principle to other institutions such as the Central Office for the Fight against Unfair Competition, which in turn has the right to take legal action, and proceeds accordingly.

In 1973, the German Press Council, which had been founded in 1949 by publishers' and journalists' associations as an 'organ of self-responsibility for the press' and which was newly constituted later in 1985 by publishers' and journalists' associations, came out with its 'Press Codes of Conduct', which were passed in cooperation with the press associations and which were intended to 'safeguard professional ethics'. The document stipulated among other things that:

> The press has a responsibility to the public to ensure that editorial contributions must not be influenced by the private or business interests of third parties. Publishers and editors must reject such attempts and supervise the clear separation between editorial texts and texts for the purposes of advertising. Advertising texts, photos and drawings are to be signified as such.

Moreover, 'Guidelines for journalistic activity' were published regularly (until 1986 as 'Guidelines for editorial work according to the recommendations of the German Press Council') and in 1992 explicitly condemned 'plugs in editorial contributions'. These guidelines, which took into account specific pages and supplements, stated that:

> Editorial contributions which are free of charge but draw the readers' attention to companies, their products, services and events must not cross the boundary into 'plugs'. An offence is particularly likely when the publication goes beyond reasonable public interest or the interests of the readers as regards information. The credi-

bility of the press as a source of information demands particular care in dealing with public relations texts as well as in writing editorial advice. Special issues are subject to the same responsibility by the editors as in all other cases.

In accordance with these guidelines, the German Press Council has also argued for the 'separation of editorial and advertising sections' (Deutscher Presserat yearbooks for 1960, 1976 and 1990), and against 'malpractices concerning invitations and gifts' (1961) and for 'keeping the textual and visual reporting of sports events free from plugs' (1974).

Finally, the separation principle indirectly enforced by the Federal Mail which, in order to secure a pluralistic and free press, transported at low cost only those papers and magazines which were aimed at informing the public about current events, topical questions or subjects which promoted the ideas of clubs, associations and other bodies; and which contained at least an overall 30 per cent, or a constant 25 per cent of 'press-like reporting'. The Central Inspection Office of the Postal Newspaper Service at the Postal Newspaper Office Berlin (West) based its decisions mainly on the guidelines outlined above in order to be able to distinguish 'press-like reporting' from advertisements and contributions with an advertising character. In 1975, for example, it rejected 38 out of 257 applications because the share of reporting fell below these acceptable proportions. In the period before the structural reform of the postal service, the postal newspaper service was 'reorganised according to private law' as early as 1991. The basic allocation of the postal delivery of newspapers was substituted by general business conditions. However, the above selection criteria mostly remained in force in order to prevent an undifferentiated access to a postal newspaper service which customarily operated at extraordinarily low prices which did not cover expenses. In order to further legitimise financial support by the state in these times of ongoing privatisation of the Federal Mail, it will become more and more important for it to disclose its ways of checking the contents of papers admitted to its postal newspaper service.

Current activities

The principles of the separation of advertising and programming which exist within media law, professional codes and unfair competition legislation have helped retain the autonomy and credibility of the public media. They secure their independence from advertisers' influences, which are camouflaged as neutral editorial statements in papers, magazines, radio and TV, and may, therefore, not be revealed. They prevent market rivals from suffering unfair competition. Thereby they serve and are beneficial not only to the advertisers, but also to all communication professions concerned – publishing, broadcasting, advertising, public relations, journalism – and the general public.

On the basis of these considerations, it seems reasonable to attempt to identify systematically what approaches, solutions and results may be expected from the communicators who are active and wield influence in the field in Germany today.

Advertising

According to the managing director of the Central Association of German Advertising Business, Volker Nickel, the 'successfully' functioning advertising business has proved its value, not only as a 'constitutive part of the market economy' but also as an important basis for the existence of the public media. The after-tax profits of advertising in the media have more than doubled over the past ten years from DM14 billion to DM31 billion (Nickel 1994a: 3). Simultaneously, the increasing number and variety of media, which has been due to dynamic technical developments as well as to the changes in behaviour of consumers of television, press and radio, and the increasing dissatisfaction of media planners with the current media opportunities available, have resulted in increasing uncertainty within the media industry. Some media commentators have even characterised the industry is being in a state of 'crisis'.

Doubting the effectiveness of traditional advertising, the advertising business has turned to 'new' solutions of 'total communication' and 'integrated communication'. Here, they refer to a marketing concept which favours the harmonisation of all communication activities within a company, organisation or institution, arguing that in this way, 'additional synergistic effects' will be unleashed. Among other things, sponsorship and product placement are seen in this context as innovative advertising forms. They are constituents of the so-called communication mix of an organisation, and are used in combination with other communication tools. According to the Head of the Marketing Institute of the European Business School, Manfred Bruhn, sponsorship now competes with the traditional communication instruments – advertising and sales promotion. This is because sponsors invest money in order to gain advertising effects as a return on their investment. Here, product placement is seen as a form of sponsorship which attempts to have products and trademarks appear within films and other productions.

In practice, so-called full service agencies are prepared to adopt and implement these concepts. Apart from these agencies, specialist agencies have emerged in recent years which supervise sponsorship systematically and make it possible to coordinate the placement of products in the media which are to be advertised and which are also required for film and television productions.

Against this background, offences against the separation principle cannot just be taken as *faux pas* or oversights. They are inherent in the system, a constituent of the integration of communication strategy. From the beginning, Manfred Bruhn, one of the originators of this concept, has explained it as follows:

> The development of sponsorship and of product placement very distinctly shows an increasing mutual permeation of economic and societal processes, particularly in the leisure activities of people. The incorporation of brands into societal life and the involvement of business companies in the promotion of sports and culture have found new 'network' forms of communication. A clear distinction between advertising and leisure/entertainment will not be possible in the future.
>
> (Bruhn 1988: 227)

At the same time, reasonable forms of networks are called for, forms which are beneficial to all participants – i.e. companies as sponsors, the groups supported in sports, culture and society, as well as the media. The following quote which appeared in 1988 has for today's reader an almost prophetic note:

> The media have an especially important role to play in the advertising effects of sponsorship. The stations subject to public law have a specific problem here because their 'programme licence' stipulates a separation of advertising and programming. But it is hardly comprehensible that for public television, this so-called programme licence should be the reason for shying away from the market economy and new forms of TV advertising. The public TV stations rely too much on their viewing figures, which are high, compared to private channels, and see no reason for turning away from their rigid stance. With a change in viewing audiences in the next few years, a change will come also for them.
>
> (Bruhn 1988: 226)

Publishers and broadcasting stations

In the context of fundamental offences against the separation principle discussed above, editorial marketing and communication
marketing in publishing houses, and increasingly in broadcasting too,
has developed thematic connections between editorial and advertising
sections. These have become customary instruments within the
broadcasting industry. As far as the print media are concerned, these
policies have, in fact, already been accepted and condoned by the
Supreme Court. On 23 January 1992 the Federal Supreme Court
ruled that placing an advertisement in a related editorial context
cannot be seen as an extra service by the publishers through which
they would gain competitive advantage. The Court referred to the
'now usual practice' of an advantageous placing of an advertisement
which is more or less expected. Consequently, a neutral observer of an
advertisement that is incorporated into an objective factual editorial
context within the same topic field may not take this to be an extra
service and thereby an illegal benefit offered by publishers for advertisers (verdict of the Federal Supreme Court of 23 January 1992, I
ZR 129/90).

Paradoxically, the 'commonsensical' presupposed influence of the
attention given to particular advertisements by their placement adja-
cent to related editorial fields has not been proved empirically either
for daily newspapers and magazines or for broadcasting. Even the
advertising industry admits that knowledge about consumer behaviour
is still very limited (e.g. Nickel 1994b: 12).

It may be worthwhile in this context to return to the study
discussed earlier of consumers' ability to distinguish editorial-style
advertisements, and to focus attention on some of the marginal findings. The study found that 60 per cent of respondents (126 out of 212)
indicated that they had read the newspaper (of 25 January 1986) from
which the test page was taken, before the survey. Twenty per cent of
the overall number of respondents (43 out of 212) said they had read
something on the page from which the text was taken. However, no
significantly higher number of respondents from this group than the
other (27 out of 43 against 49 out of 83 respectively) recognised that
the page they had read was an advertising page (cf. Table 9.3). On the
other hand, the group of 50 readers of this issue of the newspaper who
had not recognised the advertisement page did not include significantly more voluntary readers of the test page than the group of 76
readers who had recognised the advertisement page as such, i.e. 50 to
16 against 76 to 27 (Table 9.3).

Table 9.3 Cross-tabulation of the recognisability of test page 1

	Test page 1: WAZ/NRZ		
	Recognised	*Not recognised*	*No. of respondents*
Earlier page contact			
Yes	27	16	43
No	49	34	83
No. of respondents	76	50	126

The same holds for those 15 per cent (19 out of 126) who confirmed having read or looked at not only the whole test page, but also an advertisement presented by the interviewer. This group also did not recognise that the test page was an advertisement page significantly more often. On the other hand, the 50 readers of this issue who had not recognised the advertisement page had not looked at the selected advertisement significantly more often (Table 9.4).

Examining this partial analysis from the opposite perspective of copy tests which have been ordered by prospective customers, the ability to discern the material as an editorial-style advertisement was not found to be that important; rather, what is important was the attention paid to it. From this viewpoint, 34 per cent (43 out of 126 readers) had established a real contact with the page. This is a low value compared to average copy test results – they are around 88 per cent for regional subscription papers. Also, the advertisement attention value of 15 per cent here (19 out of 126 readers) appears less significant, because for comparatively large advertisements which are not in editorial style a figure of 28–36 per cent was recorded.

The view that advertising attracts more attention if it comes in the form of editorial contributions does not stand the empirical test, though it may seem plausible at first sight. Editorial-style advertisements do

Table 9.4 Cross-tabulation of the recognisability of test page 1 as an advertisement page with earlier notice

	Test page 1: WAZ/NRZ		
	Recognised	*Not recognised*	*No. of respondents*
Notice of advertisement			
Yes	13	6	19
No	63	44	107
No. of respondents	76	50	126

not gain more attention than other advertisements do but, on the contrary, gain less. This undermines the belief that the separation principle is important.

Public relations

In the summer of 1991, the topic of product publicity, which the German PR industry had repeatedly marginalised, again appeared on the agenda of the public relations profession. Though not compatible with the professed self-image of the industry, which sees itself as 'the management of communication processes for organisations with their publics' (DPRG/GPRA 1990), product publicity seeks to persuade editors to mention and endorse companies as well as advertise and describe their products and services, completely independently of advertising and payments.

The discussions were triggered by editorial advertisements and the subsequent admonitions of the Berlin Association for Social Competition, which were directed towards three well-known producers of proprietary articles as well as a publisher. These charges were confirmed in court. The Association of Public Relations Agencies (GPRA) hurriedly ordered a legal report (GPRA 1991). This report did not contain any more information than would already have been available to practitioners from existing documentation (and also from PR handbooks). Subsequently, the GPRA set up a 'symposium' for its members to discuss the matter. The professional associations advised their members to re-examine their practices of press relations, to advise them to avoid 'advancing their own interests too much' and not to overdo the discussion of the separation principle, since this would discourage customers. In taking this action, the public relations industry yet again wasted the chance to distinguish itself explicitly from advertising through a well-founded discussion of the reduction of public relations to product- and service-oriented promotion. The worse-case scenario that the newsletter *Public Relations Report* envisaged, which saw the end of public relations if the separation principle were adhered to, suffices to illustrate how superficially the topic was dealt with:

> Public relations for products would be virtually banned. ... And indeed ... a widely-known practice which is part of the service of almost all papers and magazines would cease to exist. Consider, for example, the motor pages, in which new cars are introduced, or reports on trade fairs, in which product innovations are presented.

This would, of course, also hold good as regards television! The readers would have to do without these suggestions and public relations would lose all influence with editors. The consequences are barely conceivable.

(Recht 1991: 1)

Against this background, a survey which had important implications for the PR industry appeared which touched on the core of the subsequent problems regarding the supply of editorial material. However this survey gained little attention. In February 1993, the highest civil court in Germany issued the following judgement regarding the responsibility of informants with respect to unfair competition:

A company that informs the public about its products promotionally, but objectively, is generally not guilty of unfair competition even if a press organ adopts the information and ignores the precept of objective reporting and presents the product in an advertising-style.

(Verdict of the Federal Supreme Court of 18 February 1993, I ZR 14/91)

This ruling meant that the stream of news could continue to flow without being inhibited and without discarding the principle of separation of advertising and programming in the future. The ultimate responsibility for decisions regarding selection of material for inclusion in editorial would lie with the editors.

Journalism

According to the latest studies on the self-image of journalism in Germany in 1993, journalists are perceived as neutral mediators between the outside world and the editorial sections of the media. The majority of journalists indicated that they want to inform their audience quickly (73 per cent) and precisely (74 per cent) and to explain complicated issues (74 per cent) (Weischenberg *et al.* 1994: 65ff.). More than half of them indicated that they find press releases 'important' and 'stimulating' for their work. However, less than half of them characterised the information obtained via press relations as 'reliable' and only a third indicated that they thought press releases tempt journalists to uncritical coverage, while a quarter said that press releases serve as a substitute for their own investigations (ibid. 68).

In 1988, the Club of Science Journalists, a study-circle of media publicists to which most journalists in responsible positions in daily newspapers, periodicals, broadcasting and television are affiliated, expressed 'dissatisfaction' and complained about 'PR proliferation', particularly on the part of public relations agencies. In a survey of journalists that preceded the study, 60 per cent criticised the actionism, 55 per cent the activities of deeper-probing, 58 per cent the disproportionate travelling and 60 per cent the attempts to get publication confirmation even before the event. Moreover, half of the journalists from the circle had the impression that PR agencies propagated the idea that journalists are easy to manipulate, as an argument to stimulate client business 'for product promotion by way of press relations'. The journalists claimed that press releases were useful only if they provided information instead of advertising, and research results instead of product information (PR, Public Relations and Science Journalism 1988: *passim*).

To what extent advertising does, in fact, find its way into the editorial sections through PR activities without being filtered, has rarely been investigated in the German-speaking countries, and then mostly by way of case studies (Heck 1993; Hänecke 1990). On the question of what editors know about the separation principle and how they use it, there is not a single study. Some editors with whom we talked found the separation principle 'old-fashioned', since their readers expected and desired, for instance, sources of supply to be mentioned. A systematic study of the consumers' needs, which would be of help for editors in this context, does not exist. All the same, in 1994 the information service Der Wirtschaftsredakteur ordered the Wickert Institutes to investigate whether consumers of business programmes on television see reports on new products and their producers as 'information' or as 'plugs'. Following the results of the survey, two-thirds of the West German respondents and as many as nine-tenths of the East German respondents accepted that the mentioning and visualisation of new products and their producers was 'information', while every fourth West German and every fourteenth East German regarded the mentioning of products and producers as 'plugs'.

Currently, the German Journalists' Association, DJV, regularly informs its members about the problems of the separation principle, not only through publications in the association's organ *Journalist*, but also by way of regional meetings of professional groups. As early as the beginning of 1986, the association had announced that it would examine the separation principle more closely. In particular, it wanted to oppose all forms of contributions that appeared to favour a particular party. At the same time, sponsorship and product placement in broadcasting were debated. On this occasion, the board of the DJV backed the view that coverage and advertising should be separated from one another in a way that was to be clearly recognised by readers, viewers and listeners. It was pointed out that journalistic work must not be abused for the purposes of advertising. In addition, in East Germany, the Association of German Newspaper Publishers organised events where editors were instructed about the separation principle. In spite of these measures, self-descriptions of companies and institutions (which are free of charge) continue to appear in the editorial sections. This is not only due to the fact that differentiated and consumer-friendly journalistic coverage of company affairs and products is difficult, but also because of resource limitations and lack of knowledge of the subject in question. Despite the development of Supreme Court legislation in favour of public interest, which is, however, still disputed, protection is not legally guaranteed, and there is some risk concerning claims of compensation and liability for journalistic statements which could be considered injurious to the interests of a company (cf. for example, Ott 1987).

On societal effects

To sum up, it is clear that individual interests which seek short-term advantage are in danger of losing out in the long run, since editorial sections may become so minimally editorial that they will not be attractive to companies seeking editorial 'plugs'. Second, there is inadequate proof of actual disregard for the separation principle, and its after-effects. Where there is no plaintiff, there is no judge. Where competitors do not take legal action, offences against norms go unnoticed. Control through competition has not served as a catalyst for tighter regulation as expected, and pressure which is supposed to bring about citizen-friendly solutions has not been generated. On the contrary, 'detrimental coalitions' come about, acting according to the principle of give and take, which turns out to be counter-productive to the needs of readers, viewers and listeners. Thus what we once took for granted is in danger of being lost: the right, at least, to know the origin of a piece of information.

References

Baerns, B. (1979) 'Redaktionelle Werbung im Wettbewerb von Tageszeitungen: Probleme und Befunde einer Untersuchung zur Trennung von redaktionellem Text und Anzeigen', in H-D. Fischer and B. Baerns (eds) *Wettbewerbswidrige Praktiken auf dem Pressemarkt: Positionen und Probleme im Internationalen Vergleich*, Baden-Baden (=Materialien zur interdisziplinären Medienforschung 7).

Baerns, B. and Lamm, U. (1987) 'Erkennbarkeit und Beachtung redaktionell gestalteter Anzeigen: Design und Ergebnisse der ersten Umfrage zum Trennungsgrundsatz', *Media Perspektiven*, 3, 149–58.

Baum, H. (1986) 'Im Grenzbereich von Werbung und Redaktionellem: neue Werbeformen im kommerziellen Hörfunk', *Media Perspektiven*, 11, 699–706.

Bente, K. (1990) *Product Placement. Entscheidungsrelevante Aspekte in der Werbepolitik*, Wiesbaden.

Breunig, C. (1994) 'Programmforschung – Kontrolle ohne Konsequenzen. Projekte der Landesmedienanstalten 1988–1994', *Media Perspektiven*, 12, 574–94.

Bruhn, B. (1992) *Integrierte Unternehmenskommunikation: Ansatzpunkte für eine Strategische und Operative Umsetzung Integrierter Kommunikationsarbeit*, Stuttgart.

Bruhn, M. (1988) 'Die Entwicklung neuer Kommunikationsformen: Möglichkeiten zur Erweiterung des Werbevolumens durch Sponsoring und Product Placement', *Markenartikel* (Wiesbaden), 50, 224–7.

Bücher, K. (1926a) 'Die Grundlagen des Zeitungswesens', in K. Bücher: *Gesammelte Aufsätze zur Zeitungskunde*, Tübingen.

——(1926b) 'Die Reklame. From Zeitschrift für die ges. Staatswissenschaft, Vol. 1917/18', in K. Bücher, *Gesammelte Aufsätze zur Zeitungskunde*, Tübingen, 235–68.

Deutscher Presserat (1994) Jahrbuch 1993 (Bonn) 'Deutsche Public Relations-Gesellschafte. V. and Gesellschaft Public Relations Agenturen e.V.: Public Relations', *Das Berufsbild Öffentlichkeitsarbeit*, Bonn: DPRG/GPRA (1990).

Lange, P. (1991) *GPRA Rechtsgutachten. Product Publicity – Verbot redaktioneller Werbung*, Bonn.

Groth, O. (1928–30) *Die Zeitung*, vol. 3, Mannheim, 4 vols.

Hackforth, J. (ed.) (1994) *Sportsponsoring. Bilanz eines Booms. Studie zur Präsentation und Wirkung von Werbung im Sport*, Berlin (= Beiträge des Instituts für Sportpublizistik 3).

Hänecke, F. (1990) 'Presse und Sponsoring. Auswertung einer Befragung von Deutschschweizer Verlagen und Redaktionen über ihren Umgang mit Sponsoring. Zürich 1990 (Diskussionspunkt 18)'. Abbreviated: 'Die Trennung von Werbung und redaktionellem Teil. Ergebnisse einer Schweizer Studie zu Presse und Sponsoring', *Media Perspektiven*, 4, 241–53.

Heck, A. (1993) 'PR-Beiträge, Sponsoring und Sonderwerbeformen des Bayerischen Privatfunks. Versuch einer Bestandsaufnahme', unpublished diploma thesis, University of Bamberg, 1991. Abbreviated: 'Werbung als Programm', *Journalist*, 3, 21.

Heide, W. (ed.) (1940) *Handbuch der Zeitungswissenschaft*, vol. 1, Leipzig.

Hohmeister, K. H. (1981) *Veränderungen in der Sprache der Anzeigenwerbung. Dargestellt an Ausgewählten Beispielen aus dem 'Gießener Anzeiger' vom Jahre 1800 bis zur Gegenwart*, Frankfurt am Main.

Jarren, O., Marcinkowski, F. and Schatz, H. (eds) (1993) *Landesmedienanstalten – Steuerung der Rundfunkentwicklung? Jahrbuch 1993 der Arbeitskreise 'Politik und Kommunikation' der DVPW und der DGPuK*, Münster (=Beiträge zur Kommunikation in Politik und Gesellschaft 1).

Kiock, H. (1972) *Kommunikations-Marketing: Die Technik journalistischer Anpassung*, Düsseldorf (=Gesellschaft und Kommunikation 12).

Kübler, F. (1992) *Postzeitungsdienst und Verfassung*, Berlin.

Landgrebe, K. P. (1976) *Anzeigenumfeld und Anzeigenwirkung. Vermutete und nachweisbare Einflüsse des Werbeträgers Zeitschrift auf Umfang und Art der Wirkung des Werbemittels Anzeige*, Hamburg.

Lerg, W. B. (1963) 'Die Anfänge der Rundfunkwerbung in Deutschland', *Publizistik* (Bremen), 8, 296–304.

——(1980) *Rundfunkpolitik in der Weimarer Republik*, Munich (=Rundfunk in Deutschland 1).

Löffler, M. (1983) *Presserecht. Kommentar. Volume 1: Landespressegesetze der Bundesrepublik Deutschland mit Textanhang*, Munich.

——(1968–9) *Presserecht: Kommentar*, 2 vols, 2nd revised edn, Munich. Vol. 1: *Allgemeine Grundlagen, Verfassungs- und Bundesrecht* (1969). Vol. 2: *Die Landespressegesetze der Bundesrepublik Deutschland mit Textanhang* (1968).

Martens, E. (1989) '*Bild am Sonntag*: Roman mit Werbung. Mannesmann: Tochter gesucht. Triumph-Adler: Umstrittener Gewinn. Manager und Märkte', *Die Zeit* (24), 9 June, 36.

Meyer, B. (1985) 'Zur Akzeptanz des "Anzeigenblatts" als publizistisches Medium. Systematische Darstellung des Argumentationswandels in der Rechtsprechung und in der publizistischen Praxis 1949–84', unpublished MA thesis, University of Bochum.

Nickel, V. (1994a) 'Der Einfluß der Werbung auf die Medien. Aus der Sicht der Werbung', paper presented at a convention of Russian and German journalists at the Evangelische Akademie Mülheim/Ruhr on 11 May, *Medienspiegel* (29), 18 July, supplement.

——(1994b) 'Werbung am Pranger. Merkmale einer unendlichen Debatte über die tatsächliche oder vermeintliche Sozialschädlichkeit von Marktkommunikation', paper presented at the Convention of Advertising, 18 March, Dortmund/Hohensyburg.

Ott, K. (1987) 'Geld und Presserecht', *Journalist*, 11, 38.

'PR, Öffentlichkeitsarbeit und Wissenschaftsjournalismus. Eine Erklärung des Arbeitskreises Medizinpublizisten', Klub der Wissenschaftsjournalisten, June 1988, Bonn.

'Produkt PR. Abmahnvereine: Die GPRA will aufklären und abklären/Derweil geht das EV-Spielchen weiter', *Public Relations Report* (1297), 25 July, 1.

Prüfer, K. (1937) *Handbuch des Anzeigenwesens*, Berlin.

Recht (1991) 'Produkt-PR per EV verboten/Abmahnverein kontra Verlage', *Public Relations Report* (1296), 18 July, 1.

Rodekamp, H. (1975) 'Redaktionelle Werbung. Die tatsächliche und rechtliche Problematik der Trennung von Text- und Anzeigenteil in Druckerzeugnissen', doctoral thesis, Münster.

Rühl, R. (1991) 'Die Kriegserklärung an klassische Werbewege', *W&V Werben und Verkaufen* (19), 10 May, 12, 16 18; (20), 17 May, 38ff.; (21), 24 May, 72ff.; (22), 31 May, 46ff.; (23), 17 June, 44ff.

Schiwy, P. and Schütz, W. J. (eds) (1994) *Medienrecht: Stichwörter für die Praxis*, 3rd edn, Neuwied and Frankfurt am Main.

Stolte, D. (1986) '"Es wird kein Product Placement geben", ein Textintern-Gespräch über Werbung, Film und Zuschauerforschung', *Textintern* (93), 14 November, 6–9.

Weischenberg, S., Löffelholz, M. and Scholl, A. (1994) 'Journalismus in Deutschland: Merkmale und Einstellungen von Journalisten', *Journalist*, 5, 55–69.

'Wirtschaftsberichterstattung in Deutschland – Ergebnisse einer Exclusiv-Befragung', *Der Wirtschaftsredakteur. Wirtschaft, Wissenschaft und Medien Aktuell* (29) (1994), 16, 15 August, 1–3; 17, 1 September, 1–3; 21, 2 November, 1ff.

Wöste, M. (1991) 'Programmquellen privater Radios in Deutschland. Rahmenprogramme, Beitragsanbieter und PR-Audioagenturen', *Media Perspektiven*, 9, 561–9.

Wuttke, H. (1875) *Die Deutschen Zeitschriften und die Entstehung der Öffentlichen Meinung. Ein Beitrag zur Geschichte des Zeitungswesens*, Leipzig, 16–20. Unrevised version from 1st edn of 1866.

ZAW (Zentralausschuß der Werbewirtschaft) (ed.) (1984) *Schleichwerbung. Fallbeispiele, Rechtsprechung, Richtlinien*, Bonn.

——(1994) *Jahrbuch Deutscher Werberat 1994*, Bonn.

Subject index

social-interpretative public relations 172–4
socialisation 91, 169
sociology 18, 101–2
spanning capabilities 65
sponsorship 240, 242, 246–7, 253
sports, advertising 240–1
stakeholders: attracting 75; public relations 38, *41*; relationships 33, 67, 77, 79
stereotypes, gender 112, 115n12
strategic management: competitive advantage 34–6; decentralisation 74; environment 32–4; externalities 36–8, 44, 59; levels 39–40; mission 32–3; public relations 39–43, 67–72, *73*, 78–80; publics 79; situational theory 38–9
strategy 62–3, 72–4; adaptative 27, 60, 61, 62–3; classicists 170–1; competitive 63–7, 76–7; evolutionists 171; externalities 59; interpretive 60, 61, 62–3; language 121; linear 60, 61, 62–3; planning 26–7; processualists 171; public relations 67–70; rhetorical 131–4; systemic approach 171
structuration theory 18
structured flexibility theory 184
supplier relations 15
supply and demand 14
Sweden 45
Switzerland 165–6
symbolic action 128

task environment 33–4
team discipline 139
Tech USA 139
television: advertising 239–40; programme licences 247; sports coverage 240–1

Three Mile Island affair 133
Tomorrow's Company (RSA) 148–9, 153
training 150, 173, 193, 200–1
transaction cost theory 14, 15
trust 18–19, 44, 166
Truth, Sojourner 114n3
Turkey 187
two-way symmetrical philosophy 188, 193–4, 197, 198–9

U-form companies 15
UK *see* Britain
uncertainty 32
unconscious 163
Union Carbide 134, 181
United Arab Emirates 105
USA: Catholic bishops on nuclear arms 125–6, 134; competition 14; cultural bias 12, 44; ethnocentrism 197; and German public relations 216, 218–19, 221–2; management concepts 24–7; public affairs departments 29–30; public relations 12, 147, 161–2; sexism 108
utilities 81

VDZV 233–4
Vogel, Dieter 226

WAZ 230, 231
Wilson, Woodrow 218
wine industry 234–5
women's issues, journal publication 101
workplace, sexism 99

ZAW 244
ZDF television 226, 242
Zeit, Die 220

Author index

Ohmae, Kenichi 45–6
Olasky, M. N. 28, 100
Olson, L. D. 103
Oppenheim, A. N. 147
Ott, K. 253
Ovaitt, F. Jr 47, 182, 183

Park, R. 159
Pauly, J. 191, 192
Pavlik, J. 147, 179, 190
Pearce, J. A. II 33, 39
Pearson, R. A. 126, 129
Peters, T. J. 27, 169
Peterson, T. R. 133
Pettigrew, A. M. 60, 63
Piekos, J. M. 107
Pigou, Arthur C. 37
Pimlott, J. A. R. 147
Pincus, J. D. 28, 115n16
Pinsdorf, M. K. 181, 189
Pires, M. A. 190
Popper, K. 174
Porter, M. E. 18, 34–6, 37–8, 39,
    42, 64, 65, 71
Post, J. E. 34
Prahalad, C. K. 14, 15, 64, 71
Pratt, C. 100
Pratt, C. B. 104
PRSA Task Force 102
PRTV Training Video 152
Prüfer, K. 236
Putnam, L. L. 91

Rakow, L. F. 110
Raucher, A. R. 147
Rayfield, R. E. 28, 99
Recht 251
Redding, W. C. 124, 125
Reed, J. M. 189
Repper, F. C. 22, 23, 29, 38, 67, 78,
    79, 80
Ricks, D. 183
Rieger, F. 192
Ring, P. S. 33–4
Robertson, R. 184
Robins, J. A. 15
Robinson, R. B. Jr 33, 39
Roethlisberger, F. J. 169
Roggero, G. A. 12

Ronneberger, F. 212, 222
Rose, M. 189
Rosengren, K. E. 165
Ross, I. 146
Rossman, G. B. 191
RSA 148
Rühl, M. 161, 212, 222
Rumelt, R. P. 13, 15, 16, 26, 32, 33
Russel, D. 46

Samuelson, P. A. 13
Saxer, U. 212
Scharf, W. 212
Schein, E. 169
Schiller, H. I. 17
Schmid, A. P. 188, 190
Schneir, M. 114
Scholes, K. 74, 78
Schuster, M. 93
Scrimger, J. 99
Seitel, F. 173
Selnow, G. W. 99
Sen, F. 181
Sharpe, M. L. 187, 192
Siehl, C. 169
Signitzer, B. 164, 166, 221, 222
Simon, H. 91
Simon, H. A. 14, 21
Slater, S. F. 76, 81
Smith, G. D. 97
Smith, G. G. 68, 69, 82
Smith, Hough 28
Smith, R. C. 92, 93
Søndergaard, M. 168
Sorge, A. 169
Spicer, C. H. 104
Sproule, J. M. 121, 129, 135
Sreberny-Mohammadi, A. 162
Sriramesh, K. 12, 105, 167, 168,
    169–70, 188
Stacey, J. E. 30
Stadler, G. 212
Starbuck, W. H. 81
Stark, K. 172, 173
Starrett, D. A. 36
Steiner, G. A. 33, 59
Stewart, L. J. 102
Stolte, Dieter 240
Sturdivant, F. D. 30